Cambridge Between
Two Wars

Cambridge Between Two Wars

T. E. B. Howarth

COLLINS
St James's Place, London
1978

William Collins Sons & Co Ltd
London · Glasgow · Sydney · Auckland
Toronto · Johannesburg

First published 1978
© T. E. B. Howarth 1978

ISBN 0 00 211181 0

Set in Garamond
Made and Printed in Great Britain by
William Collins Sons & Co Ltd Glasgow

To
Alan (King's)
Frances (Girton)
David (Magdalene):
and never forgetting
Peter

Illustrations

Contents

Preface

Not all the omissions in this book are involuntary. In particular, the reader will find relatively little about the administration of the University or the Colleges. This is not because I underestimate its importance. E. A. Benians of St John's, Vice-Chancellor in 1940, surveying the two inter-war decades in that year, rightly pointed out that there had never before been so rapid an increase in so short a time 'in the number of teachers and students, in facilities for research in the arts and sciences, or such a multiplication of buildings by University and Colleges'. To chronicle adequately the administration of so peculiarly complex a society as an ancient university in the twentieth century would require another book of comparable length. Again, I am fully aware that experiment and research in any one university are not carried on in isolation from what is happening elsewhere in other places of learning, both in this country and abroad. However, to do justice to that theme would again stretch my canvas beyond its limits, which are those of a historical sketch and not of a history with any pretensions towards the 'definitive'.

I am much indebted for the use of unpublished material to the Vice-Chancellor and the Council of the Senate, who allowed me to inspect the papers of the Sex Viri relating to the Haldane divorce case, and to the Master and Fellows of Magdalene College for permission to use hitherto unpublished extracts from the diaries of A. C. Benson. I have been generously favoured with advice and assistance by Dr Walter Hamilton, Professor I. A. Richards, Lord Snow, the late Lord Adrian, Lord Butler, Professor P. W. Duff, Dr T. E. Faber, Mr T. C. Nicholas, Sir Desmond Lee, Mr C. W. Crawley, Dr G. H. W. Rylands, Dr R. Robson, Professor Michael Oakeshott, Lord Annan, Mr P. F. Radcliffe, Mr Hugh Sykes Davies, Professor H. C. Darby, Mrs Peter Stadlen, Mr J. H. Doggart, Mr A. B. Beaumont, Mr J. P. T. Bury, Lord Vaizey,

Preface

Mrs Lettice Ramsey, Mr G. R. Hamilton, Mr L. J. Russon, Professor H. L. Elvin, Dr B. C. Saunders, Dr N. Boyle, Mr D. B. Welbourn, Miss Bridget Jennings, and Mrs Christine Madden. Mr Tim Young and Mr Roger Sewell helped me greatly at an early stage in my researches. Mrs Ruth Easthope devoted many hours of spare time to typing my manuscript with apparently unfailing cheerfulness.

During the last stages of this enterprise, there has been much public speculation about the identity of a hypothetical 'fourth man' believed to have recruited Philby, Maclean and Burgess as Soviet spies. Though I am not without my suspicions in the matter, I doubt if the final truth will be revealed without access to Soviet sources. Since betraying one's country, except under intolerable physical torture, seems to me so heinous an offence, I have not been prepared to speculate on the matter in print without evidence which is not in my possession. However, just as nature is said to abhor a vacuum, so history dislikes unsolved mysteries. Now that the period is being intensively studied, it would not be surprising if more light were soon to be shed on these murky corners. Perhaps a few glimmers may be found in the following pages.

Magdalene College
Cambridge
1977

Prologue

———◆◆◆———

CEDANT ARMA TOGAE

Now no more of winters biting,
Filth in trench from fall to spring,
Summers full of sweat and fighting
For the Kesar or the King.

A. E. Housman
(Last Poems VIII)

Cambridge is mostly flat, although, as F. L. Lucas observed, much of it lies intellectually at the glacial altitudes of the higher brow. A little to the south lies a low range of hills about two hundred and thirty feet high, the Gog Magog Hills. The Gogs, as they are called, were in the mind's eye of Second Lieutenant R. G. Ingle of the Lincolnshire Regiment, while he was writing up his diary at half past five on the evening of 24 June 1916, a week before the 'Great Push' on the Somme. Ingle was a clever man who had read Classics at Queens' College and been placed in the first class in the same year as two of the most prominent Cambridge Classical dons of the inter-war years, F. E. Adcock and J. T. Sheppard. The entry in his diary reads:

The bombardment for the 'Great Push' has just begun; I am sitting out here on an old plough in a half-tilled field watching the smoke of the shells rising over the German lines. There is a very wide view from here such as you get from the top of the Gogs, and you can see quite a wide front – our own bit of front and a mile or more to left and right . . . It is a pleasant, rather cloudy day, after a night of heavy rain; and the light breeze blowing from the West lessens for us the sound of the guns, besides being a protection, as far as we know, against gas. There are poppies and blue flowers in the corn just by – a part of the field that is cultivated, and on the rise towards the town is a large patch of yellow stuff that might be mustard and probably isn't. On the whole the evening is 'a pleasant one for a stroll' – with the larks singing.

A week later he wrote:

I have just got back from the trenches, which were squelching with mud, and had something to eat. We are moving up to the Chateau to-night and having breakfast there at 3.30 a.m. We moved 200 rounds from dug-outs to our gun emplacements this afternoon, which took from 3.0–5.30. Our guns were firing all the time and the Huns making some return.

It was a lovely afternoon with a fresh wind blowing: some of the trenches were badly knocked about. I looked over into Hunland as I came out – the wood in front looking like currant bushes with the blight.

Some trees were down in our wood. I passed the cemetery as I came back and looked at Rowe's grave. I am moving up by myself at 8.30, having a little time here to wash and have a meal. I had three letters to-night and the *Observer*, rather delayed, all posted on Sunday.

This ends the diary before 'the push' as I must pack up.

He was killed at 7 a.m. the following morning, 1 July.

The number of Cambridge men killed in the Great War was 2162 together with 2902 wounded, nearly a third of all who served. Of their quality and that of others of their generation, Lieutenant J. B. Priestley, who had served throughout the war in the Duke of Wellington's Regiment and came up afterwards to read English at Trinity Hall, wrote: 'Nobody, nothing, will shift me from the belief, which I shall take to the grave, that the generation to which I belong, destroyed between 1914 and 1918, was a great generation, marvellous in its promise. This is not self-praise, because those of us who are left know that we are the runts.'

The first part, at any rate, of his thesis is not difficult to substantiate. As an example, Geoffrey Hopley of Trinity went down in 1914, by which time he had secured a double first in the History Tripos, passed all his Bar examinations in one year, won a cricket blue and a heavy-weight boxing blue. He died of septicaemia after being shot by a sniper. In the very last months of the war Geoffrey Tatham, Fellow and Junior Bursar of Trinity and already a historian of distinction, was killed as a mere Captain aged thirty-four; James Woolston of Pembroke, a Professor of Mathematics in South Africa, died of wounds as a Lance-Corporal; D. L. H. Baynes of Clare with a first in Mathematics and another in Natural Sciences was killed aged thirty-two; Allan Parke of Jesus was killed just over a month before the Armistice, having been wounded at Suvla Bay in 1915 and twice in France on the same day in 1917; Philip Bainbridge, killed in September 1918 as a Second Lieutenant, had won a first in both parts of the Classical Tripos; Donald Innes, a Classical Exhibitioner at Trinity, went to the front as a Second Lieutenant in the Black Watch in August 1918 and died of wounds aged nineteen on 6 October; of Jesus College's 150 war casualties one, Francis Storrs, was killed on 10 November, the last day of the war.

The Reverend H. F. Stewart, for many years Dean of Trinity and the effective founder of the new Modern Languages Tripos, was a Pascalien and not generally a sentimentalist, but in his Commemoration sermon at St John's in the summer of 1919 he exemplified both the mood and the idiom of the day. 'I take the War List and I run my finger down it. Here is name after name which I cannot read and which my elder hearers cannot hear without emotion – names which are only names to you, the new College, but which to us, who knew the men, bring up one after another pictures of honesty and manly beauty and goodness and zeal and vigour and intellectual promise. It is the flower of a generation, the glory of Israel, the pick of England; and they died to save England and all that England stands for.'

Not surprisingly, when the end came on Monday, 11 November, 'jubilance swept through the town'. The sober columns of *The Cambridge Review* recorded that 'there was a very creditable pre-war bonfire in the Market Place, fed chiefly with packing-cases round which there was dancing; but not all the dancers performed with two sound legs. A lady who looked like a bedmaker said regretfully: "It's *something* like old times; but not quite." ' However, in one hitherto cloistered area of the University, there was something of a bonfire of convention and inhibition alike.

Girton College had been prudently sited in 1873 by its founders at a sufficient distance from the centre of Cambridge to minimize the risk of social and moral temptation for its students. However by one o'clock on 11 November, the bonds of decorum snapped and the girls emerged *en masse* to join the afternoon revels. As the College magazine put it –

Rowdy merrymaking was not the only way in which we showed our joy on that never-to-be-forgotten Monday. At five o'clock we almost all went to the Thanksgiving Service at King's, and, as we stood in the dim candlelight of that wonderful chapel, it seemed as if Earth and Heaven were no longer divided, and as if Time and Eternity were one . . . Then after Hall, when we had toasted the King, the Navy, the Army, and the future League of Nations, we had our own service in Chapel, which ended fittingly with Kipling's Recessional 'Lest we forget'.

And so to bed – having experienced in one day a range of emotions not felt by many in a lifetime . . . At about one o'clock we were awakened by an extraordinary pandemonium. At first we thought that the freshers had seized upon the occasion as a unique opportunity for the performance of their rag, and, turning over, we murmured sleepily, 'Strenuous beggars.' . . . To our astonishment we found that it was not our own enterprising freshers engaged in nocturnal celebrations, but a Cambridge party which had come to give us a share in the fun. With repeated adjurations of 'Wake up! Wake up! *Don't* you know the war's over?' they urged us to 'come out and have a bonfire,' but, owing to the lateness of the hour, this project was quite unfeasible, and when the merrymakers had sufficiently exhausted their animal spirits – incidentally giving us a notion of what a real Cambridge rag might be like – they formed fours and marched down the drive, singing us 'Good-byee'.

The next evening there was a great bonfire in the capacious College grounds and the male undergraduates were back again, even penetrating the bottom floor of the College, before being ejected by the Proctors, the university disciplinary officers, and their attendant constables or 'bulldogs'. Later in the week the Mistress, Miss Jex-Blake, invited the 'raggers' to a dance, which it is recorded passed all too quickly – 'even those thrilling but exhausting Lancers . . . But never has Girton, and, I think I may venture to say, its guests, so enjoyed a dance, and never was there a dance that ended in such an atmosphere of universal pleasure and satisfaction.'

Not all the Armistice celebrations were characterized by

this almost Arcadian innocence. One of the most remarkable
Cambridge characters of the day was Charles Kay Ogden.
Bernard Shaw considered that Ogden should have been
awarded a peerage and a princely pension, but he was fated to
spend his life, despite his intellectual brilliance, in a state of
relative penury which he characteristically described as hand-
to-mouth disease. By the time the war began he had urged his
most celebrated disciple I. A. Richards to abandon his abortive
studies in medicine and history in order to read Moral Sciences,
the name by which Cambridge philosophy was known during
the inter-war years. It was at Ogden's suggestion that the
embalmed corpse of Jeremy Bentham at University College,
London was given a new suit of underclothes and it was
Ogden who put into circulation the allegedly Chinese description of an American university as a social and athletic
institution, where opportunities of study are provided for the
feeble-bodied. He also sought to popularize an ozone machine,
which he claimed would make available the salutary air of
Brighton as an antidote to the miasma of the Cambridge fens,
and succeeded in ridding Kingsley Martin, the future editor of
the *New Statesman*, of the residual Christianity with which he
arrived at Cambridge, teaching him to appreciate Cézanne as a
makeweight.

At the outbreak of the war Ogden was the editor of a
modestly original weekly called the *Cambridge Magazine*, the
general tone of which might be described in relation to today's
journalistic standards as *eau-de-rose New Statesman*. The advent
of the war gave it a new notoriety. In the aftermath of the
retreat from Mons, and the day after Antwerp surrendered to
the Germans, Ogden's editorial observed in a manner far
from consonant with the prevailing national mood: 'We hear
suggestions in certain quarters that there is a danger of undue
pressure being brought to bear on Freshmen to join the
Officers' Training Corps this term. We do not really believe
that any College authorities will be so foolish as to jeopardize
the chances of producing a really efficient body of officers by
action so illegal and unjustifiable.' From October 1916 the
magazine carried a very extensive – if wholly uncritical – digest
of foreign (including enemy) newspaper opinion translated
by Mrs C. R. Buxton, so extensive and convenient that it was

regularly used surreptitiously by the Foreign Office. Sir Frederick Pollock, the most eminent jurist of the day, with the support of the Shakespearian scholar Caroline Spurgeon and the Tibetan explorer Francis Younghusband, waxed indignant about the welcome always to be found in the *Cambridge Magazine* for the opinions of those less than enthusiastic about the prosecution of the war. 'Week by week Mr Lowes Dickinson pours gentle streams of lukewarm water upon patriotic enthusiasm, steadily strengthening the impression that there is not much to choose between ourselves and our enemies.' However Thomas Hardy, Gilbert Murray and Arnold Bennett were all stout supporters of Ogden, and the author of *Three Men in a Boat* thought the *Cambridge Magazine* the only readable paper in Europe.

As the war went on, the shortage of paper presented Ogden with a problem which he characteristically solved by buying up all possible penny dreadfuls and pulping them as the need arose. At the height of his enterprise he owned shops, which he used as storehouses, at 6 and 10 King's Parade, 63 Bridge Street, 12 Benet Street and 1 Free School Lane. His headquarters was in a fantastically cluttered office over MacFisheries in Petty Cury, called Top-Hole.

Shortly after 11 a.m. on 11 November 1918 a mob of students, predominantly medical, started to smash Ogden's windows, and paintings by Duncan Grant, Vanessa Bell and Roger Fry were hurled into the street, as Philistia and Bloomsbury came to blows. Late that evening Ogden and Richards met to determine whether Richards could identify any of the perpetrators. Half-way down the stairs, Ogden made a reference to a recent article in *Mind*. They talked for an hour or more by the flickering light of a gas-jet. By the time they parted in the small hours, they had given birth to one of the most characteristic books to appear in Cambridge during the inter-war years, *The Meaning of Meaning*.

Although the *Cambridge Magazine* very understandably commented later that week that in Britain at any rate violence had not yet been recognized as the proper method of obtaining communal ends, there were at least two further incidents of the sort before a general revulsion set in. On 7 March 1919 at a debate between the Cambridge Socialist Society and the

Cambridge Independent Labour Party (the sort of exercise in fissiparous fraternity which so happily characterizes the intellectual Left in England and France), three Socialist speakers were forced by ex-officer intruders to stand on a table. They were then made to sing 'God Save the King' and subsequently ducked in the river. A contributor to the *New Cambridge*, signing himself 'Old Timer', commented on the proceedings somewhat subjectively as follows: 'The meeting was a scream – a nice, good-humoured show, which did us all a power of good. How splendid it was to hear Messrs A, B and C singing "God Save the King"! Looking at Messrs A, B and C though, one couldn't help feeling that they were poor creatures . . . It is the womenfolk who follow these poor specimens who annoy me. It will be a long time before I forgive the three women who stayed through the meeting. In the first place, they took advantage of their sex to hurl insults at a large number of Naval and Army officers and secondly they refused to stand up when everybody sang "God Save the King". They added a further insult by laughing in the face of an officer in uniform who was standing at the salute.'

A year later, Norman Angell, a founder member of the Union of Democratic Control, author of *The Great Illusion*, a Nobel Peace Prize winner in 1933 and the most assiduous pacifist of the epoch, was denied a hearing in Cambridge and only rescued from immersion in the river by police intervention. This prompted much correspondence in the university press, including a dignified protest from Lowes Dickinson of King's against the impropriety of attempting to silence unpopular opinions by force, and a letter to *New Cambridge*, pointing out that if people such as Philip Snowden, Ramsay Macdonald, Norman Angell or George Lansbury attempted to address meetings in a town like Cambridge they would inevitably be labelled as Bolsheviks and regrettable riots and man-hunts would ensue. Another correspondent felt that the episode demonstrated that those who had fought in the war were not going to have Bolshevism preached to them by a miserable sub-man who was frightened to fight for his country.

We have the authority of the *Cambridge University Handbook* to assure us that by the end of the year 1920 all the normal activities of the University had been resumed. That in itself was a very remarkable feat of resilience. What would never be restored were the tone and tempo of the pre-war period. Ten days after the Armistice *The Cambridge Review* published a notice of Rupert Brooke's *Collected Poems*, which evoked a now vanished world – his 'life slips by like a panorama of earth's loveliest experiences. There are the happinesses both intellectual and athletic of a great public-school; the fascinations literary, dramatic, exploratory of a great university; the charms of an old riparian country vicarage; a bouquet of rare friendships; travels which end in dalliance among South Sea islands and clear lagoons; the trumpets of war; confessions and night-marches; a death amid the isles of Greece. Through it all, Rupert moves like the ideal knight, splendid of feature and spirit alike. Laughing, loving, weeping, dreaming, thinking, writing, playing – even swimming!' Escapism of that sort was soon to be wholly out of fashion. Furthermore, as George Dangerfield's *The Strange Death of Liberal England* has demonstrated to us clearly, the Great War was in a sense only an interlude interrupting a variety of social conflicts which had already reached a formidable pitch of intensity by 1914.

The debates in the Cambridge Union constitute a very erratic barometer of political and social opinion amongst undergraduates. But attendances in the inter-war years, relative to the total student body, were often surprisingly high and the choice of motions and of distinguished visitors invited is frequently indicative of preoccupations and social trends. The first post-war debate, a thinly attended affair, was significantly on the subject of Guild Socialism, with Hugh Dalton of King's speaking very much to the point, but the left-wing economic historian C. R. Fay inclined to stress the merits of the Machine Gun Corps to an extent detrimental to the strict relevance of his discourse. In due course the Union heard Stanley Baldwin pointing out that he would deeply regret it if politics became a contest of Labour *v.* the Rest, since political cleavages should be vertical and not horizontal and the propaganda of class warfare filled him with depression, since it brought not life but death. A prominent undergraduate debater was Sub-Lieutenant Lord Louis Mountbatten, one of whose speeches was described in November 1919 as 'full of beans and enthusiasm and though he certainly did talk to some extent through his hat, still, never mind. It was a great effort.' The following April a rather less indulgent *New Cambridge* parody of his debating style read: 'I'm frightfully bucked to have a chance of blowing the gaff for half a jiff.' The *Granta* reporter sorrowfully felt forced to admit 'I don't know why, but politics are undoubtedly not this speaker's forte.' About Winston Churchill on the other hand there were no reservations. In February 1920 'our visitor gave us one more glimpse of what a really big personality can do. We didn't believe all he said; but there is that magnetic, boyish over-the-hills-and-far-away touch of greatness that made us shout for joy very much like the morning stars.' Opposing the motion that the time was now ripe for a Labour government he proclaimed himself much in favour of freedom of speech. 'Let's have sarcasm, argument, invective, or any weapon known to human ingenuity, but don't threaten to take away a man's coal.' The trouble with Labour was that it not only made men equal, it kept them equal. '. . . Men didn't work harder for the State. Superhuman altruism would lead to a dead level of equality. We had advanced a little from such palaeolithic doctrines.' In March 1920 Colonel Josiah Wedgwood (in a vote of confidence debate), attacked the coalition government for causing high prices by depreciating the currency. 'The Labour party knew what to do and would do it. All expenditure must be cut down.'

Arguably the greatest Union debate of the inter-war years was that of 21 October 1919, when S. C. Morgan of Trinity moved 'that this House considers the League of Nations to be worthless as a guarantee of international peace, and to be a radically unsound and dangerous project'. The President, J. W. Morris, subsequently a Lord of Appeal, described the atmosphere as being reminiscent of a Crystal Palace cup-tie. Over a thousand members were crowded into the chamber, i.e. nearly a fifth of the undergraduate population. The Duke of Northumberland made what Lord Robert Cecil called a brilliant presentation of a bad case. For the Duke, there was one invariable test of whether a thing was noble or not: the amount of sacrifice it cost people. What effort and sacrifice had we made for the League? Was it not merely the excuse for avoiding the burden of national defence? The old hypocrisy was that war was unthinkable: the League set up a new organized hypocrisy in which visionaries saw a realization of their idle dreams. As between a nation of armed savages and a nation of slaves, he would be for the former. Not so Lord Robert Cecil, for whom the evening was a triumph. He made such a moving appeal to the idealism of youth that it 'vibrated to the very soul of his audience'. An utterly dedicated Christian, he nevertheless committed himself to the heretical proposition that men naturally prefer good to evil, although perhaps he was thinking of his generation of the Cecil family rather than of the majority of mankind. The next day amid great enthusiasm and a nice letter from the Chancellor, Mr Balfour, a Cambridge branch of the League of Nations Union was founded. The following May, Earl Haig, who had been somewhat too vigorously carried shoulder high through the streets with Viscount Jellicoe when they received honorary degrees, addressed the Union in sombrely prophetic tones: 'Do not think for a moment that I am not in favour of the League of Nations, for I am a hearty supporter of the ideal; but it is yet in its infancy, it takes much time, and there are so many selfish people in the world that we must at least be armed, not for aggression but for legitimate defence. See to it that we do not again have to improvise . . .'

Even before the twenties were really under way, one young man, who would develop into Cambridge's leading polemicist in the inter-war years, had already made his mark in the Union. This was Maurice Dobb of Charterhouse and Pembroke, who joined the Communist Party of Great Britain on its foundation in 1920. Fair-haired, pink-cheeked, always smartly dressed and polite and considerate in debate, he regularly earned encomia such as 'clear and delightful as usual; his is always a real contribution to the debate'. He was elected to the committee at the end of 1920. Dobb was particularly adept at presenting radical views in a relaxed and unalarming manner, observing for instance on one occasion that 'national ownership does not involve bureaucracy', so that *Granta* recorded that it was mainly due to him that 'the old unreasoning hatred of the Labour Party is dying down in the University'. In this he was very much more successful than Kingsley Martin who earned the rebuke – 'the member for Magdalene ought to know that a series of superior sneers forms no answer to the arguments of opponents'. An equally predictable note may be detected in the report of a visit by Oswald Mosley, still then a Conservative, who in a debate on India in November 1920 'seemed to many there present to stir up deliberate race-hatred among the Indian students'.

While post-war attitudes and opinions were being hammered out in discussions on the capital levy, the power of the unions, the position of women and the impropriety of men wearing shorts in tearooms, the primary business of the University, the advancement and transmission of learning was rapidly returning to normal. After four largely barren years, there was a rapid influx of senior and junior members of the University. The numbers of undergraduates in residence had fallen from 1178 in 1914 to 235 in 1916. By January 1919 the number was 2635; by May 3844, including 190 United States servicemen on a short course and 400 naval officers whose education had been interrupted at Dartmouth by the demand for them as midshipmen on active service. Kipling celebrated their arrival in a poem of which one stanza reads:

> Nay, watch my Lords of the Admiralty, for they have the
>   work in train;
> They have taken the men that were careless lads at Dart-
>   mouth in 'Fourteen',
> And entered them in the landward schools as though no
>   war had been.
> They have piped the children off the seas from the Falklands
>   to the Bight,
> And quartered them in the Colleges to learn to read and
>   write.

Two of them were to acquire great fame – Mountbatten and P. M. S. Blackett, the physicist. Although the last of the naval officers left in 1923, veteran college porters were wont to describe a bacchanalian evening in the late thirties as 'nearly up to the standard of the naval gentlemen, sir'. Sub-Lieutenant

E. W. Bush and a friend in Trinity climbed across the roofs of Nevile's Court and the hall and planted the White Ensign on the lantern above the hall. It was removed the following day after a similar feat of athletic virtuosity by two of the most eminent Trinity dons of the inter-war years, E. D. Adrian and R. H. Fowler. Other ex-servicemen were unhappily less mobile, being dependent on the good offices of the Cambridge Provisional Limb Depot where they could obtain a free peg-leg, 'a much lighter article than the usual Roehampton jointed limb'.

Demobilization brought back to Cambridge many dons who were to be specially prominent in the inter-war years: in History, J. H. Clapham from the Board of Trade, H. W. V. Temperley, captain in the Fife and Forfar Yeomanry and J. R. M. Butler serving with the Scottish Horse; in Economics, Maynard Keynes from the Treasury, A. C. Pigou from ambulance driving and D. H. Robertson, decorated in the Middle East fighting; in Mathematics J. E. Littlewood, a Lieutenant in the Royal Garrison Artillery; in Modern Languages Donald Beves, chief instructor at the Central School of Drill; in Law, H. A. Hollond, Deputy Assistant Adjutant-General at Haig's Headquarters; in Classics J. T. Sheppard, a Deputy Assistant Censor and F. E. Adcock from Room 40, the centre of the spider's web of Naval Intelligence; among divines, Milner White of King's, who assumed command of his unit when all the officers were killed, and so earned a severe admonition from the Chaplain-General for acting as a combatant, and C. E. Raven of Emmanuel, a zealous chaplain on the Western Front, soon to become Cambridge's leading pacifist; in Physics James Chadwick, returning from internment throughout the war and G. I. Taylor from aeronautical research, involving the practice as well as the theory of parachuting; and in Engineering, the redoubtable Donald Portway, who commanded troops in the retreat from Mons, as he would once again command them in the withdrawal from Dunkirk. Among those who stayed behind, Sir Arthur Quiller-Couch, 'Q' to many subsequent generations of admiring undergraduates, wrote from Jesus, in the dark days of 1915, that 'when dusk has fallen and the Mayor and Corporation leave the world to darkness and to me', he would walk in the Fellows' Garden carefully hiding the ardent tip of his cigarette (lest it should attract a Zeppelin) and think of the day when 'the familiar streams' would flow again. Sir James Frazer in Trinity continued to work out the consequences for mankind of the sinister story of the King of the Wood in the Arician grove of Diana on the sylvan shores of Lake Nemi. A. E. Housman, also in Trinity, had sent most of his savings to the Chancellor of the Exchequer at the start of the war, but by the summer of 1919 was beginning to spend money on himself 'instead of saving it up for the Welsh miners'. More strenuously, E. J. Rapson of St John's, the Professor of Sanskrit, marched four miles to Histon every Sunday morning throughout the war to drill the volunteers, returning in time to sing in the depleted College choir at eleven o'clock, where he always sang on the note, though 'vibrato was anathema to him'.

One very prominent pre-war figure did not however return, and another, who was to earn remarkable celebrity in post-war Cambridge, had been a combatant on the enemy side. Bertrand Russell had been appointed in 1910 to a College lectureship at Trinity in Logic and the Principles of Mathematics at a stipend of £210 a year. With another mathematician E. W. Barnes (later to be Bishop of Birmingham) prominent in his support, the College planned to elect him to a fellowship in 1915 when his lectureship expired. Just as this was about to happen, Russell applied for leave of absence for what would have been the first two terms of his fellowship and nobody had any doubt that he would apply the time available to pacifist politics rather than to mathematical logic. The thirteen members of the Trinity Council thereupon decided that he should not be elected to a fellowship but that his lectureship should be renewed for five years and that he be granted leave of absence. Shortly afterwards Russell wrote a leaflet in support of a St Helens' schoolteacher called Everett, of which he publicly admitted the authorship in his celebrated letter to *The Times* headed *Adsum qui feci*. He was fined a hundred pounds. On 11 July 1916 the Trinity Council agreed unanimously that 'since Mr Russell has been convicted under the Defence of the Realm Act, and his conviction has been confirmed on appeal, he be removed from his lectureship in the

College'. This in turn precipitated an article in the *Cambridge Magazine* headed: 'Trinity in Disgrace – America's opportunity.' Russell's own comment on the episode was to the effect that since all the younger fellows had obtained commissions in the armed forces, the older ones naturally wished to 'do their bit' by depriving him of his lectureship.

It was generally held, and certainly by Russell, that the prime movers were the idealist philosopher McTaggart and the bibulous historian R. V. Laurence. At any rate twenty-one fellows remonstrated against the Council's decision in relatively measured terms and they included men whose eminence is in itself a remarkable index of Trinity's academic distinction at this time – A. N. Whitehead, A. S. Eddington, F. M. Cornford, G. H. Hardy, J. E. Littlewood, C. D. Broad, A. S. F. Gow, F. A. Simpson, D. A. Winstanley, J. R. M. Butler, R. H. Fowler, D. S. Robertson, E. D. Adrian. Early in 1918 the incorrigible Russell was once more in trouble for pacifist propaganda, this time involving offensive remarks about the Americans, and was incarcerated in Brixton prison for six months during which he wrote his *Introduction to Mathematical Philosophy*. His activities at this period and indeed generally throughout his life perfectly exemplified Maynard Keynes's judgement: 'Bertie in particular sustained simultaneously a pair of opinions ludicrously incompatible. He held that in fact human affairs were carried on after a most irrational pattern, but that the remedy was quite simple and easy, since all we had to do was to carry them on rationally.'

The war over, twenty-seven fellows wrote a letter to the Council, drafted by the lawyer Harry Hollond, urging Russell's reinstatement, of which the vital paragraph reads: 'It is and always has been the sincere intention of every one of the signatories of this letter, in the event of this proposal being rejected, to preserve in the fullest possible way the amenities of social intercourse. But it is inevitable that the further exclusion from the College, in consequence of conduct for which he has already suffered heavily, of a former colleague for whom many Fellows have a warm affection, would produce a continuing soreness of feeling on their part, which would make the maintenance of harmony depend on conscious effort rather than on the spontaneous sympathy which membership of our Foundation should imply.' As a result the Council offered Russell a five-year lectureship from 1 July 1920, though he resigned shortly afterwards owing to one of his periodical marital crises.

Two illuminating attitudes to the Russell affair are contained in a letter to Hollond from A. E. Housman and an article in the magazine *Old Cambridge* of July 1920. The former reads as follows:

Dear Hollond,

I am very much obliged to you for taking the trouble to write to me about the Russell business. Russell is a great loss to the College, not merely for his eminence and celebrity, but as an agreeable and even charming person to meet; on the question of conscription I agreed with him at the time, though I now see I was wrong, and I did not feel sure that the action of the Council was wise, though his behaviour was that of a bad citizen. So far therefore I am nearly neutral: what prevents me from signing your letter is Russell's taking his name off the books of the College. After that piece of petulance he ought not even to want to come back. I cannot imagine myself doing so; and my standard of conduct is so very low that I feel I have a right to condemn those who do not come up to it.

I am writing this, not to argufy, but only in acknowledgement of your civility in writing to me. I hope I shall not be able to discover 'conscious effort' in the amiability of yourself or Hardy when I happen to sit next to you in the future. I am afraid however that if Russell did return he would meet with rudeness from some Fellows of the College, as I know he did before he left. This ought not to be, but the world is as God made it.

Your party has a clear majority, and you ought, quite apart from this question, to vote yourself on to the Council as opportunities arise. There is not nearly enough young blood on it.

Yours sincerely,
A. E. Housman

The magazine article, after an account of Russell's war-time activities, concluded: 'This man has been through the war comforting the King's enemies. To bring him back to Cambridge would be an insult to all loyal citizens, and it would confirm the impression which has been made everywhere outside Cambridge, that the University is rotten with false doctrines and disloyalty.'

The handsome Austrian Ludwig Wittgenstein, who always reminded I. A. Richards of Lucifer both in appearance and in his capacity for engendering discord, had been Russell's protégé at Trinity for five terms from early in 1912. As a private in the Austrian army he had much enjoyed the war until confined to a prisoner of war camp at Cassino, from which he sent his celebrated postcard to Russell in March 1919 – 'I've written a book which will be published as soon as I get home. I think I have solved our problems finally.' The *Tractatus Logico-Philosophicus*, of which the English translation would appear in 1922, despite its assertion in the preface that 'the truth of the thoughts communicated here seems to me unassailable and definitive', was not destined to prove the last word for Russell or for philosophy or even for Wittgenstein. But for the moment Cambridge philosophy remained unperturbed by his strange genius, while McTaggart continued to propound idealism in huge volumes, succinctly described by Russell as advocating the remarkable view that 'mind alone is real and reality consists of Thought thinking about thought. All else is illusion including the sea, the sun and moon or the great nebula in Orion.' Richards, at that time training to be a philosopher (or moral scientist, as the Cambridge description then was), found McTaggart a less than stimulating director of studies. His supervisions were always timed for two o'clock, and Richards tip-toeing up the stairs would listen outside the door until he heard a sufficiently reverberating snore, whereupon he tip-toed down again and resumed his reflections on the difficulties involved in reconciling meaning with metaphysics.

The *ancien régime* in philosophy was about to yield to the revolution, but in physics there was an essential continuity with the pre-war era, which would soon blossom into a golden age. In 1919 Sir Joseph John Thomson succeeded Montagu Butler as Master of Trinity and resigned the Cavendish

Professorship, which he had held since 1884. One of his successors, Sir William Bragg, wrote of Thomson: 'He, more than any other man, was responsible for the fundamental change in outlook which distinguishes the physics of this century from that of the last.' His successor at the Cavendish laboratory was the New Zealander Ernest Rutherford.

Part I

———◦◦◦———

THE TWENTIES

'The nineteen-twenties were a time of general optimism, and rightly so. In spite of the many baffling problems at home and abroad, there seemed no reason to doubt that the evolutionary processes which had served us so well in the past would continue to operate in the future.'

(Harold Macmillan,
Winds of Change 1914–39)

——◆◆◆——

CHAPTER ONE

Men, Women and Manners

The Jubilee celebrations at Newnham College on 21 July 1921, described by A. J. Balfour, the Chancellor of the University, as a gathering commemorating noble achievements and rich in solemn memories, proved, like the Duchess of Richmond's ball, to be a festive prelude to a very nasty battle.

In 1881 the Senate had admitted Girton and Newnham undergraduates to the Tripos examinations and their names appeared in the class lists. In 1887 Agnata Frances Ramsay of Girton secured the only first class in the Classical Tripos. Not surprisingly, there soon developed a movement to allow women to assume the titles of the degrees which they might reasonably be declared to have earned. The Senate, comprising resident and non-resident Masters of Arts, voted against the proposal in 1897 by 1713 votes to 662. Only in Emmanuel was there a majority in favour of the women among resident members. A leading anti-feminist was the Disney Professor of Archaeology Sir William Ridgeway, an Irishman who gloried in his descent from Cromwellian settlers. An unusually combative Conservative, he was always spoiling for a fight. He much disliked the portrait of himself in Gonville and Caius, because it lacked animation, the reason being that the artist had what Ridgeway always called 'all the right views'. In the sitter's opinion had the artist been 'a damned Radical' it would have been a much better portrait. Ridgeway concluded his speech to the Senate in the 1897 discussion with the dire warning: 'Our pilots have given ear to the sirens of Girton and Newnham and unless we take heed will wreck this great University.'

By the Michaelmas term of 1919 the sirens were singing again in considerable chorus and some important pilots were beginning to wobble on their course. In the spring of that year there had been insistent calls for the reopening of the whole question of the position of women in the university and for the setting up of a syndicate (or committee) to make appropriate proposals to the Senate. The women's cause was known to be supported by Cambridge figures as weighty as Henry Jackson and R. St J. Parry, Jackson's successor as Vice-Master of Trinity, 'Q' Frederick Gowland Hopkins, A. C. Pigou, McTaggart, Stewart and J. N. Keynes, the Registry (head of the university administrative service), with the lively support of the classicists J. T. Sheppard, F. E. Adcock, T. R. Glover and F. M. Cornford, the historians J. H. Clapham, H. W. V. Temperley and C. R. Fay, the mathematician G. H. Hardy, and Maynard Keynes. Seven heads of houses were known to favour at least a reopening of the question.

More conservative elements were much disquieted. *The Cambridge Review* addressed itself editorially to the problem in June 1920 as follows: 'It is one of the strongest characteristics of the intellectually dyspeptic that they will never submit to a government by sound precedent; but to the plain man a definite ruling pronounced by a sober-minded body of voters is quite sufficient to forbid any further discussion now . . . Not that we wish in any way to appear unchivalrous or to minimize the good work often done by women students; but "so long as the sun and moon endureth" Cambridge should remain a society for *men*, and any sister institution should by its own arrangements procure a charter, and, as a separate institution, confer its own degrees. The convenience of common examinations could, of course, be retained.' Warming to the theme, the editorial went on to deplore the prevalence of young married fellows in Colleges and recommended the imposition of a period of at least ten years' celibacy on election. 'After all – in spite of any 1882 statute* – our original founders were not fools and had possibly studied their Semonides (of Amorgos) with greater diligence than modern reformers.' It is indeed conceivable that a modern reformer in 1919 might not have had handy on his shelves a copy of Semonides of Amorgos, a seventh-century BC poet. The surviving fragments of his iambics reveal him clearly as the prototype of what we call in our contemporary cant 'male chauvinist pigs'. He likens different types of women to

* Before 1882 fellowships had to be resigned on marriage.

different species of animals in a markedly unflattering way, concluding: 'For this is the greatest ill that Zeus hath made, women. Even though they may seem to advantage us, a wife is more than all else a mischief to him that possesseth her; for whoso dwelleth with a woman, he never passeth a whole day glad.' Even a modernist divine like J. F. Bethune Baker was concerned that the 'dreaded ghost' of a woman Vice-Chancellor might materialize (as it eventually did fifty-six years later), although he felt that Cambridge, if it could not always lead, might at least represent the life and thought of the nation as a whole.

The awkward truth of the matter for the anti-feminists was not only that the nation at large, judging by the bulk of the national press, was against them, but that Oxford also was rapidly proceeding to sell the pass. Before the end of 1920 the admission of women to full membership of Oxford University had been approved by Convocation without a division. Furthermore, the reformers kept reassuring everybody that there was no likelihood in the foreseeable future of any possible outcome which might involve men's colleges in actually admitting women. Parry of Trinity confidently affirmed that no advocate of the admission of women to membership of the University had contemplated their admission to men's Colleges – 'it is obvious that it is not desirable; nor as far as I know has it ever been desired by any responsible person'. So a syndicate was appointed by the Senate at the end of 1919 to report, as it eventually did, at the end of the Easter (summer) Term of 1920. Its constitution was interesting in that it numbered six conservatives and six liberals. Of the former, Will Spens of Corpus combined a Disraelian pragmatism with many of the attributes of Warwick the Kingmaker; Claude Elliott of Jesus was to be successively Head Master and Provost of Eton; Sorley was a professor of the sort of philosophy which was going very rapidly out of fashion at Cambridge; and R. V. Laurence was a *bon viveur* and political ultra, at that time much in the limelight as tutor to the under-graduate princes, later to be George VI and the Duke of Gloucester. The coolest head amongst them apart from Elliott's, which was always unusually cool, was probably that of E. C. Pearce, successively Master of Corpus Christi and in 1928 first Bishop of Derby, who observed that in his view women could not be admitted on equal terms simply because they were not content with equality. They mean to rule, he thought, and usually do in the end. The liberals, apart from Parry, included the legal luminary A. D. McNair, J. R. M. Butler and the decidedly radical economic historian C. R. Fay, who combined rather uneasily his enthusiasm for the character-forming merits of the Machine Gun Corps with his idealistic socialism. In February 1920, while the issue was being debated behind closed doors in the syndicate, a private business meeting of the Union considered the possibility of membership of the society for Girton, Newnham and the Cambridge Training College. The result enabled *The Cambridge Review* to comment, in a vein of evident relief in such a parlous situation, that fortunately for the society this attempt to put the clock on had been thwarted by a considerable conservative majority.

In May 1920 the syndicate reported, predictably, that it was wholly unable to agree. The liberals produced Report A, recommending that women should be admitted to full membership, but excluded from men's colleges. There were some rather imprecise suggestions about limitation of numbers. The conservatives in Report B proposed the establishment of a new women's university, initially centred on Girton and Newnham. In an argument designed to buttress this solution, it was contended that if women were concerned with the academic management of the university they would use their influence in favour of women's abilities, which were, it was held, better suited to routine rather than to original work. Spens, for whom complex administration was a lifelong passion, signed Report B, but proposed a federal system in which there would be separate but at times conjoint male and female houses of the Senate.

Girton and Newnham not surprisingly preferred Report A. The Senate discussion in October was a lively affair. Sorley quoted Ernest Barker, the political philosopher soon to be the holder of a Cambridge professorship, to the effect that: 'Women in a university of their own could have a life of their own. In a mixed university they may lean on men and follow the curricula and models of men. In a university of their own they are independent. They can develop their own type of life.' J. H. Gray of Jesus pointed out that women had hitherto been admitted on the Cambridge Higher Local examinations and so escaped the (far from exacting) Cambridge Previous (or Little-Go) examination with its surviving requirement of two classical languages and mathematics – 'in fact, if he might put it so, they did not cross the *pons asinorum*. They had a private *ponticulus asellarum*, a structure far too delicate to be tested by the weight of the male animal.' Clapham for the liberals pointed out that nobody seemed prepared to specify what part or parts of Cambridge teaching were unsuitable for women. Sir Geoffrey Butler remarked that the Natural Sciences Tripos endured for three weeks, which entailed a physical handicap for women students, so that if the admission of women to full membership of the university led to a move-ment to curtail the unnatural length of the Natural Sciences Tripos it would serve a useful end in itself. Fay castigated Report B as in reality offering women full sovereignty in a high school and nothing more. But the man of the hour was Professor Sir William Ridgeway, whose enthusiasm for the anti-feminist cause had in no sense abated with the passing of the twenty-odd years since 1897. As he put it: 'It has been said that the old Tories in Cambridge do not wish women to have degrees. Not a bit of it. They do not care if they are covered with degrees from head to foot. But they do not want them to interfere with the university and the education of their men students.' He used, he continued 'to have great hopes of some of our women students carrying on research, but the best researchers all get married, and those who do not get married seem to do nothing.' It was, he felt, important for the university to think about the men – 'it is men who have to bear the burdens and the struggles of life'.

Despite strong affirmations to the contrary by Miss Jex-Blake of Girton and Miss Stephen of Newnham, the con-servatives continually played up the possibility, in the short or long term, of women seeking to invade men's colleges. As Report B warned, 'for the moment they may be content with having stormed the walls of the university, but in time – probably in a very short time – they will be heard knocking loudly at the gates of the colleges'. In vain, W. E. Heitland of

St John's in Newboltian heroic verse mocked the fears of the conservatives:

Lock the gates and bar the windows. Strong our college walls and wards.
Let them gossip in the Senate, let them chatter on the boards.
And for us another glass of '78.
Oh, bestir yourselves to fight;
You will hear ere fall of night
The thunder of their knocking at your close-barred college gate.

In May, J. T. Sheppard, ever a liberal though not a ladies' man, had secured a majority of ninety-nine in the Union for full equality and separate colleges, despite P. L. Babington of St John's putting the opposing view that 'the effect of co-education in the University will be the end of all we treasure in university life today'. But gradually opinion began to harden. Though J. R. M. Butler would just live long enough to see the Trinity statutes altered to permit the admission of women, he maintained stoutly towards the end of the Michaelmas term of 1920 that 'the chimera of female control is an absurdity as great as that of women entering men's colleges'. However, increasing attention was paid to Spens' argument that tripos results showed that the Cambridge examination system was not suited to women and to Sorley's rather curious opinion that women suffered from being assiduous note-takers, unable 'to manifest the polite indifference of men at lectures', a point which assisted him to secure the reversal of Sheppard's victory at the Union in May with an anti-feminist majority of 423 to 337 in November. Just before the final vote in the Senate a poll of undergraduates showed a majority of 2329 to 84 against Report A. The issue was scarcely affected by a letter to *The Times* by Rutherford and W. J. Pope, Professor of Chemistry, urging the need for more laboratory space for the women students whom they would welcome.

8 December was a raw and foggy morning. By 11.30 non-resident voters were arriving in Cambridge from Liverpool Street. Both sides fetched their supporters from the station,

in one instance in a Red Cross ambulance. Gowns were available on loan. According to *The Times*, some of the costumes were scarcely academic, one cleric wearing a soft black hat, his MA gown, black puttees and yellow boots. Another might have been the Rev. Bute Crawley 'come up for a jolly day from Crawley-cum-Snailly' in a very rustic pair of leather gaiters. The result was a defeat for Report A by 904 to 712 and there was no point in going on with Report B, as it was known perfectly well that the women would have nothing to do with it. An analysis of the voting on Report A shows King's with a substantial majority and Trinity with a small one in favour; Corpus Christi voted 48–8 and St John's 116–77 against; in Emmanuel 34 voted for and 34 against. Among the successful opponents of Report A were J. B. Bury, Elliott, Spens, Kenneth Pickthorn, J. J. Thomson and D. A. Winstanley. What was to happen now?

Before the Senate vote E. D. Adrian and the influential Trinity law don Harry Hollond had issued what is called in Cambridge a fly-sheet, a document asking for supporting signatures, which normally represents the previously canvassed views of people anxious to see something done which is different from what they fear the Council of the Senate and its supporters are trying to achieve. Adrian and Hollond felt that Report A was not explicit enough about controlling the number of women. They therefore proposed that this should be rectified but that women should after all be given titular degrees – which the ribald described as the B.Tit – and that as time went on further privileges for women could be introduced. By March it became clear that the matter could not be decently concluded as a result of the December voting and it looked as if the choice now lay between the Adrian/Hollond proposals and a simpler alternative put up by the Master of St John's, R. F. Scott, born in 1849, who suggested titular degrees, limitation of numbers and no loose talk of further privileges. However under the Vice-Chancellor, P. Giles of Emmanuel, the defeated supporters of the original Report A produced a very similar scheme including a limitation of numbers to 500 but with virtually full membership of the university. By the Michaelmas term of 1921, it had been agreed that this would be put before the voters as Grace I (as Cambridge administrative terminology has it). The Scott scheme would be Grace II and the count would take place on 20 October. The voting was a slow process but by the evening there was a substantial mob of undergraduates outside the Senate House bawling 'we won't have women'. It fell to J. H. Clapham in his usual measured tones to announce the result – Grace I (for virtual membership) defeated by 214; Grace II (for titular degrees) carried by 642. At this point a Corpus Christi MA, the Reverend Howard Percy (Pussy) Hart, Vicar of Ixworth, assumed the role of Camille Desmoulins, whom he otherwise did not resemble, on Bastille day by yelling 'Now go and tell Girton and Newnham.' The mob set off down King's Parade and eventually some three hundred arrived outside the bronze memorial gates of Newnham. There were police in the grounds of the College but they made a tactical miscalculation about the probable point of entry. As the undergraduates began to smash in the gates, using a loaded hand-cart as a battering ram, a Newnham don appeared and apparently made herself heard over the cat-calls and howling. In spite of her plea that they should go and damage anything else but not the memorial gates, since they were what Newnham cherished most, she was answered by one of the 'leaders': 'We know that; that's why we are doing it.' As even the ultra-conservative *New Cambridge* observed: 'there must have been some cads in the crowd, but that young man was a master-cad'. A number of freshmen were sent down; Pussy Hart was brought before the University disciplinary committee, the Sex Viri, and severely reprimanded; the most prominent figures in undergraduate life, whose biographies appeared weekly in *Granta* under the heading 'Those in Authority', led by the Rugby internationals G. S. Conway and R. R. Stokes and the President of the Boat Club H. S. Hartley, whipped up a subscription to help repair the damage; and Donald Portway described the affair in meiotic terms, wholly characteristic of the period, as 'altogether rather a bad show'. A quarter of a century later Cambridge came into line with Oxford by admitting women to full membership of the University.

Under the new statutes of 1926 women became eligible for teaching posts. However, the old orthodoxies died hard. In

February 1924 Mr Justice Parry delivered what he no doubt considered a profound series of reflections on the subject to the University Law Society. The meteoric rise of women to a status of independence and equality he considered to have been one of the outstanding events of the last hundred years. Yet women, he felt, were not really able to face the full glare of what he liked to call the Seven Lamps of Advocacy – honesty, courage, industry, wit, eloquence, judgement and fellowship. 'Honesty and courage women have, but industry crushes them. Wit they admire, but do not possess. Eloquence they suspect, judgement they lack and fellowship is alien to them.'

The Colleges of Girton and Newnham, the institutions at the heart of this controversy, were certainly not devoid of some peculiarly Anglo-Saxon, if not anachronistic, attitudes. As late as 1924 two Newnham undergraduates wrote as follows to the editor of the Newnham magazine: 'We would like to propose a reform. At present many people rush off to games immediately after lunch. From the point of view of health it would be much better if there were an interval between the mid-day meal and violent exercise. We therefore suggest that organized games should never begin before two o'clock and that the games authorities should strongly discourage individuals from arranging tennis or fives for 1.45 or even 1.30 as often happens now. Even if this means a shorter time for play, we believe that the standard of the game would be much improved.' In the Michaelmas term of 1920 it was reported that Newnham was 'inundated with Freshers, numbering nearly a hundred, all sparkling with brains and eagerness. However, they are being strenuously exercised by the Lacrosse and Hockey clubs.' In the previous summer the Newnham VIII all weighed between nine and twelve and a half stone and the nine-stone cox, B. Clarke, was very sensibly enjoined to remember not to lean out of the boat at corners.

However even Angela Brazil's imagination would have been considerably exercised to envisage a form of torture which both colleges inflicted on themselves throughout the twenties. This was the Fire Brigade. The Girton Fire Brigade had been founded in 1879 and trained by Captain Shaw, so movingly apostrophized in *Iolanthe*.* The freshers were particularly involved in doing their bit. In November of 1919 we read that 'the Fire Brigade novices are becoming proficient tyers of knots and runners with hoses. They practise between the hours of 7.30 and 8 a.m. It is pleasant to lie in bed and listen to their energetic movements in the chilly corridors.' It was not all character-building – there were lighter moments, as for instance the Girton Fire Brigade dance of 1919 which 'fulfilled all expectations in the way of cheerfulness, if not of rowdiness. The team lancers were perhaps a scene to be forgotten, but then we do not win the Newnham match every day!' For the same occasion two years later the hall was decorated not only with flowers and evergreens but with ropes, hydrants and hoses and an effigy of H. F. G. Murphy, not only Captain of the Fire Brigade but Captain of Games, in the act of effecting a gallant rescue. Protests were apparently of no avail, including a particularly poignant one in Newnham addressed to the editor of the College magazine in 1920 from 'One who lives very near the rattle.' She wrote:

I am sick of the Fire Brigade; I hate it, despise it, and am perpetually irritated by it.

For generations, this infamous institution has warped and blighted our life at college, an insult to a community of thinking women. Is this a reason that it should exist a moment longer?

We have fought a four years' war to oust the spirit of militarism from Europe, but here in our midst Junkerism is still alive.

We are at the mercy of Captains, Lieutenants, codes and drills, all the paraphernalia of a Prussian discipline. I have watched the masterful bullies who delight to see Freshers fly half-choking from a hardly-touched lunch; who gloat over bent backs and straining sinews rolling hoses to a stop-watch; who order their victims on to the dizzy heights

---

* 'Oh Captain Shaw,
  Type of true love kept under,
  Could thy Brigade
  With cold cascade
  Quench my great love, I wonder!'

of parapets at hideous hours of the morning. These are not sights to forget . . .

We want dignity in our students. Is not the sight of puffing, sweating creatures dashing upstairs to extinguish imaginary flames a ludicrous and painful spectacle?

We want the rule of common sense. Is it right to spend hours attaching hoses that are known to leak too badly for any water to reach the actual blaze, or to rise at dawn to practise rolling up these very hoses in a quicker time limit than that of the fellow company?

I sum up thus – the Fire Brigade is a criminally insensate and inhuman organization, a source of constant nervous strain to every member of the College.

By March 1922 when the Newnham hockey report records the names of the first XI, 'with the number of years they have held their girdles' one begins to fear that Angela Brazil is about to collapse into the arms of Arthur Marshall. Mercifully, femininity began to reassert itself. The Girton Debating Society voted by 128 to 29 that it is better to have loved and lost than never to have loved at all. It is possible to feel that the ice is cracking as one reads: 'Irene's chief weakness is that she can never find the stopper of her hotwater bottle' or in 1927 that 'Nita has always been something of an enigma', although even as late as that year there is a somewhat grim finality about a character sketch reading: 'Joyce has the safe solidity and comfort of an English country town.'

By then Rosamond Lehmann and her daring friend Grizel Buchanan had created for us the Girton of *Dusty Answer*, and Miss Jex-Blake with her plain alpaca bodice and full long skirt had ceased to be mistress after thirty-one years. Her successor Bertha Phillpotts resigned after less than three years in 1925 because 'her father needs her and she feels she must go' – as striking evidence of the survival of male dominance as can be imagined. Miss Major, who reigned at Girton for the rest of the twenties, used to address the 'freshers' on problems of Cambridge deportment. The half-way mark for the girls on the long march into Cambridge was Storey's Way, at which point Miss Major recommended that they should put on hats and gloves, warning them to 'remember, my dears, that the eyes of the Cambridge ladies will ever be upon you.'

Girton, about which Kathleen Raine writes in the relevant volume of her autobiography *The Land Unknown*, was changing fast under the surface towards the end of the twenties. She arrived as a science exhibitioner from an Ilford grammar school in 1926. She emerged as a Communist, a friend of Malcolm Lowry and William Empson, and was soon to marry successively Hugh Sykes Davies and Charles Madge. Yet she wrote of her early days in Girton – 'We were only too glad to live in that college, the very realization of Tennyson's *The Princess*; to visit one another's rooms, like schoolgirls, for sophisticated coffee, or homely "jug" (cocoa at 9 p.m.). Most of us were still virgins at the end of our three years; nor was it the virgins among us who were neurotic, restless, dissatisfied and liable to breakdowns, but the "emancipated" minority who were not.'

Downstairs as well as upstairs, Girton commanded a re-markable loyalty from many of its inmates. Gladys Crane, who worked as a gyp or maidservant at the college for fifty years, wrote of the twenties: 'in those days we were full staff between forty and fifty and twenty-six of them housemaids. We used to work very hard but we were a merry little crowd, more like one big family and we all had our little bits of fun . . . At tripos time, the first years used to get up in the morning about seven o'clock and make tea, and take a cup to each student in their subject who was taking tripos. Sometimes we would give them a horseshoe cut out in cardboard and covered with silver paper just for luck. There used to be crowds of students and dons to see them go off by bus at 8.30 a.m., and the last day students of the same subject used to sit on the gate waiting for their return, then provide a very nice tea for them in one of their rooms. Sometimes the cook would dish up the potatoes in the shape of a horseshoe for we were in those days very interested in our students, we used to be very proud if ours got a wrangler or a first. We were often to be seen on the hockey field when a cup match was being played, and how excited we were if our college won.'

But there was a long way to go, as is evident from the elegiac conclusion to *Dusty Answer*: 'Farewell to Cambridge, to whom she was less than nothing . . . Under its politeness, it had disliked and distrusted her and all other females; and now it ignored her. It took its mists about it, folding within them Roddy and Tony and all the other young men; and let her go.'

One much interested in the foibles of his fellow men and a connoisseur of the passing pageant of Roddys and Tonys was A. C. Benson, Master of Magdalene, a compulsive writer of ephemeral novels and belles-lettres who managed also to write a diary of some four million words, despite an energetic existence and highly precarious mental health. Although a much loved figure in the social round of Cambridge, which still demanded a gargantuan intake of food and drink, and equally admired as host or guest, his diary during the last years of his life is often atrabilious and occasionally vitriolic. It affords us some remarkable glimpses of the senior members of the university in the first half of the twenties.

A great weekly institution in term-time was the University sermon on Sunday afternoons. In October 1923 Benson attended it for the first time since 1883 to hear Canon Mason of Canterbury, who 'began weakly, but there was a fine apostrophe to the Church, in the style of Newman – "Wherefore, my mother, do they prepare for thee a bill of divorcement, that thou art not worthy to be the Bride of Christ?" I looked round. Stanton's head was embedded in his chest; Parry asleep with a look of uplifted piety, Nairne's skull-like head dangling on his thin neck, one of the Bedells asleep, his head pillowed on the other's shoulder. I was aroused by a sharp sound to my left; Hadley, rigid with sleep, snored and struggled . . . A disgraceful scene of infinite futility and grotesqueness. We scuttled away.' Stanton and Nairne were successively Regius Professors of Divinity, Parry Vice-Master of Trinity and Hadley Master of Pembroke. The Esquire Bedells are University officials of great dignity who wait upon the Vice-Chancellor. *The Cambridge Review* invariably printed the University sermon in full, thereby stabilizing its income, since clerical Masters of Arts, of whom we may perhaps assume Pussy Hart to have been one, utilized the material of the sermons as inspirational background for their Sunday morning homiletics in country parishes throughout England and Wales. Yet when the editor suggested that the practice of printing the sermon in its entirety should be discontinued, an immediate letter of protest carried amongst others the signatures of Thomson, Durnford (Provost of King's), Sheppard, Spens, Clapham and Laurence.

The fact was that religion in Cambridge in the twenties was a very live issue. In the Lent term of 1920 a mission led by Charles Gore attracted between two and three thousand undergraduates to prayer meetings in the Guildhall. A similar mission in 1923 appeared again to be a great success, as recorded by the Bishop of St Albans in a rhapsodic account in which he wrote: 'Again and again I thought to myself, I should like to have a few of those silly old croakers and cynics who go about wagging their silly old heads (and tongues too), just as if there was anything in them, and solemnly telling everybody that Christianity is played out and that the Church is finished, and that the Church of England is as dead as the dodo. Played out? Finished? Dead? A pretty vigorous form of death anyway, so far as I could judge from this week.' Perhaps the most sought after preacher in the Cambridge of the twenties was Inge, the Dean of St Paul's. Long queues would form along King's Parade when he came to Great St Mary's. Benson, himself the son of an Archbishop of Canterbury, comments on other celebrated divines of the period. Of Headlam: 'A hard and repellent man, unpleasing to look at, dogged and sour. In these days when dogmas and records are so uncertain that the intellect cannot submissively accept them, a sermon isn't of much use unless it touches the heart; and this sermon was like the rustling of wind in a leafless wood.' Of William Temple: 'A stout man, with small eyes and mouth in the middle of a great globular face – a voice like a mechanical timbre. As he stood in the pulpit he seemed half roly-poly pudding, half trombone. But it was a *very* fine sermon, *admirably* phrased, and would have been very moving but for the awful evenness of tone.'

The Evangelical tradition in Cambridge traces its history to the appointment of Charles Simeon to Holy Trinity in 1783. It was fostered in a strenuous and rather exclusive fashion in the twenties by the Cambridge Inter-collegiate Christian Union or CICCU. During its jubilee celebrations in 1927 CICCU set forth its somewhat uncompromising doctrinal position as follows:

(1) The CICCU rejects the so-called liberal view of the Scriptures and denies the outlook and results of the higher critics.

(2) It can find nothing in common with sacerdotalism, which appears to it, among other departures from the primitive faith, to place the priest where Christ as mediator should be found.

(3) It stands for creation and rejects evolution.

(4) It cannot find any authority for a belief in the success of attempts by social or political action to make the world a better place, and suspects that the unconscious purpose of such efforts is really to make the world a more comfortable place for the human race to go on sinning in.

(5) The Bible most unmistakably teaches both the existence and the superhuman power of a personal evil agency, whom Christ called Satan and described as the prince of this world.

(6) The CICCU cannot be enthusiastic about schemes for bringing world peace by means of political bodies such as the League of Nations, or social uplift by methods of reform.

CICCU's evangelical techniques were as effective as they were disarming, as for instance in this announcement in *The Dial*: 'The Christian Union is by no means as alarming as its name implies; it is composed of perfectly normal people and embraces every shade of opinion, so that no member of College need feel that his views will not meet with sympathy.'

A champion of a more sacerdotal approach to the Christian faith was Eric Milner White, Dean of King's. A double first in history, he was well suited to King's in that it was said of him that in a moral crisis he was a leader of liberal opinion. He was not a person with whom to take liberties. When the Jesus Boat Club invaded King's one bump supper night he treated the occasion as a courtesy visit, getting their president to line them up and shaking hands with them politely as he saw them returned to the darker purlieus of Cambridge. Six weeks after the Armistice he introduced on Christmas Eve a service of nine lessons and carols, first broadcast in 1928 and subsequently listened to annually by innumerable infidels on the radio. Keynes' wife, the ballerina Lydia Lopokova, considered that Milner White's organization of processional services revealed him as 'the greatest choreographer of us all'.

What was known in the period as the Social Gospel was also beginning to make an impact. In a University sermon of 1925 Welldon, Dean of Durham and ex-Headmaster of Harrow, perhaps rather prematurely observed that the day when the upper social class, as it is called, could afford to amuse itself with selfish luxury had gone by and he hoped and prayed that it had gone for ever. Two years later Canon Peter Green from the same pulpit more vividly told his congregation: 'I wish I had the power of a magician that I might bring England's working boys before you, that you might see them, hanging on to a rope at the back of a van or a lorry, or pushing a heavy hand cart, sweating in a ragged shirt or corduroys in the glare of the glass furnace or the moulder's shop, or working, stripped to a cotton vest and drawers, as a little piecer in one of our Lancashire cotton mills.' In 1928 no less a body than the Marshall Society, the social meeting point of the economics faculty, discussed 'The Need for Religion in Social Work', it being considered by one of their speakers that 'the intelligence of the working class is not up to that of the Cambridge undergraduate and some spur to goodness, other than the purely material, is therefore necessary'. In that same year Michael Ramsey, a former president, returned to the Union to argue the merits of disestablishment as a means of revivifying the Church of England, claiming that 'innumerable enactments of the past two hundred years have made Establishment more and more obsolete and now the only logical course is to complete the process'.

The great medieval historian G. G. Coulton of St John's, the leading anti-Roman Catholic controversialist of the day, whom Hilaire Belloc, usually worsted by him in argument, immortalized as the 'remote and ineffectual don that dared attack my Chesterton', conceded that 'the belief in this crucified carpenter has taken more men out of themselves than any other thing in all recorded history'. It was a courageous remark in that it was made to a Cambridge society known as the Heretics, conspicuous in its heyday in the twenties for total freedom of thought, the sort of emancipated irreverence which one associates with the eighteenth-century *philosophes*, and general moral free-wheeling. The twenties was the age of exclusivity *par excellence*. More exclusive than the Heretics – though only just – and probably a great deal less lively (and certainly less heterosexual) were the Apostles. The Society, as it was known to its members, was in this period, as has been related *ad nauseam*, more or less the Cambridge branch of Bloomsbury. Fortunately, its proceedings were so secret that it is not possible, even were it desirable, to chronicle every least heart-throb and *éclaircissement*, as is now the vogue among the residuary legatees of the Bloomsbury epic. So closely guarded was the security of the Apostles' proceedings that when Tom Driberg went to see a former member Guy Burgess in Moscow in the fifties, the latter, although he had been perfectly prepared to betray his country, felt it a point of honour not to reveal any of the Apostles' secrets.

Like other Cambridge institutions in 1919, the Apostles were in need of some post-war reconstruction. Not that there was any shortage, quantitive or qualitative, of 'Angels', as the senior members were called, including as they did G. E. Moore, Russell, McTaggart, A. N. Whitehead, Lowes Dickinson, Keynes, Forster, Roger Fry, Gerald Shove, Eddie Marsh, Leonard Woolf, Sir Frederick Pollock, G. M. and R. C. Trevelyan, Lytton Strachey, Walter Raleigh and J. T. Sheppard. In 1912 Sheppard had examined F. L. Lucas, then a boy at Rugby. After being wounded on the Somme and later gassed, 'Peter' Lucas came back to Trinity to graduate. His brilliance as a classic was such that, before he had completed his tripos in June 1920, Lowes Dickinson, Keynes, Pigou and Sheppard had persuaded the fellowship electors at King's to snap him up and he became a fellow in 1920. He and Sheppard were enthusiastic recruiting sergeants for the Society. In Sheppard's view a measure of male pulchritude in addition to intellectual promise was no bar to a candidate's prospects of enlistment. Lucas's first pupil was an Etonian freshman George Rylands, whom Sheppard immediately cast as Electra in his production of the *Oresteia*. Amongst the new post-war generation of Apostles as well as Lucas and Rylands were W. J. H. Sprott, the psychologist, two future professors of philosophy in

R. B. Braithwaite and Ludwig Wittgenstein, Frank Ramsey, the mathematical genius who translated Wittgenstein's *Tractatus Logico-Philosophicus*, two future schoolmasters Cecil Taylor and Francis Cruso and a prominent Cambridge games player who became an outstanding eye-surgeon, James Doggart. Meetings were held on Saturday evenings. Coffee and sardines on toast, known Apostolically as whales, were provided. A paper was then read, after which lots were drawn and members 'took the hearth-rug' and discussed the paper or indulged in spirited digressions. An annual dinner took place, often in a private room in the Ivy restaurant in London, usually culminating in a speech by Pollock, the doyen of the Angels.

The atmosphere at the Heretics' was much breezier. Meetings were advertised in the local prints and members were not in the habit of calling each other 'dear boy' (it is believed that on one occasion Sheppard thus addressed an undergraduate within the precincts of King's, only to receive the rejoinder: 'I'm not your dear boy, I'm in Selwyn'). Founded in 1909, the Heretics sensibly elected the ever energetic Ogden as president in 1911 and he held the post till 1924, when he was succeeded by the economist Philip Sargant Florence. Law 4 of the society required members to reject all appeal to authority in the discussion of religious questions, a position which led to much Cambridge epigram-coining, as for instance F. M. Cornford's statement that theology was already taking its place as a branch of anthropology or Russell's view that the Ten Commandments should be approached like a Cambridge examination paper on the basis that 'only six need be attempted'. Dora Black, a Girton don, who married Russell in 1921, was secretary in 1918 and 1919 and wrote enthusiastically to Ogden: 'I wish we could all be Bolsheviks quick and have done with it.' But psychology (with Ernest Jones on narcissism in 1922) and anthropology were more exciting than politics in the twenties. Sargant Florence tells us that 'the word sociology being a Latin-Greek hybrid was not used in polite academic society, but many subjects discussed were essentially that'. With Braithwaite and Frank Ramsey as prominent members, philosophy was a popular topic. I. A. Richards' young literary protégé, William Empson, was president in 1928. In 1927 Roger Fry unveiled to the society the secrets of 'the quasi-monumental, semi-geometrical expressionism of Picasso and the exquisitely harmonious arabesques of Matisse'. Later on in that year the Heretics satisfied themselves that they had demolished the twenty-year labours of the revisers of the prayer book in twenty minutes, and in 1928 the theory was advanced that if Winston Churchill had been allowed to play with toy soldiers in childhood he would not have become so temperamentally bellicose. In 1927 Richards undermined Aldous Huxley's reputation by describing him as the freshman's philosopher. There was originally an economics section in 1921, which was inevitably addressed by Maurice Dobb on 'The Decline of Capitalism', and heard a celebrated paper by Mrs Braithwaite and Joan Robinson, a young Girton economist, in which the joint authoresses retold the story of Beauty and the Beast in orthodox economic jargon with much reference to margins and increments. By the end Beauty and the Beast lived happily ever after, 'constantly keeping in mind their higher ideals and maximizing their satisfaction by equalizing the marginal utility of each object of expenditure'. But this was eventually hived off in 1927 to become the Marshall Society, an altogether more serious affair.

Perhaps the greatest Heretic of all was J. B. S. Haldane, in whose complex and fascinating personality the capacity to outrage contemporary canons of respectability was surpassed only by his brilliance as a biochemist and, in later years, hi devotion to the Communist cause. An Eton scholar with a first in mathematics and another in Greats at New College, Oxford, he became an officer in the Black Watch and was described by Haig as 'the bravest and dirtiest officer in my army'. Like Wittgenstein on the opposing side, Haldane clearly enjoyed the war. He was soon afterwards to make a great name for himself as a biochemist despite the fact that he never had a science degree. Gowland Hopkins offered him a readership in biochemistry and Trinity gave him a bed and dining rights. During the ten years from 1923 when he held that post not infrequent attempts were made by his supporters, notably Adrian, to secure his election to a fellowship. Any such efforts were effectively frustrated by Haldane's habit of discussing the most intimate details of his life in his booming voice in the hearing of everyone at High Table. On one occasion, Adrian was convinced that prospects were at last looking bright, only to observe with dismay that Haldane, hurrying into dinner from his laboratory, had brought into Hall with him a gallon jar of urine, forming part of his current experiment, which he had placed on the table amid the college silver.

It was not only the college authorities of whom Haldane fell foul. In 1924, he fell in love with a clever and unhappily married young Fleet Street journalist Charlotte Burghes. Haldane never kept such matters to himself. William Bateson, director of the John Innes Horticultural Institution once commented in exasperation: 'I am not a prude, but I don't approve of a man running about the streets like a dog', and C. D. Broad delivered himself of the aphorism that Haldane was never a man not to blow his own strumpet. Neither Haldane nor Charlotte, his future wife, had any doubt about the rectitude of their plans to secure a divorce for Charlotte from Mr Burghes, who, according to statements later made in court, did not work to support his wife and child, lived on his wife's earnings as a journalist (some of which he spent on an actress), gambled, drank, pawned her jewellery and refused to provide her with grounds for divorce. Consequently, it became necessary under the prevailing divorce law for Haldane and Charlotte to commit adultery in an overt manner, which they did. In December 1924, before the divorce proceedings, Haldane had told both his professor, Sir Frederick Gowland Hopkins, and the Vice-Chancellor, A. C. Seward of Downing, of his intention to commit the necessary adultery. Hopkins thought it a pity but made it clear he did not wish to lose his outstanding assistant in the biochemical laboratory. Seward was said by Haldane to 'have hummed to some extent' without committing himself one way or another.

On 28 October 1925 Seward wrote to Haldane:

A meeting of the Sex Viri was held today and as the meeting was not a full one it was decided to hold another next week. It is only fair to you that I should tell you that the clearly expressed opinion of the members present leads me to advise you, in your own interests, to resign the readership.

Should you be disposed to take this course the usual method is for you as Reader to inform me as Vice-Chancellor that you wish to relinquish your office.

I wish to make the situation clear. If you resign, the resignation would take effect as an ordinary resignation. If, on the other hand, you prefer to leave the matter where it is and the Sex Viri should decide on deprivation their decision would be published in the Reporter.

The Sex Viri comprised, as the name implies, six senior members of the University, Pearce, Master of Corpus Christi, Lord Chalmers, Master of Peterhouse, Henry Bond, Master of Trinity Hall, described by Benson as 'a very peaceable and kindly Master, not emphatic or impressive' and three professors of Law (C. S. Kenny, W. W. Buckland and H. D. Hazeltine) under the Vice-Chancellor. Their function was to act as the ultimate guardians of morals and discipline in the university. At this meeting none of the lawyers was present (Kenny indeed being confined to a nursing home), which perhaps explains why they made the disastrous mistake of proceeding as far as they did without hearing Haldane's side of the case. On 6 November Haldane did appear before them and defended his actions on the ground that the divorce had been in the best interests of Charlotte and her child. On 12 December the Sex Viri met again in Kenny's nursing home. Pearce proposed, and Chalmers seconded, a motion depriving Haldane of his readership on the ground that he had been guilty of gross immorality within the meaning of the University Statute B, chapter XI, section 7.

The fat was now in the fire. To begin with, Haldane had a right of appeal and proposed to exercise it. Secondly the sentence which had been passed, combined with the wording of the statute, would require the appeal tribunal to uphold the judgement that Haldane's action had been in fact tantamount to *gross* immorality. Nothing short of gross would do.

Procedurally, the Council of the Senate now had to nominate five Judges Delegate (two with legal experience), who then had to be approved by the Senate. Seward's correspondence at this moment reveals signs of haste, if not panic, accentuated by the fact that he had no great confidence in the university's solicitors, whose senior partner 'is not always up to date; he declined to have a bathroom in his house for some time and I do not know that he has one even now'. Keynes produced a list of six nominees, including G. M. Trevelyan and Sir Charles Darwin, none of whom was selected. Eventually, the following names emerged: Sir William Bragg, Sir Walter Morley Fletcher of the Medical Research Council, J. J. Withers, MP for Cambridge, M. R. James, Provost of Eton (who wrote 'it is a most unpleasant job and one of a kind of which I have no experience') and as president, the celebrated 'hanging judge' Mr Justice Avory.

They met in London on 17 March 1926. Haldane's counsel was Stuart Bevan KC. He called as witnesses Hopkins and Haldane's father, himself a very eminent scientist. The university was represented by Sir Malcolm Macnaghten KC, MP. Bevan sought to establish that Haldane was a good influence on the girls in his laboratory and that Hopkins considered his own daughter was not at risk in Haldane's company. He read out in court a testimony from Littlewood, the Trinity mathematician, to the effect that it must be obvious to anybody that Mr Haldane was a man of very wide ability and that Cambridge was quite obviously the proper place in which to develop it. The main burden of the defence, however, rested on the concept of gross immorality. 'Gross immorality, in my submission, imports something other than mere immorality . . . Every co-respondent is immoral; it is not every co-respondent who is grossly immoral.' Macnaghten had, of course, to argue a contrary view: 'The offence that Mr Haldane committed was the offence of adultery, and the submission I have to make is that adultery must always be gross immorality.' Rather elaborately he developed the theme that there can only be one standard of morality in these matters, equally appropriate to a reader in biochemistry as to a professor of moral philosophy or to a professor of divinity. He imagined an undergraduate 'caught in the toils of a woman, and brought up by the Proctor, the Proctor reprimanding him, and the young man saying: "I am not so bad as 'so and so'. After all, I was only going to commit the offence of fornication. The professors and readers of the university can commit adultery without rebuke." '

The tribunal was out for fifty minutes and returned the verdict 'That the majority of the Court is of the opinion that in view of all the circumstances of this particular case, which have been more fully before us than they were before the Sex Viri, the appeal should be allowed; but this decision is not to be taken as any expression of opinion that adultery may not be gross immorality within the meaning of this statute.' Kenny wrote to Seward that the decision surprised him greatly and Seward, after visiting the solicitor, wrote 'I saw Francis today in his kitchen-midden; he did not tell me anything fresh but said that in his opinion Avory, Bragg and Fletcher were the majority.' Haldane returned to his biochemistry and he and Charlotte lived happily for some time after, setting up a progressive salon at Roebuck House, Old Chesterton, unkindly described by Malcolm Lowry as 'Chaddy Haldane's addled salon'. Visitors tended to get a disagreeable surprise from a large white cat which Haldane had trained to jump unexpectedly on to their shoulders from a door-top.

The first issue of the *New Cambridge* in January 1919 proclaimed confidently: 'The life of new Cambridge should differ but little from the old. There is not much to be altered. It must be more strenuous. It must be more serious, in many ways, than it was before. It must be more progressive.' By November 1920 a note of editorial disquiet on the part of A. V. Burbury of King's is discernible: 'There are various small cliques which we won't mention, who know just the strings to pull to spread their propaganda – several for ragging, one or two definitely political, one ultra-intellectual circle for a most skilful form of Soviet subversion. They don't amount to much really; but they will continue to be a nuisance as long as people will follow on without asking themselves in each case the question they can always answer: "Is this one of the things that's not done?" . . . If only there were someone like the Prince of Wales here, someone whom we could all watch and all would imitate – to show us the immense number of things that *can* be done; and the few that simply *cannot*!' Certainly, when that mercifully inimitable character the Prince of Wales did pay the university a visit in May 1921 he received a vociferous welcome – 'We enjoy flag-wagging and we wagged flags to our hearts' content; we enjoy shouting insanely, and we shouted all day with the limitless gusto of a well-fed and conquering army.'

Instincts of this sort are inseparable from an illiberal or actively hostile attitude to those excluded from the herd. In 1925 two Indian tennis stars, D. R. Rutnam and S. M. Hadi, were both turned down for the captaincy of the university team, which should have gone to one or other of them in point of ability and seniority, on the ground that there was 'an unwritten law that gentlemen of colour should not be elected'. Both refused to play that season and *New Cambridge* commented under the headline 'A Disgraceful Situation' – 'This colour snobbery is much too frequent in Cambridge and is only a sign of ill-breeding.' Yet the next year a film critic in the same magazine was guilty of the most crass anti-Semitism – 'I never have liked Jews and I never cared for the productions of Carl Laemmelle; but at the end of *His People* I respected the chosen tribe with reservation and revered Mr Laemmelle. The film was excellent and its proof lay in the manner in which the producer succeeded in making us enjoy the film, unfettered by racial prejudice.'

There was no lack of emphasis on the purifying and en-nobling qualities of team sports as an agent of moral rectitude. Benson was much incensed at the reluctance of the President of his college, A. S. Ramsey (father of Michael and Frank), to allow the handsome cricketer E. W. Dawson to play for Leicestershire in term-time, so as to enhance his confidence – 'Ramsey is rather absurd about it all – fears we shall lose our reputation for strictness if we give him any rope. He won't see that to have a thoroughly good and delightful boy here in the Cambridge XI is worth more than any repute for strictness. He won't or can't face facts.' 'Old Timer' thought that even if you were no oarsman you were a poor fellow if you didn't produce a police rattle and run alongside your college boat in the Lents. We learn in 1920 that 'in Pembroke there is a large element of hearty athletic "Public School Products" and the attitude towards them is shown in the fact that some of the best rooms in the college have been allotted as a "Blues' Staircase", but, however one may look at the question, no one can deny that just this type is one of the most valuable solid elements, here or in any place, and it is in this type that the backbone of sound English horse-sense is found in British public and private life.' R. A. Butler of Pembroke was once tackled from behind in broad daylight and brought to the ground in one of the college courts by a valuable solid element. As to horse-sense, a racing correspondent commented on the 1925 undergraduate point to point at Cottenham: 'bad language – and we regret to report that some of it was very bad – is not one of the aids to getting a horse over a jump.'

Fortunately, the quality of Cambridge athletics in the twenties, linked to some extent with the number of undergraduates who were not required to take honours degrees, was a great deal more impressive than the inept moralizing to which it often gave rise. So impressive in fact that throughout the inter-war years games-playing captured the imagination and loyalty of a great many undergraduates and dons alike, but without usually reaching the level of organized mania found in many American universities. However, rowing was something of an exception. In the early twenties the custom prevailed in Downing that nobody could get up from dinner in Hall until the President of the Boat Club had finished his savoury sardine. In 1924 when Rutherford gave a talk in St John's on atoms and their structure 'the Lady Margaret Boat Club ten o'clock law saved the lecturer from the usual cross-examination'. 'No special ritual' was followed at Jesus Boat Club meetings except that 'when a certain toast is proposed after a club dinner in Little Hall, the members turn to the east to drink it, facing a portrait. It is a portrait of Steve Fairbairn.' Fairbairn was the legendary rowing coach of the period.

The advent of the new technology threatened at one point to add a regular Oxford versus Cambridge air-race to the contests already conducted on land and water. The first and last race took place in July 1921 when three SE5 planes with light blue tails and three with dark blue set off from Hendon aerodrome for a race of 140 miles round a triangular course taking in Harrow, Epping and Hertford, whose unsuspecting inhabitants had not been warned. The proceedings were conducted at 120 miles per hour at 100 feet. The last circuit was described as a most unpleasant affair, a confused mixture of roaring engines and shrieking wires with everyone's engines 'racing far beyond the safety mark and pouring out hot oil and steam'. Cambridge had the first three past the post with W. S. Philcox of Caius the individual winner. N. Pring of New College 'did not finish', but there seems to be no record of where he landed.

Notwithstanding the extent of what was called at the time manly endeavour, change was in the air. By 1925 the *New Cambridge* even had an editorial recording a decline in athleticism to the extent that 'it is even possible to prefer Correggio to cricket and hold one's head up'. A novel of the period, *Break of Day* by Ian Macartney, while not flinching from the true rigour of the cult of manliness has certain undertones suggestive of a slight trembling of the upper lip. A characteristic pice of dialogue runs:

'Hello, Dixie! Good blind at Oxford?'

'Marvellous, thanks awfully.' Dixie could give a peculiar, thrilling value to the word 'marvellous'. As he said it now, it suggested cocktails and caviare and rivers of champagne.

'Good. By the way, you can take your hockey colours. Congrats, and that. I'm just going over to put up the notice.'

Shy and awkward, they shook hands in the dark passage. 'Thanks awfully, old thing!' (What the hell did one say at such moments?)

'Does that mean I'm allowed to wear one of those jolly blazers?'

'That's right' said Guy. Very British and unromantic, thought Dixie.

It was the opinion of *The Cambridge Review* in 1919 that a few fines would soon dispel the 'unwholesome' notion that untidiness is the sign of a 'sport'. Not only was the wearing of a gown without a cap seen as 'a repulsive practice', but it was becoming more and more difficult to find anybody prepared to wear anything on their head at all – 'the apparent disappearance of any form of headgear, even among the *bene*

vestiti of Jesus Lane,* is a fashion which we trust will not
appeal long to those who come from the better Public Schools'.
By the spring of 1921 the rule that gowns need not be worn in
the streets throughout Sundays was rescinded. In 1922 the
Tutorial Representatives, a blameless and indeed somewhat
conservative committee of college tutors, whose arrival on the
university scene prompted a former vice-chancellor Sir
Arthur Shipley to comment that Cambridge was gradually
passing under the rule of a Soviet government, gave much
attention to these matters. It was recorded in their minutes
that no college would allow a man to go into Hall in a brightly
coloured blazer, but that the practice of colleges differed in
respect to the wearing of knickerbockers. An unusually laconic
entry in Benson's diary sums up a college meeting early in
1923 with the phrase 'absurd strife about knickerbockers'.

Whereas knickerbockers and the grotesquely wide 'Oxford
bags' were compatible with generally conformist attitudes and
indeed became in themselves the outward manifestation of
what was known as the done thing, the early twenties saw the
emergence in Cambridge of a new type of plumage and some
much more exotic birds. Among the St John's freshmen of
1923 was the Harrovian Cecil Beaton who arrived in Cambridge
wearing an evening jacket, red shoes, black-and-white trousers
and a huge blue cravat. He started busily planning to buy for
his rooms green curtains, green cushions, green china and
tall, twisted, wooden candlesticks. As the weather got chillier,
he brightened the Cambridge scene with an outfit comprising
fur gauntlet gloves, a cloth-of-gold tie, a scarlet jersey and
Oxford bags. Soon he would be enjoying 'highly aesthetic
lunches' with his more scholarly Trinity friend Steven Runciman, whom he described as wearing heavy rings, carrying a
parakeet on his fingers and having his hair cut in an Italianate
fringe. Successively a starlet and then a star of the Footlights,
Cecil Beaton seems to have been less moved to pity and terror
than more serious Cambridge playgoers by the Amateur
Dramatic Club's *Oedipus Rex* of 1923, since he tells us: 'everyone laughed when Herbage as Jocasta insinuated himself on
to the stage. His salmon-pink gauze dress was a travesty; his

* A reference to the 'socially' exclusive Pitt Club.

bosoms had been padded as large as balloons.' Despite which, the only Cambridge theatrical club during the twenties to admit women was the Mummers, largely the creation of Alistair Cooke of Jesus. This was in part attributable to the stringent gate hours applied to the inmates of the women's colleges, which rendered joint rehearsals virtually impossible. By 1929 a *Granta* journalist was writing a weekly article (certainly not produced in Girton or Newnham), which would characteristically begin with a phrase like: 'My dears, I've gone all Gallic in the Long . . .'

A correspondent, signing himself *Festina Lente*, wrote to *The Cambridge Review* in 1919: 'We owe greatly to the proctorial system, from the point of view of morality, the fact that our two great universities are the cleanest in the world.' The Proctors who in those days patrolled the streets after dark, accompanied by their 'bulldogs' prepared to give chase to a suspected malefactor, were described in the Students' Handbook as 'taking cognisance in general of any violation of morality or decorum'. The same compendium reminded undergraduates that to be out after midnight without leave was regarded in colleges as a serious breach of discipline. T. R. Glover, a proctor immediately before and after the war, described his proctorial functions as requiring him to be 'on the prowl at night on the track of erring youth'. It was not only their nocturnal duties which they took seriously; in May 1921 the Proctorial Syndicate was much exercised as to whether persons taking their degrees should or should not have their trousers turned up. And, as can be imagined, their preoccupations intensified as the jazz age developed. The Lent bumping races were followed in 1925 by 'serious disturbances' in the town, but when the Proctors suggested that colleges should keep their men in after bump suppers, Downing complained that they had only 36 out of 140 living in college. In 1928 the Tutorial Representatives discussed disturbances in the streets after club dinners. In the opinion of the Senior Proctor the new cocktail habit with the consequential late hour at which dinners started was an important contributory factor. The truth was that the young men were often noisy, obstreperous and ingenious. Noise, a problem about which academic persons are very sensitive, was a subject of complaint in the early post-war years in respect of barrel organs or hurdy-gurdies, playing 'I'm looking for the Ogo-Pogo', or occasionally the raucous shouts of newsboys. But these minor irritants were soon drowned by the motor car. Seward told the Senate in 1925 that 'the motor habit, when it becomes an obsession, induces a state of mind out of harmony with the best traditions of Cambridge', and in that year freshmen were forbidden cars. Another trouble was that the motor car conferred on undergraduates a new and alarming mobility. In 1925 there was a vigorous discussion on the danger of undergraduate immorality being stimulated and facilitated by the use of motor cars after dark. One point of view advanced was that if undergraduates do want to go and be immoral it is at least arguable that it is better they should go and be immoral in Bedford than that they should go and be immoral in Chesterton (an adjacent village). The view of the Proctors was that 'if men who can afford motors are to be allowed to attend dancing halls in Huntingdon and Bedford without let or hindrance, then the sooner the edict which prohibits their poorer brethren from attending similar places in Cambridge is repealed the better. Cambridge may then accept the newly discovered principle that it is not the business of the Proctors to control the morals of undergraduates and come into line with the newer universities by confining its efforts to the giving of lectures and allowing its students to do as they like . . .' The thin black line was under pressure but it would hold for some years yet. Always useful in the firing line was the ever formidable Portway of St Catharine's. It was widely believed (and has indeed appeared in print) that when this former boxing blue was patrolling the streets as a proctor he repelled an attack on his bulldogs by three drunken RAF officers by felling all three and inviting the police to dispose of their bodies. For fourteen years he was either Proctor or Motor Proctor. In the last capacity he toured the streets in a Daimler on the look out for unregistered undergraduate cars.

Undergraduate ingenuity was not infrequently exemplified by elaborate jokes like the Pavement Club, which resulted in large numbers of undergraduates sitting on the ground for prolonged periods, or the perpetration of hoaxes. Perhaps the most successful hoax occurred in 1921. Many senior members of the university were invited to the Guildhall to hear a special lecture on psychic phenomena by Sir Arthur Conan Doyle. The seated audience were confronted by a blank stage and after what seemed an interminable delay, an under-graduate announced regretfully that Sir Arthur had not materialized. Not unnaturally, the distinguished audience was very angry, though their ruffled tempers were partially soothed by some undergraduates entertaining them with 'a few simple ballads'. Some four years later what purported to be the Don Cossack choir rode into the Market Square from the station on horseback. Amongst those decked up for the occasion in Clarkson costumes and false beards was the celebrated writer of film scripts T. E. B. Clarke, then at Clare, whence he departed after one adventurous year, spending his last night in Cambridge with two friends impersonating a proctor and his retinue and booking twenty members of the university for the offence of being out after dark without cap and gown. Others who achieved subsequent notoriety, after failing to secure a degree in the twenties, were Christopher Isherwood of Corpus Christi, the best history scholar of his year, and perhaps predictably Cecil Beaton, who recorded in his diary in 1925: 'Daddy didn't seem to mind my coming down from Cambridge without a degree, but he's been getting in rather a state since then.'

The Cambridge Gownsman commented unfavourably in 1926 on the annual bacchanalian revels on 5 November: 'a rag is a matter of careful organization, and not mere hooliganism. This university is a university for gentlemen.' If the word gentle-men is defined in terms of the class structure rather than in those of Cardinal Newman, this was no longer wholly true. In the two years before the war fifty per cent of the Oxford and Cambridge scholarships went to boys from the cheaper boarding schools and day schools and twenty per cent to boys from day schools charging either no fees or less than ten pounds a year. Eight hundred between the two universities matriculated as commoners on money from various local authority or private sources. A new system of State Scholarships began in 1920 and to some extent broadened the ladder of access. At St John's, fourteen out of fifty scholarships and exhibitions awarded in 1919 and 1920 went to candidates not from public schools. College scholarship funds were imaginatively used to assist the needy scholar at the expense of the rich. In Trinity as at other colleges from 1926 a £100 scholar under the new statutes could only receive £30 unless he was in financial need, and we learn from the *Annual Record* that 'the payments to be made in each case are fixed by a small committee, after considering strictly confidential information provided by the tutors'. In 1925 sixty-two State Scholarships were held at Cambridge at a cost of £14,085, of which some £6000 came from the Board of Education and the rest variously from parents, schools, local authorities and the colleges themselves.

It was still a narrow ladder, but one firmly based on a very old Cambridge tradition. The force of this can be discovered from an undated memorandum written by Giles, Master of Emmanuel just after the war: 'It has frequently been complained that the cost of education in the residential universities of Oxford and Cambridge renders access to them possible only for the rich. This was never true, and at all times the bulk of students were drawn from the sons of clergymen, doctors and other professional men whose means were often enough strained to provide their sons with a university education. At all times the colleges set aside part of their emoluments for necessitous students, but the number who could be substantially helped in this way was not large because the resources of the colleges themselves were often scanty. At all periods eminent scholars have sprung from the poorer classes. George Green the mathematician had been a miller before he came to the university, Samuel Lee, afterwards professor of Arabic, was a carpenter, Porson was the son of a Norfolk hand-loom weaver. But it was not till the County Councils began to encourage education that a large number of the sons of working men began to come to the university.'

College attitudes varied. Entry statistics for Sidney Sussex, not a college over-concerned for its 'social' image, were as follows:

Year	Number of Freshmen admitted	Public School	Non-Public School	From Abroad
1923	35	25	10	0
1925	51	33	14	4
1926	51	32	14	5
1929	51	34	13	4

At the 1924 meeting of the Incorporated Association of Headmasters the secretary stated that it was much more difficult for a poor boy to get to Oxford or Cambridge than before the war. But the St John's economist, C. W. Guillebaud, writing in the early twenties recorded that 'there has been an immense increase in the proportion of the men entering Cambridge who come up from the elementary and smaller secondary schools, as a result of the extension of scholarships given by county councils and the state'. He reveals the system at work when the admissions committee at St John's was considering a border-line candidate in the lowest part of the exhibition class. One member noticed that the candidate's father was an engine driver and that a £30 exhibition would not help much. Another member expressed the view that after all, if the worst came to the worst, he could always come up *in loco parentis* – despite which donnish sally, the necessary money was scraped together from various trust funds. The necessary money in the twenties was about £235 a year with initial expenses of £70. Spens was almost certainly right when he said in a lecture on the English college system in 1933 that at many colleges nearly half the students were in receipt of financial assistance and a considerable number wholly supported.

What then were the grant-aided undergraduates like? B. L. Manning, a Jesus historian, wrote in 1936: 'I make bold to say this after nearly a quarter of a century at Cambridge: no schools send to Cambridge better boys than the county grammar schools; no boys do better in work or later careers; no boys appreciate more the peculiar advantages of the older universities; no boys are better treated by the older universities.' H. M. Burton came up to Fitzwilliam Hall in 1920 from Latymer Upper School on a Board of Education teacher training grant of £80, supplemented by a London County Council scholarship. He was the son of a Fulham house-painter earning thirty shillings a week. In his autobiography *There was a Young Man*, he tells us that there were some thirty other boys from Latymer Upper in Cambridge, all in receipt of college awards ranging from £100 to £30, but nearly all heavily supplemented from other sources. He thus describes himself and some of his friends: 'These unpublicized, ant-like scholars, who scurry from lecture to lecture, sport their oak* in order to work, purposefully tramp to Grantchester or some other "grind" every afternoon, summer or winter, and drink cocoa or Ovaltine before going to bed, are really among the happiest of undergraduates. At last they are in a community which does not despise them for being unable or unwilling to play games, nor write them off as mad because they are genuinely interested in their studies . . . For seven years these boys rose at half past seven or earlier – by artificial light in winter – breakfasted hurriedly, gathered their books and their packets of sandwiches, and set off by bus, train or bicycle to their secondary school. At six they were home again to a high tea, and then settled down nightly to their homework . . . Whatever they do with their future they have arrived through their own toil, the sacrifices of their parents and often of their brothers and sisters . . . The back street boy who played hopscotch on the pavement, dropped his aitches and maybe wiped his nose on his sleeve, has become the civilized young man in the absurd garb of a Bachelor of Arts, kneeling before the Vice-Chancellor and receiving his passport to reasonable comfort, freedom from anxiety and a clean job under cover.' Burton recalled two of his contemporaries among the non-collegiate students at Fitzwilliam House, opposite the Museum, in the days when it was striving under W. F. Reddaway, its Censor, to become a college. One, from a very poor Liverpool home, became a colonial bishop; another, the son of a railway engine cleaner, secured a double first in mathematics and after teaching in public schools went into the City, acquiring first a silk hat and eventually a knighthood. One of the reasons why social reformers are so hostile to meritocracy is that it tends to increase respectability and conservatism.

* Lock the heavy outer door of their room.

Harold Davenport from Accrington Grammar School became a fellow of Trinity in 1932 and the undisputed leader of the British school of number theory. He was frequently heard to proclaim with vehement conviction in North Country accents 'all changes are for the worse'.

In contrast with the rigorous examination for scholarships and exhibitions, other methods adopted by various colleges for admitting undergraduates could fairly be described as idiosyncratic. We obtain a glimpse of the interviewing procedure at Magdalene in 1923 from Benson: 'We only see candidates for five minutes each and the only chance is to put them at their ease and ask them vague questions about professions etc. But R[amsey] thinks we ought to test attainments. So he says in a loud indignant voice: "How do you make chlorine gas?" The candidate stares, silently ruminates – and when he gives an erroneous answer three of the five minutes are gone.' Armitage, the Senior Tutor of St John's, who once unsuccessfully tried to borrow money from Benson, admitted Cecil Beaton, according to the latter's account, because he recalled the charm of the candidate's father and this despite the fact that the college was full.

In those days an undergraduate could be admitted without having taken the Previous examination or Little-Go. This could be attempted in October, December, March or June. Tripos candidates (i.e. those aiming at an honours degree) nearly all had this requirement out of the way before arriving, having secured the necessary credits in the School Certificate. The Little-Go required Latin and Greek or another modern language, mathematics (very elementary), slightly harder mathematics or physics and chemistry, an essay and précis and scripture or history. The first question in the mathematics 'A' paper in 1922 required candidates to find the rent of 19·57 acres of land at £2 13s 8d an acre to the nearest penny. By 1930 the Clare physicist Henry Thirkill, an immensely influential Cambridge figure, was complaining that the Little-Go was not only easier than Responsions, the Oxford equivalent, but easier than the School Certificate. Two Cheltenham housemasters thought that: 'Little-Go Latin is ludicrous. Half-wits can pass.'

If the dividing line between 'valuable solid elements' and half-wits was sometimes a narrow one, involving some subjectivity on the part of different admissions tutors, neither the hearties nor Burton's Ovaltine drinkers were necessarily the predominant element in college life. The Michaelmas Term entry of 1918 at Gonville and Caius included Joseph Needham, a product of Sanderson's Oundle, biochemist and sinologist, who would one day hold the Chinese order of the Brilliant Star, and be Master of the College; A. B. Cobban, a great historian of France; R. Cove Smith, an outstanding rugby international, who became a celebrated paediatrician; Hamish Hamilton, the publisher, who stroked a British Olympic crew; two notable Olympic athletes in Harold Abrahams and H. B. Stallard, who became Hunterian Professor of the Royal College of Surgeons; a future star of the musical comedy stage, Claude Hulbert, and a notable radio producer Eric Maschwitz; and G. F. Hopkinson, perhaps the most daring and original paratroop commander of the Second World War, dropped into the sea off Sicily and picked up by a boat commanded by a fellow member of the Caius First VIII.

The Cambridge of 1919 differed radically from that of 1930 in matters of literary and aesthetic taste and feeling. In 1930 honorary degrees were awarded to Barrie, Masefield and Galsworthy, but by that time all three were very much *vieux jeu*, as far as the intelligent and/or fashionable young were concerned. Indeed, by 1924 Benson had laid aside *The Forsyte Saga* with the comment 'a dry, ugly book but with a lot of interesting things, but too much crowded with uninteresting people, not enough different to be so precisely recorded'. By 1929 J. M. Reeves, then an undergraduate at Jesus, solemnly pronounced the final epitaph on Georgian poetry in *Granta* as follows: 'I suppose the last word on Georgian poetry has been said a great many times, albeit one still lacks a succinct formula in which to dismiss it. Its main faults are that it is facile, sentimental, socially and politically non-significant, fit for people of all ages and above all popular . . . the erudition and obscurity of the poetry which is now considered good in Cambridge have at least this in their favour, that they are bound to limit the circle of a poet's real admirers.' The age of

exclusivity had arrived with a vengeance. F. L. Lucas, reviewing T. H. White's undergraduate poems that year, felt
that the cackle about Art going on in the University was
enough to break the voice of a nightingale.

Yet, less than ten years previously, *The Cambridge Review* had
written of Flecker's *Hassan*: 'it would be hard to find a more
impressive piece of dramatic literature in modern times' and
Cecil Beaton had found *Dear Brutus* 'too tragically beautiful,
all so fresh, spontaneous, polished, intricate . . . I walked into
Leicester Square with tears on my cheeks'. In 1922 *The Cambridge Review* noticed the emergence of a new literary quarterly,
containing what it loftily dismissed as several pages of 'what
is presumably intended for poetry by Mr T. S. Eliot'. Basil
Willey, then a young English lecturer, wrote of the early
twenties: 'Of the major corrosives of the century, of Marx and
Freud, for example, hardly more than a soupçon had as yet
trickled through into our fool's paradise. I shall never forget
the amazement, the incredulity, with which I first heard from
one of my own pupils (who was a Communist or about to
become one) that a poem, an image, an emotion or an ideal
could be bourgeois . . . I remember what a joke we all thought
it when Ernest Jones psycho-analysed Hamlet . . . I can hear
Q's snort to this day.' Willey recalls his colleague Tillyard
casually observing at the end of a walk round Grantchester
that there was a new chap called T. S. Eliot for whom one
should be on the look-out.

The development of critical attitudes towards Ronald
Firbank was symptomatic. An early post-war *Granta* reviewed
Valmouth with a mixture of puzzlement and moral indignation
as 'a book with a strange nastiness, and the nastiness is so
elusive, being so overshadowed by vivid characterization that,
though I tried hard, I could not piece it together . . . Mrs
Thoroughfare's son, a naval officer, marries a negress. I
imagine Mr Firbank has better information from the Admiralty; for I am certain that an N.O. and a black wife would
not be tolerated nowadays by My Lord Commissioners . . .
This book will not enhance the author's reputation. It is hard
to find a descriptive word, but I think "unhealthy" is sufficiently near.' In 1928 the same review column held *Prancing
Nigger* to be a 'pretentious, pleasing booklet' and in 1929

praised *The Flower beneath the Foot* as 'a chic and sensuous cadenza'.

Another reviewer, generally ahead of his time in 1922, was loud in praise of *Ulysses*, although warning his readers that 'it is untrue, however, emphatically untrue, that the book is of use to the pornographic reader'. That D. H. Lawrence had not yet been universally accorded his later Cambridge status as a major prophet is attested by an irreverent 1927 reviewer who quoted with derision, perhaps not wholly unjustified, the following sentences from *Glad Ghosts*: 'The Colonel's breast is white and extraordinarily beautiful, Mother, I don't wonder poor Lucy yearned for it, to go home into at last. It's like going into an orchard of plum-blossom, for a ghost.'

By 1926 the battle against J. C. Squire and what would now be called the literary establishment was well and truly joined. For James Smith of Trinity, Squire's criticism was a matter of picking holes in gossamer, rumpling Aurora's bed, crushing butterflies and pilfering from angels. He had no weapons left, thought Mr Smith of Trinity, to 'hurl against a rising hostile army'. By the end of the twenties the rising hostile army among Cambridge undergraduates had divided itself into two camps, themselves engaged in mostly friendly rivalry. Two *avant-garde* literary magazines made their first appearance in the autumn of 1928.

The less iconoclastic of the two was called *The Venture*. The editors were Anthony Blunt of Trinity and Robin Fedden and Michael Redgrave of Magdalene. Redgrave would win great praise during his Cambridge stage career in the roles of Edgar, Prince Hal and Captain Brassbound under Rylands' direction, but he also wrote a great deal of verse and in 1930 delivered a paper on the desirability of poetry being obscure to the Kingsley Society in Magdalene, a club which discussed topics as wide-ranging as the ataraxy of the cultured Chinee, or, under the stimulus of Michael Ramsey, the sentimentality of the English hymnal. Apart from Redgrave, *The Venture*'s poets included Blunt's old school friend at Marlborough Louis MacNiece, John Lehmann, and Cambridge's new importation from Bloomsbury, Julian Bell, son of Clive and Vanessa. Bell contributed in particular a long and brilliant poem in Drydenesque couplets entitled: 'An epistle on the subject of the ethical and aesthetic beliefs of Herr Ludwig Wittgenstein (Doctor of Philosophy) to Richard Braithwaite Esq. MA (Fellow of King's College)', which still repays students of the Wittgenstein problem posed by the lines:

> In every company he shouts us down
> And stops our sentence stuttering his own;
> Unceasing argues, harsh, irate and loud,
> Sure that he's right and of his rightness proud.

It concludes:

> Ah Richard, why must we, who know it vain,
> Seek value through this tortured mass of pain;
> Who so easily in matter find
> Every delight of body and of mind.
> I pity Ludwig while I disagree,
> The cause of his opinions all can see
> In that ascetic life, intent to shun
> The common pleasures known to everyone.

Anthony Blunt instructed Cambridge taste on the Gothic revival, the delights of Johann Michael Fischer and Bavarian rococo, and the work of Brueghel, only lately considered a quaint painter of peasant customs.

The last number of *The Venture* in 1930 held out a hand of friendship and reconciliation to its more fiery rival *Experiment* by including two of *Experiment*'s most controversial contributors, William Empson and Malcolm Lowry, so that 'the cacophony between the horns of elfland and the furious klaxons' might abate. Empson's 'Sleeping out in the Cloister' described how

> The creepiness of Cambridge scenery
> In the same way, consists in having trees
> And never, from any view-point, looking 'wooded' –
> What was once virgin forest in safe hands.

Lowry's piece, which one might describe as maritime Joycean, displayed his usual acuity of vision: 'The barmaid with long fingers, refined and sensitive, mopped the swimming bar with a slobbery rag which she wrung out into a bucket.'

In an earlier number of *Experiment*, Empson had first published his celebrated poem 'Camping Out' with its dramatic opening line 'And now she cleans her teeth into the lake.' Other contributors included T. H. White, Humphrey Jennings, the film producer, Richard Eberhardt and Kathleen Raine, who concluded one of her poems somewhat emphatically as follows:

> Does he know that my thoughts are crouching spider-like,
>   with cold glittering eyes lest his pursue?
> No, no, no, no, no, no.

Prominent also among this group were Hugh Sykes Davies, soon to be a fellow of St John's, who found that the only place in which it was possible to supervise Lowry was in a pub, and the Jesus scientist Jacob Bronowski, who was an assiduous Cambridge journalist and a highly ambitious versifier. One of his contributions (*The Venture* No. 2) strikingly testifies to the pervasive, if possibly unconscious, influence of Eliot. It begins:

> We have come to the latter season of the year
> When kingdoms tremble

and ends

> Let us be patient, that have no certainty
> but of the end, and steady fetlocks treading.
> Keep us from fear
> turn us to this last penance
> we are dry, we are brittle crackling brass:
> let us retire from the public streets
> and pray in winter.

As Empson, a scholar in mathematics, observed, 'modern lines are finite, though unbounded'.

In music, in art, in drama, the speed of change was similarly vertiginous. Sir Charles Stanford was still Professor of Music in 1924, having held the chair since 1887. But there was no Music Tripos until 1945, and in 1920 he only turned up for four afternoon lectures a year and was non-resident, which was not surprising as he enjoyed a stipend of only £200 a year. Stanford considered that the truest test of all the best musical composition is 'the unconscious but inexorable emotion which we British call water down the spine', a point of aesthetics readily communicable to a generation much given to cold baths. In the college chapels we learn that Gray in A, Noble in B Minor and Macpherson in G were the general favourites immediately after the war. J. B. Priestley, turning an honest penny as a music reviewer, described a 1921 popular concert at the Guildhall, in which 'Miss Adela Verne began with a dashing Chopin scherzo, but before she had finished, she was rattling off patrols, imitations of old music boxes and what not, to the great delight of her audience . . . Mr Fraser Gange, who began with a capital rendering of "The Two Grenadiers", [the party piece of the philosopher G. E. Moore], moved all hearts with "Sands of Dee" and Tosti's "My Dreams".' Priestley saw no reason why persons 'who would shrink from describing themselves as music lovers should not visit and enjoy this series of concerts'. Yet a more professional critic, the poet W. J. Turner, was able to say by 1922 that in his view Cambridge was the most musical town in England.

If this was true, it was largely the work of Cyril Rootham of St John's, who had become conductor of the Cambridge University Music Society (CUMS) in 1912, and E. J. Dent, who succeeded first Stanford and then Charles Wood as professor in 1926. Under Rootham, CUMS performed Purcell's *Fairy Queen* in 1920, its first performance as a stage work since the end of the seventeenth century. In 1925 came Handel's *Semele*, hitherto not played as an opera, but as a secular oratorio. All but one of Rootham's orchestra for this performance came from Cambridge. On the last Sunday of the Lent Term of 1925 undergraduates found themselves 'weighing up Palestrina at Christ's against Mozart and Borodin at Queens'.' In 1929 came the first English performance by CUMS of Honegger's *King David*. In the second number of *The Venture*, Dent wrote that the progress of music needed leaders, both as

Girton undergraduates in 1921

The General Strike 1926. Undergraduates of Queens' College driving a tram in Hull

composers and listeners, and Oxford and Cambridge, he thought, were, as they ought to be, the main breeding ground of these leaders. Some of them would congregate in deckchairs at the Informal Music Club, presided over by one of Cambridge's two great *salonnières*, the kindly Mrs Gordon. Her rival, Mrs Prior, provided better wine, and the musical entertainment, as befitted the wife of a professor of French, might include Mrs Prior singing 'l'heure exquise' and a Mr Moncrieff's rendering of Grétry's 'O Richard, O mon Roi'.

The transition in taste from Sir William Orpen to Picasso was more rapid still. An exhibition of modern art in King's Parade which included works by Sickert, Paul Nash, Mark Gertler and Duncan Grant earned a decidedly lukewarm notice – 'on the whole the exhibition is rather pathetically disappointing; it represents so many hopeless and befogged aspirations, and is so little aware of the glorious clarity it might have revelled in. We feel that modern art is in crying need of sentiment. At present its nearest approach to any such thing is a cynical introspection, that welcomes ugliness for its own sake.' The Cambridge-Bloomsbury nexus, with Roger Fry a frequent visitor, was particularly influential in creating new canons of taste, although entrenched philistinism in many of the public and grammar schools (at St Paul's the 'drawing' school served as a detention centre) was a severe handicap to overcome. Undergraduates continued to decorate their rooms with reproduction hunting prints and magazine pictures of Bugatti racing cars. A notable evangelist of the *nouvelle vague* was Gertrude Stein, who from time to time addressed select gatherings of undergraduates. Sitting very four-square in her heavy tweed skirt, her legs well apart, with Alice B. Toklas crouched at her feet looking sharply corvine, she would proclaim that Picasso was the only *real* artist (with the exception of Beethoven), in that all the others allowed a measure of intellectualization to come between the molten inspiration and the finished product.

An article on architecture in *The Cambridge Gownsman* in 1926 recorded with satisfaction that 'gone at last are the crockets, finials, cusps, canopies, traceried windows, perforated ridge tiles, and the wealth of spikes and architectural extras which clothed the monumental edifices of our Victorian ancestors'.

If Cambridge architecture in the twenties had in theory thrown over the old, it had not yet in practice discovered the new. There was much strenuous building in the vicinity of Downing to accommodate the increased demands of the natural sciences – biochemistry (1924), pathology (1927) and the pale purple brick Low Temperature Research Station (1928). Sir Nikolaus Pevsner dismisses it all sadly in the phrase: 'a great chance of generous planning for the laboratories and institutes of a modern university has been missed'. There were some skilful developments at Jesus; Magdalene was expanding felicitously across the street with Redfern's adaptation of whitewashed brick houses for collegiate use; less successfully, Peterhouse's new wing might, in Pevsner's view, have made a good post office. Rapidly approaching completion were two large collegiate buildings, both expressing the confidence and solidity of a proud imperial present – Lutyens' Benson Court at Magdalene and Sir Giles Gilbert Scott's very handsome Memorial Building at Clare, its view to the west soon to be foreclosed by the vast mass of the same architect's University Library.

The English in the twenties had an inordinate passion for dressing up. Cambridge did this to considerable dramatic effect and by no means everybody shared Charlotte Haldane's view that an atmosphere of infantile cleverness, of 'cute' puerility, of archness and self-conscious precocity was inseparable from Cambridge amateur theatricals. To begin with, Sheppard's Greek drama and Frank Birch's ADC productions set an early post-war pace. Birch, a fellow of King's and later a professional producer, drilled his actors with an almost Prussian precision, but Sheppard varied his interpretation with every rehearsal and on one occasion instructed an athletic Old Etonian Cassandra to perform first like a flame and then like a lily. In a triennial series from 1921 to 1930, comprising the *Oresteia*, *The Birds*, Sophocles' *Electra* and the *Bacchae*, Sheppard and his collaborator J. Burnaby of Trinity, later Regius Professor of Divinity, won considerable acclaim. Soon after his arrival in Cambridge George (Dadie) Rylands had a great *succès d'estime* as Electra, and shortly afterwards in 1924 as the Duchess of Malfi. Benson, much devoted to him at the time, went along to see the performance, but evidently found Jacobean drama little to his taste – 'to see Rylands strangled on the stage and put kicking and mewing in a great black coffin was grotesque. Then Wormald, very limp and faint, was strangled, expostulating, and the audience laughed. Then four people were stabbed. The whole thing was sickening, and not redeemed by any art or beauty – the very motive of all this crime obscure.' Rylands continued to take the boards himself (he acted Emilia as late as 1932), but before the end of the twenties he was establishing himself as an outstanding producer at the ADC and the Marlowe Society. Of the four productions of *Lear* which he staged at Cambridge, the 1929 performance with Michael Redgrave as Edgar was perhaps the most distinguished. Other undergraduates in his productions, who later became celebrated professional actors, were Robert Eddison and Basil Bartlett.

In June 1919 the first post-war May Week revue of the Footlights Club was appropriately called *Reconstruction*. Soon the future dress designer Victor Stiebel would be following Cecil Beaton and Norman Hartnell as 'the girl of the year'. By 1929 the dramatic critic of *The Cambridge Review* was assuring his readers that 'altogether this year's Footers' show is going to be a wow'. As to the first act finale: 'The Boy Scouts' and Girl Guides' chorus has a rousing marching tune and some not unkind satire on those two wonderful national movements.'

From 1926 onwards, Cambridge drama for the more sophisticated came to mean week by week throughout term attending the Festival Theatre, successively managed by Terence Gray and Anmer Hall. Gray was an enterprising and original impresario with a black spade beard and a black Rolls-Royce, who advertised his new Festival Theatre as the most progressive theatre in England, and justifiably so. By 1929 Flora Robson and Robert Donat were acting there and Tyrone Guthrie producing. As described by *The Girton Review*: 'The stage is left bare in contrast to a few powerfully designed masses, built up of neutral coloured blocks, on which light is playing giving them an architectural quality. The whole scene is vitalized by the continual slight variety of pools of coloured light blurred and splotched with shadows. The back drop is abolished and in its place coloured lights are thrown on a plaster dome.' The stage could of course revolve. 'Players start up from their seats beside us, move about in our midst and call across our heads. The hot breath of drama is on our necks.' The repertoire drew extensively on the Abbey Theatre and on Scandinavia and Russia, the programmes were printed in white on black paper so that they could (theoretically) be read in the dark, and the Grill Room in 1928 was 'decorated in the Modern Spirit, under the direction of Doria Paston, down to the red trousers and green shirts of the waitresses'.

The habits of senior members of the University still occasionally exemplified the personal and functional eccentricity of which one reads in the works of Winstanley and E. F. Benson about earlier Cambridge epochs. Indeed, Housman once observed that having been at Cambridge for twenty years he had come to realize that it was an asylum in every sense of the word. A. J. Stevens had been elected a fellow of St John's in 1868 without the obligation to perform any particular duties. He occupied a set of rooms on the ground floor of the Third Court from 1883 to 1930 but held no college office and took very little part in college affairs. His one learned paper on 'The Repulsion of Solid Bodies referable to Radiation' had appeared in *The Engineer* in 1876. A frequent participant in discussions in the Senate House in the early post-war period was the Reverend Dr James Mayo. He invariably prefaced his contribution to debate by stating that he knew nothing about the subject in question. Living in Cambridge, he enjoyed the sinecure living of Buckland-next-Faversham from 1873 to 1920. Year after year he took Special Examinations, twelve in all, being invariably placed in the first class. In the early days of wireless he took legal action against his next-door neighbours on the grounds that they were inflicting bodily injury on him by sending rays through his person. He enjoyed pushing perambulators off the pavement, without overmuch concern for the comfort of their occupants.

Although far from demented, G. G. Coulton was decidedly eccentric in his habits. He reached Cambridge by a very unconventional route. He had taken an aegrotat degree, taught in a preparatory school and at Sherborne, Sedbergh and

Dulwich (where he took the Army Class) and had once attempted suicide. His rooms in St John's were high above the Third Court, which necessitated coal being dragged up sixty-three stone steps. On arrival, a visitor encountered indescribable confusion. Coulton's main sustenance was a special brand of cocoa from which he removed the fat with strips of newspaper. When dining in Hall, he could be seen to transfer a chicken bone for his cat into an envelope which he kept for the purpose. On one celebrated occasion he argued a theory so vehemently at a history tea-party that he emptied the contents of his cup down the corsage of a lady don dressed in white satin.

A certain acerbity of discourse is a notorious feature of higher academic societies, although Benson was over-stating the case in remarking that 'the characteristic of the place is dry pecks rapidly delivered at hard-shelled but singularly empty intellectual nuts'. A not infrequent method of discourse was that of W. H. Macaulay, Vice-Provost of King's, and the last fellow of that college to follow the old practice of keeping a horse and riding regularly to hounds – 'he would act as if the merest allusion would put *you* in possession of all he knew himself, whilst purporting to know nothing on *his* side which had not fallen under his own observation or had been related to him in the plainest language'. The classic example of Cambridge felinity, Housman's remark to Sheppard, 'I hear your lectures are very well attended, so I know they must be bad' is a pre-war one, but some of Benson's thumb-nail sketches in the diary are remarkably malicious. 'Clapham came to dinner – rather loud, egotistical, indiscreet. Disturbed at Pigou's worship of one undergrad. They are always together. The undergrad reads the lessons in chapel and Pigou who *never* attends appears in his place and the undergrads giggle . . . Clapham no doubt counts on being Provost; but will he be elected? He browbeats undergrads and is not popular with his colleagues – that eternal righteousness of Nonconformists. The strong Protestant type is very unpleasant in ordinary life, though it may be the moral backbone of the country. A man like Clapham needs culture and art, not a varnish of them, but to live a little in such things and to care about them. A man like that knows nothing of the possible beauties of life.

He was however very friendly and full of goodwill, pleased to be asked.' This can be contrasted with the description of Clapham by his King's colleague Frank Birch – 'his integrity was as firm as a rock, as high as a mountain, as deep as the sea'. In fact, Clapham and Pigou climbed happily together in the Alps in 1920, 1922 and 1924. Benson's judgement was heavily occluded by snobbery, a failing he shared with his friend, the Trinity historian of American extraction, Gaillard Lapsley. After a visit to Christ's, Benson wrote of the fellows as 'not rude, only rather bourgeois . . . rather plebeian looking men' and described the Master, Sir Arthur Shipley as 'a dumpy and unimpressive' man. His snobbishness was not however untinged with realism – 'the Etonians at Cambridge are amazingly nicer, easier, more accessible at first sight than boys from any other school – but when a stupid and selfish boy has the Eton stamp it's a bad mixture and almost accounts for class war'. Housman, to judge by the following extract from the diary, might positively have enjoyed class war, provided he was on the winning side – 'I said that a man could satisfy all ordinary human desires on £10,000 a year. Housman said: "No – it wouldn't enable him to buy slaves – civilization is built on slavery." I said: "It would practically". "No" said Housman "their souls would be their own".' The strangeness of Housman's character never ceased to fascinate Benson. 'I had a long and curious talk with Housman. He spoke of his youthful adoration of Napoleon III, and the Franco–Prussian war was a great shock and grief to him (then aged eleven). He spoke with contempt of writers as opposed to men of action. "Put Bismarck by Swinburne, Shelley by Napoleon III . . ." Housman then told me two of the most obscene French stories I have ever heard in my life – not funny, only abominable . . . What a queer creature he is – so prim, so kind, so passionate. I think he is really a very uncivilized man, wearing a mask because he is timid and unhappy.'

The rigours of donnish intercourse were still mitigated in true Edwardian style by the pleasures of the table. These could be enjoyed formally or more intimately. Benson describes a feast at King's in December 1923: 'I went with FRS [Salter of Magdalene] to King's. A great crowd. Very cordially received by Sheppard. Found myself next the Vice-Provost (Macaulay),

with Clapham the other side. I was much moved by the sight
of the Hall, remembering old feasts forty years ago. It is a
grand room. A great crowd of undergrads. We had a good
dinner but the waiting very inefficient . . . Macaulay spoke in a
high, reedy voice, quite inaudible – a most rambling speech
about Winchester notions [the boys' patois at Winchester].
The undergrads behaved badly, talked and cheered. Then
Roxburgh, Head of Stowe, made a loud, bawling, hearty
speech, rather vulgar. Then I made my little speech, but felt I
couldn't carry to the end of the Hall. My points well taken, but
it wasn't one of my best. I replied to *Floreat Etona*. R[yland]'s
golden head at the BA table, not seeming very happy. Then a
barrister MacBride spoke, hearty and effective. Then Adcock,
a most witty speech full of little personal epigrams. Too many
in fact. Each epigram had the same cadence and aroused much
laughter. The effect too much like a litany. Inge [Dean of St
Paul's] sat opposite in black when he ought to have been in
scarlet, deaf and ill at ease. Then Sir Almroth Wright [a
famous bacteriologist, described by Evelyn Waugh as a prize
bore] spoke – an ugly, heavy, rustic sort of man. A most
surprising speech . . . delivered with mournful cordiality and
much medical detail. Beautiful music at intervals. But the time
sped on and I grew very weary. A surprise was the sight of a
bulky smiling amiable man, with snowy hair, very dignified,
who turned out to be the ridiculous Crowder of my Eton days,
an infinite bore and philanderer and ugly beyond the power of
man to conceive. We didn't rise till past eleven.'

Gastronomically impressive, but mercifully less prone to
formal oratory, were the dining clubs. Of these, the Family
had its origin in a group of Jacobite sympathizers in the late
eighteenth century. In 1929 the membership comprised J. J.
Thomson, A. S. F. Gow, Winstanley, Laurence, H. F. Newall
(professor of astrophysics)* and Housman of Trinity; A. F.
Scholfield, the University Librarian, of King's; A. B. Ramsay,
Master of Magdalene; G. H. A. Wilson, Master of Clare;
Seward, Master of Downing; and H. D. Rolleston (Regius
Professor of Physic) of St John's. In that year Housman
entertained them to the following dinner:

* Newall in 1891 brought his twenty-five-inch telescope to Cambridge
and worked with it for the next fifty years.

Meursault	Huîtres de Whitstable
Goutte d'Or 1918	
Oloroso, Steinberg Cabinet	Croûte au Pot Parisienne
Auslese 1921	Filets de Sole Walewska
	Côtelettes de Mouton à la Nelson
Pommery 1921	Pommes de Terre Noisette
	Haricots verts au beurre
Romanée Conti 1921	Bécasses rôties sur Canapé
	Salade Flamande
	Rocher de Glace Mocha
	Petits Fours Sec
Cockburn 1878	Moëlle au Madère
Latour 1920	Fruits
Cognac Courvoisier 1869	Café

They all survived the evening with their faculties apparently unimpaired, although Laurence was beginning to show signs of cracking up; Benson had recorded sadly some five years previously: 'Somehow Laurence seems to me to be rather going to pieces. He looked incredibly old in his lofty rooms. But what has he to look forward to? He gave me oceans of port and champagne.' Of Laurence, Winstanley said 'to know Laurence is in itself a conservative education'.

Matters of ritual and precedence play a considerable part in the conservative education of academics. Despite New Testament injunctions to the contrary, they tend to preoccupy those concerned in Christian worship. Bishop Drury, who shortly after the war became Master of St Catharine's, a College at that time with only six fellows and no electric light, preached a University Sermon in 1924. It was followed by an unseemly exchange between the Masters of Peterhouse and Magdalene – 'Master of Peterhouse rather vexed with me for taking place of honour among heads. "Come, we must follow our seniority! I am a D.Litt and I am your senior." I said mildly that I was LL.D and so rank above him by faculty. He was much confused and cast down.' However, as Adcock observed: 'We should not be impatient of barnacles; for though they show where a ship has been, and not where it is going to, they are the accretion of experience, which is the beginning, if not the whole, of wisdom.'

Epitomizing in speech, as in life, not only the survival but the revival of a traditional, structured and ordered Cambridge, was the Oxonian Sir Arthur Quiller-Couch, of whom Basil Willey, a fervent though not uncritical admirer, wrote: 'All that he thought and said presupposed the unbroken continuity of the old Christian-Humanist tradition, the old class structure of society, the old sense of decorum, propriety and ceremony in human relationships as in literature.' He always lectured in correct morning dress, but was equally meticulous sartorially in donning a suit of emphatic checks and a brown bowler hat and brown leather gaiters for his not infrequent leisure occasions. His undergraduate following was enormous and he was a hero to his bedmaker, on whose observation: 'I can't do enough for you, Sir Arthur', he is said to have commented 'And to do her justice she doesn't.' An Asquithian Liberal and a romantic, he told the Union that the destinies of the world rested more safely on the shoulders of Antony and Cleopatra than on those of Mr and Mrs Sidney Webb and in 1922 observed: 'I believe that nowadays the true mission of the English Tripos is to preach the spirit of Greece.'

Yet it was in Cambridge English, no less than in philosophy and economics, that radical changes were already under way by the middle twenties which would revolutionize men's attitudes to society, as the work of the physicists would revolutionize their view of the natural universe. Cambridge was not wholly given over to feasting and the preservation of barnacles.

CHAPTER TWO

The Advancement of Learning

Before 1919 the University received no state aid apart from small sums doled out by the Board of Education for engineering, medicine, teacher training, agriculture and forestry. With the fall in the value of money, salaries were now absurdly low and lack of adequate pensions ensured that professors were not retiring even in their eighties. Furthermore, the desirability of expansion and at least a measure of modernization was generally accepted. Fears that the autonomy of the two ancient universities might be attenuated as a consequence of the receipt of public funds were considerably allayed by the known attitude of the President of the Board of Education, H. A. L. Fisher, enshrined in his dictum: 'The state is, in my opinion, not competent to direct the work of education and disinterested research which is carried on by universities.' Pending the deliberations of the Royal Commission set up in November, 1919, both Oxford and Cambridge were given a grant of £30,000 a year without prejudice.

The Commission, which reported on both Oxford and Cambridge in April 1922 was decidedly high-powered with Asquith in the chair and a membership which included Sir John Simon, Arthur Henderson, G. M. Trevelyan, Blanche Athena Clough (soon to be Principal of Newnham), Anderson, Master of Gonville and Caius and M. R. James, Provost of Eton (socially balanced by Albert Mansbridge of the Workers' Educational Association). It met sixty-six times and examined ninety witnesses. Re-echoing Fisher, the Commissioners emphasized that 'if there were any danger that grants of public money would lead to state interference with opinion in the universities, it might be the less of two evils that they should decline in efficiency rather than lose their independence in order to obtain adequate means'.

From the text of the Report it might appear that the commissioners were louder in praise of what they saw and heard than perhaps the true facts of the situation wholly justified, unless one is on the look-out for an occasional mild qualification. This can be illustrated if one italicizes three words in paragraph twelve thus: 'The sense of history and tradition in perfect harmony with the sense of progress and free intellectual enquiry seems enshrined in the quadrangles, courts and cloisters of *not a few* of these ancient colleges.' Of the undergraduates we read that 'most of the Oxford and Cambridge undergraduates are serious and hard working students, if not entirely divested on all occasions of the exuberance natural to congregated youth'. As to their seniors, 'a conscientiousness in discharge of duties that is perhaps sometimes misdirected, and occasionally almost excessive, is commoner than the old negligence'. The Commission was critical of the prevalent laxness about admission requirements and cunningly suggested that this might lead to future overcrowding, if the colleges were not more careful, since 'the highest type of university education cannot be provided wholesale'. A grant of £4000 a year was recommended for each of the women's colleges for ten years. A general cordiality of tone about this particular subject stopped short, however, of wilful imprudence in paragraph 194 – 'We desire strongly that Cambridge should remain mainly and predominantly a men's university, though of a mixed type as it already is'; and in paragraph 198, which roundly declared that 'the statutes of the university should prohibit the admission of both men and women as members of the same college or public Hostel'. There was only one section of the report which aroused violent general hostility. The Commissioners had had the bright idea of consulting Mr A. E. Towle CBE of the Midland Railway Hotels and Refreshment Rooms. As Professor Sorley put it: 'there is an exhortation to greater simplicity of living (which just shows how foolish the colleges were to invite the Commissioners to their feasts instead of to their ordinary frugal meal)'.

Before the recommendations of the Commission could be implemented much work had to be done on the statutes and a new Statutory Commission held its first meeting in October 1923 under the chairmanship of Lord Ullswater. The new statutes were approved by the King in Council on 1 June 1926 and came into force that October. The speed and efficiency with which they were drafted and approved were largely due to the outstanding skill of Hollond. Their general (and remarkable) acceptability is attested in the Vice-Chancellor's report of 1927 by G. A. Weekes of Sidney Sussex to the effect that 'no controversies have ruffled the surface of university life'.

Among other changes, the new statutes created the faculty system, thus reorganizing teaching, hitherto largely in the hands of the colleges. The teaching staffs of the various faculties were appointed and paid by the university and the fees charged to students for such teaching paid to faculty funds. Retiring ages and a proper pension scheme were introduced. Educational policy and the co-ordination of faculty teaching were made the responsibility of a reorganized General Board, sensibly small in numbers and elected by groups of faculties. Concurrent changes in college statutes ensured that stipendiary college fellowships were made conditional upon holders being engaged in teaching, research or college administration, and at least half of them were reserved for those holding university posts. University finance was strengthened by a new scheme of contributions from college endowments. The Regent House, comprising holders of university posts, fellows of colleges and certain administrative officers, became the effective legislative body and the political influence of the likes of Dr Mayo and Pussy Hart thereby disappeared. Women became eligible for university posts and the principle of supplementing the value of scholarships according to financial need was firmly established. Independently of any commission, Cambridge had taken a peculiarly momentous step in becoming for the first time a university of research with the establishment of the three year PhD degree in 1919. It seems probable that the driving force behind this decision was the desirability of not losing brilliant young scientists to European universities. The new post-graduate degree was not universally popular with the old guard. H. C. Darby, the first geographer to avail himself of it, was greeted in Hall as late as 1932 by Pigou with the words: 'Ah, Darby, they tell me you're doing a thing called a PhD. What do you want to do that for?'

In the early post-war period, one Cambridge discipline was itself the object of an external enquiry, the Prime Minister's Committee on Classics in Education under the chairmanship of the Marquess of Crewe. There was perhaps no great cause for anxiety with one out of ten boys doing Greek at St Olave's, Southwark and one out of twelve at Wolverhampton Grammar School. However, Asquith's Commissioners had seen fit to comment: 'The Historical Tripos has indeed carried off from classics the greatest number of its old clientele, but not possibly the best men in proportion.' Considerable excitement too had been generated by the decision taken in January 1919 by 161 votes to 15 to abolish compulsory Greek in the entrance examination or Little-Go, thus reversing decisions to the contrary taken in 1873, 1880, 1891, 1905 and 1906. Oxford, so carefree and liberal in admitting women to full university membership, followed suit only in March 1920 and by 434 votes to 359. Latin, however, remained and cannot always have held out much enjoyment to those who would have agreed with G. G. Morris of Corpus Christi that the set text for 1920, the *Captivi* of Plautus, was 'crabbed in style, full of archaic forms and frigid in humour'. Nor were all classical experts invariably tactful. The great J. W. Mackail of Oxford, described by Benson as 'a dry stick frosted at the top . . . no one less calculated to stir the waters and send young men on their way rejoicing', came over to Cambridge to give a lecture. According to *The Cambridge Review* he said: 'Latin is not only the finest mental training possible, but it is also at once the base and the standard of all knowledge.' It was reported that: 'he answered the question of the use of a little Latin very neatly. The fact that we do not all take the Mathematical Tripos at Cambridge does not deter us from learning that twice two is four'.

Amongst the Crewe investigators was T. R. Glover of St John's, ancient historian and Public Orator. He reported a vigorous clash of headmasters in the committee, with Alington of Eton concerned 'for those who fear that the bones of the majority of students will be found bleaching on the dreary road which leads through Caesar, Nepos and Ovid' and Walker of St Paul's thundering that 'no funicular railway can be built up Parnassus'. The Crewe findings can be summed up as expressing the belief that the classical scholar 'has had the advantage of studying a civilization in which many of the fundamental problems are the same as our own but present themselves in vastly simpler forms and on a much smaller scale . . . his powers of criticism are not deadened by custom, for though the ancient world took various wrong things for granted, they are not the same things as we take for granted now'. Glover, though perpetually one of the busier figures on the Cambridge scene, found time to write his *Greek Byways* (1932) which tells us how obsidian was mined at Milo; how Pythagoras forbade his disciples to eat beans; how Pytheas visited St Michael's Mount and Strabo the Bouches du Rhône; how Artemidorus wrote a classification of dreams; and how the Indian guinea-fowl shed tears for Meleager.

No doubt because of the very high quality of many sixth form and Cambridge classical teachers, numbers kept up well during the twenties. After 1921 the tripos was reorganized and numbers remained steady and even rose from 89 men and 11 women in Part I in 1926 to 122 men and 23 women in 1929 at a time when matriculation figures were static. But like the great empires it chronicled, the study of classics contained within itself elements which would lead to its own decay.

Looking back on the classics which he had read just before the war, Tillyard wrote 'literature in the Classics Tripos of those days was overshadowed by the superstition that textual criticism was the noblest kind of scholarship and altogether superior to the acts of literary assessment to which the settling of the textual question was supposed to lead'. The greatest textual critic of the day – indeed the greatest Cambridge figure in this field since Bentley and Porson – was of course Housman. It was not therefore particularly encouraging for those devoting a lifetime of unselfish scholarship to textual criticism to hear the great Kennedy Professor himself describing textual critics as dogs hunting for fleas. It must have been, to say the least, decidedly chilling to read his opinion that a scholar who means to build himself a monument must spend much of his life in acquiring knowledge which for its own sake is not worth having and in reading books which do not in themselves deserve to be read. Throughout half a lifetime (1903–30) Housman was editing the epic poem of Manilius, a Roman astrologer. We can cite two reactions to his lectures, one unfavourable and one favourable, one at the beginning of the twenties and one ten years later. F. L. Lucas found them impressive but repellent – 'the lecturer himself, immaculate in his starched linen and icy in his impassive aloofness as the Pole Star, seemed the awesome embodiment of a steely, mathematical precision [Benson was convinced that Housman was descended from a long line of maiden aunts]; but his faith that *all* knowledge was precious, whether or not it served the slightest human use, revolted me then, as it revolts me still. I imagine I might have felt the same rebellious repugnance in listening to the great Calvin preaching with inflexible yet absurd logic on predestination at Geneva. I sensed something morbid and unhealthy in this formidable ascetic pressing into his own skin the harsh folds of his intellectual hair shirt.' The impact on J. Enoch Powell was rather different. 'His face as he read was expressionless, and the effect, especially with the heavy overhanging moustache and bald cranium, was of a voice proceeding from the mouth of one of those masks which the actors wore on the Greek tragic stage. The only movement of the body likely to be observed was a quick prefatory wielding of the window pole to exclude the hated draught from above his rostrum. The lecture having been read – always precisely fifty minutes in length – he donned his mortar-board and stalked impassively back to his fastness above the Jesus Lane entrance to the repellent pile of Whewell's Court . . . The severity of Housman's presentation was the severity not of passionlessness but of suppressed passion, passion for true poetry and passion for truthfulness. For Housman textual criticism was the exercise of moral self-discipline, a lesson which I was later to endeavour to communicate in my own lecture-room at the University of Sydney . . . No one, I believe, ever heard Housman on Horace, *Epistles* 1.7.29, the passage where Bentley by conjecture restored *nitedula* (fieldmouse) in place of the nonsensical *volpecula* (little fox) of the manuscripts, without receiving the moral enlargement of a great sermon.' But as the last volume of the Manilius edition appeared, the editor himself expressed a doubt whether there would be a long posterity for classical studies. To quote Lucas again – 'one came away feeling as if one had been watching a disguised Apollo picking the oakum of Admetus – divinely, but oakum'.

One one occasion, however, Apollo not only doffed his disguise, but even struck his lyre. Walter Hamilton, later Master of Magdalene, recalls a dramatic occasion in the twenties when Housman was lecturing on the text of one of Horace's odes (iv. 7). Suddenly he began to read out his own English translation, and when he had finished the last line, stalked out of the lecture room, leaving his audience to consider the appropriateness of:

> Thaw follows frost; hard on the heel of spring
> Treads summer sure to die, for hard on hers
> Comes autumn, with his apples scattering;
> Then back to wintertide, when nothing stirs.

If there were any misgivings in the field of ancient history, they were only on the score of how best to marshal and publish the immense store of new material emerging in a field conspicuous for intellectual productivity. As Glover put it: 'it's a poor subject that cannot be brought into an ancient history lecture'. S. C. Roberts, in charge of the Cambridge University Press, was concerned in 1923 with the publication of the first volume of the *Cambridge Ancient History* (the last appeared in 1939) and considered that it had the smoothest passage of all the collaborative Cambridge histories, as a consequence of F. E. Adcock's tact and efficiency. His co-editors were J. B. Bury, the Regius Professor of History, until 1927, when he was succeeded by M. P. Charlesworth of St John's, and S. A. Cook. Cook was at this period a university lecturer in Hebrew, a subject which he had first learnt when he bought a one and sixpenny grammar, for which he had saved up, as a boy of fourteen in the year of Queen Victoria's jubilee. With his friend Giles of Emmanuel he contributed many chapters on the Egyptians, Babylonians, Hittites and Assyrians. Charlesworth, greatly loved as a tutor and teacher at St John's, was an expert on the economic history of the Roman Empire. Adcock, as we have seen, had served in the celebrated room 40 at the Admiralty during the war and had a large drawing of its famous chief, Admiral 'Blinker' Hall, in his rooms in King's, flanked by one of Housman. He became Professor of Ancient History in 1925 and held the chair for a quarter of a century. His many personal contributions to the early chapters were on Athens, but he also wrote extensively on the Roman Republic. As an editor, in the tradition established by Lord Acton in the *Cambridge Modern History*, he called in aid some of the most illustrious of Oxford and European scholars. But well before the *Cambridge Ancient History* was completed, doubts were beginning to arise whether the Cambridge approach to history, typified in these mammoth enterprises, was a desirable one. By the early thirties, Glover wrote: 'Surely it is time there was a reaction to a larger and profounder conception of History – to the study of movements and their causes rather than events and their dates – a study . . . more akin to biology than morphology, a study of the living rather than the dead.'*

If some small element of corrosive doubt was therefore at work both in regard to textual criticism and to ancient history, confidence in the educative merits of composition in Latin and Greek prose and verse was at its zenith. As F. M. Cornford, Professor of Ancient Philosophy, put it: 'the mere power of writing a dead language is in itself valueless. [A truism not always put in front of the toiling schoolboys of the period.] The chief profit gained by the attempt arises from the special effort which it entails. Complex ideas have to be analysed into their constituents. Those constituents which are relevant have to be distinguished from those which are not. For the elements so selected an adequate expression must be discovered in a language so different from our own that very few of the words which it uses precisely coincide with the dictionary equivalents in English. This process, as all know who have gone through it, cultivates the sense of style and is a good training in clear thought. Herein lies the peculiar superiority which composition in a long dead and therefore widely different language

* The *locus classicus* of the type of historical writing, against which Glover was inveighing, is to be found in the *Cambridge Shorter History of India* – 'Nasir Khan of Khandesh died in 1437 and was succeeded by his son Adil Khan I, who died in 1441, and was succeeded by his son Mubarak Khan I, and in 1442 Ahmad I of Gujerat, having failed to restore Masud to the throne of Malwa died, and was succeeded by his son Muhammad I, known as Karim.'

has over composition in a modern tongue. French or German has in almost all cases a sufficiently exact equivalent for even the most complex ideas.'

Trinity's first research student in 1895 was Ernest Rutherford, who became Cavendish Professor of Experimental Physics and Director of the Cavendish Laboratory in 1919. *The Cambridge Review* commented: 'by this appointment the great succession in the Cavendish Chair of Clerk Maxwell, Rayleigh, J. J. Thomson has been worthily maintained; and nothing more need be said'. In that year Rutherford, in his own words, 'made some experiments to test whether any evidence of transformation could be obtained when alpha particles were used to bombard matter'. The result – the breaking up of a nucleus of nitrogen – meant that man could now get inside the atomic nucleus and play with it if he could find the right projectiles. These projectiles could either be provided by radio-active atoms or by ordinary atoms speeded up by electrical machines. Four years later Rutherford told the British Association at Liverpool that 'we are living in the heroic age of physics'.

The triumphs of Cambridge physics in the pre-Rutherford years – among them Thomson's discovery of the electron – lie outside the limits of the inter-war years. It is no doubt true, and certainly frequently asserted, that even Rutherford's experimental genius only accelerated matters a decade or so. But it is not always a characteristic of genius to inspire an almost unqualified affection and esteem, such as Rutherford commanded among his colleagues in particular and in Cambridge in general. Sir Mark Oliphant, who worked under Rutherford in the Cavendish from 1927 to 1937, recorded his first impression as follows: 'I was received genially by a large, rather florid man, with thinning fair hair and a large moustache, who reminded me forcibly of the keeper of the general store and post office in a little village in the hills behind Adelaide where I had spent part of my childhood. Rutherford made me feel welcome and at ease at once. He spluttered a little as he talked, from time to time holding a match to a pipe which produced smoke and ash like a volcano.'

Lady Rutherford complained of a portrait of her husband by

Oswald Birley on the ground that it showed him with his mouth shut, whereas he was always either talking or smoking. James Chadwick wrote of Rutherford's volcanic energy and immense capacity for work: 'A "clever" man with these advantages can produce notable work, but he would not be a Rutherford. Rutherford had no cleverness – just greatness. He had the most astonishing insight into physical processes, and in a few remarks he would illuminate a whole subject. There is a stock phrase – "to throw light on a subject". This is exactly what Rutherford did. To work with him was a great joy and wonder.' He had too a considerable width of non-scientific interests, though sceptical about two contemporary Cambridge enthusiasms, literary criticism and philosophy. His strictures on the utility of philosophy once impelled a philosopher friend to tell him: 'You always were an amiable barbarian.'

It must be true of the team Rutherford built around him in the twenties that it contained the largest number of gifted experimental physicists grouped together which had ever been known. Almost to a man, they would have echoed Oliphant's verdict: 'He drove us mercilessly, but we loved him for it.' In the twenties James Chadwick, son of a Manchester railway storekeeper, who had worked with Rutherford in Manchester, was his second in command in the organization of the Cavendish and pre-eminently the director of research. Chadwick was as painstaking about guiding new recruits in a laboratory over Rutherford's office as he was in keeping a close eye on any work going on outside Cambridge which could be absorbed into the Cavendish programme. The triumphs of the Cavendish were significantly attributable to the pervasive spirit of collaboration, of which an outstanding example was Chadwick's persistent pursuit of the implications of an idea thrown out by Rutherford in a Royal Society lecture in 1920, which led to his own triumphant discovery of the neutron in 1932.

In an essay on the craft of experimental physics Blackett described what the Cavendish man of those days had to be. 'He is a jack-of-all-trades, a versatile but amateur craftsman. He must blow glass and turn metal, though he could not earn his living as a glass-blower nor even be classed as a skilled mechanic; he must carpenter, photograph, wire electric circuits and be a master of gadgets of all kinds; he may find invaluable a training as an engineer and can profit always by utilizing his gifts as a mathematician.' He cited an experimenter who was heard to complain that he had spent two days getting a leak in his apparatus so small that it would now take him a week to be able to find it. In the early twenties C. T. R. Wilson of Sidney Sussex, Reader in Electrical Meteorology, was in charge of a third year research class, insisting on its members doing experiments covering several weeks instead of the short problems which were then more fashionable. Blackett wrote of Wilson's famous invention, the cloud chamber – 'it can be said of most experimental methods that, if the discoverer had not discovered them, they surely would have been discovered very soon after by someone else. But if there had been no C. T. R. Wilson to begin experiments in 1896 on the formation of water drops in air and to achieve the first photographs of atomic tracks in 1911, physics might have lacked this superb experimental method for many years.' In 1927, as Jacksonian Professor of Natural Philosophy,* Wilson won the Nobel Prize in conjunction with the American A. H. Compton. The cloud chamber was instrumental in Chadwick's discovery of the neutron in 1932 and in that of the positron in the same year by the American C. D. Anderson. Yet as a lecturer Wilson was a notorious embarrassment. His delivery was hesitant, his voice scarcely rose above a whisper and anything which he wrote on the blackboard was virtually indecipherable.

Blackett of Magdalene, a tall and remarkably handsome young man, spent the twenties as a research worker in the Cavendish, developing, among other activities, the Wilson cloud chamber into an automatic instrument for the study of nuclear disintegration and working on the study of cosmic radiation which would eventually win him a Nobel Prize in 1948. At this period he observed 400,000 particle tracks in a total of 23,000 photographs taken at the rate of 270 per hour. He has told us in his own words how an experimental physicist

* The holder of this Chair was enjoined by the Founder's will in 1783 'to have an eye more particularly to that *opprobrium medicorum* called the gout'.

of that period went about his work in the laboratory – 'he must visualize an alpha particle moving in a hyperbolic orbit round an atomic nucleus, but he must know just at what speed the alpha particle ceases to behave like a particle and becomes, for a time, a wave, to recover its particle properties in time to make a bright scintillation on a screen. He must know that when two exactly similar particles collide the queerest things happen, to be understood neither by waves nor particles, unless the experimenter is prepared to follow these concepts into six dimensional space.' Contemplating which, it comes of something of a consolation to those who lack this sort of capacity to wander through strange seas of thought alone that a spirited debate was being conducted at the Cavendish in the twenties about the relative merits of Bank of England sealing wax and plasticine as a vacuum cement. It remains, however, difficult to understand quite what Chadwick can have meant when he said that Rutherford had no cleverness.

The room next door to the laboratory used by Rutherford and Chadwick was occupied by G. I. Taylor of Trinity, who was a scientist of extraordinary versatility, being a master in the fields of applied mathematics, classical physics and engineering science. Very much a man of action, he had been successively a meteorologist on an ice patrol in the North Atlantic after the sinking of the Titanic and an airman and parachutist in the 1914–18 war. He made major contributions to the theory of aerodynamics and pioneered important studies in metal physics and the turbulent motion of fluids. He was also an expert on the meteorology of fog.

Rutherford's skill as a talent-spotter was perhaps seen at its most spectacular in the recruitment in 1921 of a young Russian, Peter Leonidovitch Kapitsa. He was the son and grandson of Tsarist generals and had lost his first wife and family in the aftermath of the revolution. He was sent over to England by the Soviets to purchase scientific equipment and so impressed Rutherford that he was admitted to the Cavendish as a research student, being paid for some years by the Russian purchasing mission. C. P. Snow has described him as having something of the inspired Russian clown about him. He was undoubtedly an expert at getting his own way by a skilful combination of cajolery, bullying and flattery. He certainly surpassed himself in the art of flattery on the occasion when he observed to his friend F. A. Simpson of Trinity – 'Simpson, you must have led a very saintly life'. Kapitsa became a fellow of that college in 1925 and in 1929 was the first foreigner for 200 years to be elected a fellow of the Royal Society. He and his wife Anna retained their Russian nationality and from 1920 habitually took their summer holidays in the Caucasus. In the twenties he was working successfully on methods for producing magnetic fields of far greater intensity than had been previously available, using a large generator which he had acquired from the Manchester Tram Corporation. He helped Rutherford in the investigation of the magnetic properties of atoms and made great advances in the field of low temperature research. Initially, the other members of the team were inclined to be jealous of his closeness to Rutherford, but this soon gave way to a general appreciation of his remarkable gifts of intellect and character. It soon became a badge of promise for a young Cambridge scientist to be invited to attend the Kapitsa Club, which met in Trinity on Tuesdays. Oliphant recalls Niels Bohr addressing an alfresco meeting of the club: 'On a hot summer evening we moved outside to the Backs, and set up a blackboard on a slope near the river. When darkness fell, bicycle lamps were used to illuminate the board, but Bohr's perambulations crossed the beam of light, and his voice waxed and waned with the amplitude of his movements. His peculiar English floated to us like that of some disembodied spirit speaking through veils of ectoplasm. He had no sense of time, so that our limbs became cramped from sitting on the grass, and the bicycle lamps grew dim before he stopped at nearly midnight.'

Originally working under Kapitsa was another Cavendish hero J. D. Cockcroft, who joined as a rather mature research student from Manchester and became a fellow of St John's in 1928. The following year a Russian theoretical physicist Gamow, who had been working with Bohr in Copenhagen, visited the Cavendish and described a discovery which enabled Cockcroft to see the real possibility of a breakthrough in the search for the nuclear disintegration of light atoms by bombarding them with artificially accelerated protons. An Irishman, E. T. S. Walton, at Cambridge on an Overseas Research Scholarship, had been working without much success in this field in a semi-basement laboratory in the Cavendish. The joint efforts of Cockcroft and Walton in the next few years were to prove both dramatic and momentous even by the standards of the Cavendish.

Francis William Aston's pre-war collaboration with Thomson had obtained from experiments with neon the first evidence for isotopes, of which in due course Aston, a pioneer of the mass spectrograph, discovered 212. With his machine he demonstrated how much the mass of an atom differs from the sum of the constituent particles and classified the various elements into their different isotopes. A Nobel prizewinner in 1922, he was a fellow of Trinity but held no university post and was a somewhat eccentric bachelor, working in a particularly dingy laboratory, draped with discarded apparatus. He was an exception to the prevalent Cavendish ethos, in that he was no great collaborator and a rather spasmodic worker. When on one occasion as Rutherford's partner on the golf course, he drove a particularly bad shot into the long grass, the great man roared at him: 'What's the matter with you, Aston? Done a couple of days' work? You ought to have a holiday!'

Aston's training as a chemist enabled him to make a specialized contribution of a particularly valuable kind to Cavendish nuclear research. The same was true in another related discipline of R. H. Fowler, who became Cambridge's first Professor of Mathematical Physics in 1932. Fowler was a huge man of great personal charm, a golf blue and a county cricketer, who married Rutherford's daughter. Badly wounded at Gallipoli, he turned to scientific war work and one of his most celebrated papers 'The Aerodynamics of a Spinning Shell' was an outstanding contribution to ballistics. Unlike Aston, he was a natural collaborator, always ready to apply his outstanding mathematical gifts to the solution of experimental problems, and gathered round him a large group of theoretical physicists.

The triumphs of the experimental method in describing the nature of the physical world did not, however, seem quite so all-embracing to the astronomer, A. S. Eddington of Trinity, author of *The Internal Constitution of the Stars* (1926) and *The Nature of the Physical World* (1928) and sometimes referred to in Cambridge as the modern Archimedes. It was uncomfortable, and indeed almost insulting, for an experimental scientist to read: 'An intelligence unacquainted with our universe, but acquainted with the system of thought by which the human mind interprets to itself the content of its sensory experience, should be able to attain all the knowledge of physics that we have attained to by experiment.' For Eddington knowledge was objective only in so far as it lay beyond physics – epistemology is after all the key which will unlock the secrets of the universe. Eddington, the son of a Quaker schoolmaster, certainly compensated for the timidity of his social existence, which was much given over to solitary bicycle rides, by the daring nature of his speculations. He was a formidable pure mathematician and brilliant expositor of relativity theory as well as being an outstanding astronomer. The publication in 1928 of a paper by Dr P. A. M. Dirac of St John's, then aged twenty-six, on the wave-equation of the electron set Eddington off on the task of linking relativity, hitherto largely related to astronomy, with quantum mechanics, mostly the concern of atomic physics. In 1921 Eddington wrote: 'it is one thing for the human mind to extract from the phenomena of nature the laws which it has itself put into them: it may be a far harder thing to extract laws over which it has had no control. It is even possible that laws which have not their origin in the mind may be irrational, and we can never succeed in formulating them.' He was inclined to hold to that opinion. His undoubted eminence as an astronomer offset his activities as a metaphysical popularizer, which seemed to many to be not wholly respectable.

William Whewell, Master of Trinity, suggested in 1847 that in order to preserve the reverence of undergraduates for their professors a century should be allowed to elapse before any new discovery in science was admitted to the curriculum. Such a prescription would have been no less inappropriate for the study of biochemistry and physiology in Cambridge in the twenties than it would have been for nuclear physics. A universally revered figure of the period was Frederick Gowland Hopkins, of whom G. M. Trevelyan said: 'He might well have thought a lot of himself, but he only thought of others. And so he was loved no less than he was admired.'

Hopkins can be said to have laid the foundations of our whole modern knowledge of the biochemistry of the human body, with all the clinical applications involved. In some autobiographical jottings in 1937, by which time he was a Nobel laureate and held the OM, he wrote: 'In research I have at no time worked under or with an expert senior to myself . . . I was led at a right moment to follow a path then trodden by very few and where each wayfarer was conspicuous. It is now a crowded path on which individuals cannot fail to jostle each other.' His early career might be said to resemble a chapter from a latter day edition of *Self Help*. Brought up as a fatherless only child, he was removed at fourteen from the City of London School after a long period of undetected truancy. At sixteen he was an insurance clerk. Thereafter he spent five years as an assistant in a forensic medicine laboratory. After a London external degree and a medical qualification, he eventually reached Cambridge in 1898, at the age of thirty-seven, supervising physiology at Emmanuel as well as descriptive anatomy, which he greatly disliked. By 1914 he was a fellow of Trinity and Cambridge's first Professor of Biochemistry. In 1925 Lord Balfour opened the new Institute of Biochemistry for which the trustees of Sir William Dunn had provided £210,000. As he did so, Balfour may have remembered what he once said of scientists: 'They are the people who are changing the world and they don't know it. Politicians are but the fly on the wheel – the men of science are the motive power.'

Hopkins' pupils in the twenties were often amused by the vigour with which this essentially gentle man castigated a mysterious entity called the giant biogen. For Hopkins this was an old battle cry, recalling his early triumphs against the prevailing orthodoxy, which thought of the chemistry of the cell as something quite different to laboratory chemistry. The substance of living matter was thought to be the mysterious protoplasm – once involved in that, molecules of food and oxygen lost their identity and became incorporated in the living molecule or biogen, which made them lose their chemical characteristics. The cell, however, for Hopkins was a chemical machine, perfectly susceptible to investigation. 'I will ask you to consider whether catalysis on highly specific lines is not among the most fundamental and significant phenomena in nature.' Cell life was an ordered sequence of events governed by specific catalysts and that was to be the way forward in the study of life, reproduction, function and heredity. Already celebrated for his work on the chemistry of muscular con- traction and the discovery of vitamins, originally known as 'accessory food factors', Hopkins always derived particular satisfaction from his success in 1921 in isolating from living tissue the substance called glutathione and demonstrating its importance for oxidation in living cells.

No less than Rutherford, Gowland Hopkins was a leader of a formidable team of colleagues and researchers. Among those working with him in the twenties and attending the famous departmental tea-parties, over which 'Hoppy' presided benignly, were Haldane (1923–32), T. S. Hele, later Master of Emmanuel, Joseph Needham of Caius and his wife Dorothy (herself a fellow of the Royal Society) and F. J. W. Roughton of Trinity. When Haldane left in 1932 his readership in bio- chemistry passed to Needham. Haldane's contribution was mostly in the field of genetics, but he had a habit of experi- menting on himself in pursuit of the principles of respiratory physiology, often with alarming short-term consequences. Needham's contribution was in the development of chemical embryology and the inauguration in the department of invertebrate and comparative biochemistry, while his wife specialized in muscle chemistry. Roughton, like R. H. Fowler a scholar of Winchester, became a fellow of Trinity in 1923. He was a man of mildly eccentric habits, such as chewing his necktie while lecturing, and often presented a somewhat uncouth appearance in his shaggy plus fours. In the twenties he was working on the kinetics and mechanism of haemoglobin reaction.

Roughton was successively a lecturer in biochemistry and physiology. The buildings in which these two closely related sciences were studied were appropriately within a stone's throw of each other. The Cambridge Physiology School, founded by Sir Michael Foster in the late nineteenth century, already had a distinguished past. In the twenties a visitor might have found the professor, Joseph Barcroft, living for a week in an air-tight glass room at oxygen tensions equal to those obtaining at altitudes of 15,000 to 18,000 feet. The most popular lecturer, E. D. Adrian, was conducting brilliant experiments in electrophysiology, of which the most celebrated was derived from the minute manipulation of a single nerve fibre of the sternocutaneous muscle of a frog. From this was discovered the mechanism of the modulation of nerve messages. Much of the success of the laboratory was perhaps attributable to the fact that it boldly attacked general biological problems and only indirectly those of human physiology. Less than half the staff had had a medical training, though this was not true of Adrian.

Towards the end of the twenties one of the most spectacular of the new generation of natural scientists was J. D. Bernal, an Irishman with a Jesuit education, who was in Cambridge from 1927 to 1937. He became a pioneer in X-ray crystallography, itself a branch of physics, but of immeasurable benefit to chemistry and biochemistry, especially in the study of enzymes. Writing about chemistry in Cambridge and elsewhere, just after he had become a fellow of Christ's in 1931, C. P. Snow, whose own field was infra-red spectroscopy, summed up the position, as he then saw it, as follows: 'Our section of chemistry follows the same methods, has the same aims, as chemistry had thirty years ago. It is essential, in fact, that a lot of workers, both in Cambridge and elsewhere, should be making new and strange organic compounds, discovering their properties . . . and generally continuing research in the manner that is considered to be typically "chemical". This can yield satisfying results, both from the stand-point of appreciation and of pure scientific reasoning . . . Traditional chemistry has an essential part to fill in the wider chemistry which we now know. But it is no longer the only part. It is ceasing to be the chief part. The future of chemistry rests, and must rest, with physics.' Organic chemistry was to acquire a new lease of life, but for the moment Snow found a striking vindication of his thesis in the appointment to the new chair of Theoretical Chemistry of J. E. Lennard-Jones, Professor of Theoretical Physics at Bristol University. Snow's friend, the Tasmanian Frank Bowden of Caius, started work on a table in a basement full of dustbins in the department of Physical Chemistry in 1927 and ended his career eventually as professor of Surface Physics.

What is now known as Engineering in Cambridge came to be called Mechanical Sciences between the wars. In 1919 Charles Edward Inglis succeeded to the chair of Mechanism and Applied Mechanics, founded in the year of his birth 1875, and in 1934 became professor of Mechanical Sciences. From 1915 to 1918 the Engineering Laboratory was largely given over to the manufacture of thirteen and eighteen pounder shells and Inglis was busy designing a transportable military bridge. In 1920 there were three honours students and two others; in 1921 there were 119 taking honours and four taking specials. At the end of the war the teaching staff was six, by October 1919 it was thirty-eight. The building in Free School Lane was hopelessly inadequate, but with the aid of a gift of £25,000 from Sir Dorabji Tata, head of an Indian engineering combine, a new building in Trumpington Street was in operation by 1922. When Inglis retired in 1943 the department had become one of the leading engineering schools in the world.

It was only in 1919 that engineering had become sufficiently respectable to be allowed to run its own affairs, instead of being under the tutelage of a special Board of Mathematics. A glance at the lecture programme of the Engineering Society in 1921 suggests a technological milieu markedly different from that which obtains today – 'large bridges, grinding wheels, mountain railways, factory economics, the manufacture and use of ball bearings and the construction of electric lamps'. Inglis insisted on raising academic standards and was himself a brilliant teacher, fertile in the creation of excellent demonstration models. All his undergraduates had to take a qualifying examination in mathematics and mechanics at the end of their fourth term. Ingeniously, a substantial number decided to fail so that they could avoid the relatively exacting honours course and merely do a special, a situation which in 1924 led to there being thirty-one special and seventy-eight honours candidates. Unlike Rutherford and Hopkins, Inglis was not a leader of a research team and was notoriously critical of the PhD approach to research, though his own work in railway bridge vibration was distinguished. An interesting member of the department in the twenties was the electrical engineer E. B. Moullin, like Inglis a fellow of King's. He invented an electric torsiometer with which, as his obituarist tells us, 'he crossed the Atlantic in the liner *Franconia*, spending most of his time not in the elegant saloons but in the cramped propeller tunnels in the bottom of the ship, which even the greasers on their inspections left as soon as they could; here he tended his instruments on the spinning shafts and hoped that the weather would be severe enough for the propellers to pitch out of the water.'

Professor Max Newman of St John's, who became a University Lecturer in Mathematics in 1927, wrote of his subject that it enjoys the advantages and suffers the penalties of being a secret doctrine. Einstein began a lecture on Electricity Theory in the Framework of the General Theory of Relativity in the Senate House in May 1932 by defining his position as similar to Russell's – 'Pure mathematics is the subject in which we do not know what we are talking about and don't care.' Consequently, there is and always will be a peculiar profanity in the generalist with his heavy boots disturbing the inner recesses of this particular intellectual temple. As far as the highly selected Cambridge novitiate was concerned, the way forward was stern and uncompromising. In Part I of the Tripos in 1926 there were 120 men and 19 women; in Part II only 59 men and 16 women. Part III – the mathematical equivalent of the Jesuit tertianship – was only introduced in 1935 with 18 male candidates.

The golden age of the *Principia Mathematica* (1910–13) had passed and Russell, as we have seen, left Cambridge at the beginning of the twenties. We learn that he and Littlewood on holiday at Lulworth in 1919 would amuse themselves by discussing whether the distance from themselves to the post office was or was not the same as the distance from the post office to themselves. Littlewood began in 1912 to occupy the same rooms in Trinity which he kept till his death in 1977 and was Rouse Ball Professor from 1928 to 1950. It was often said that there were three outstanding mathematicians in Cambridge – G. H. Hardy, Littlewood and the collaborative Hardy-Littlewood. Hardy described himself as being, at his best and for a short time, the fifth best pure mathematician in the world, but considered Littlewood better. Their fruitful collaboration in the twenties had to be carried on largely by correspondence in that between 1919 and 1931 Hardy had a chair at Oxford, where he lived at New College with a large picture of Lenin in his room. A cricket fanatic, Hardy considered that the only two men in the world indubitably in the 'Bradman class' during his lifetime were Lenin and Einstein. He once travelled a considerable distance not to see J. B. Hobbs, the cricketer, batting, but to hear him make a speech.

Probably the outstanding wrangler of the vintage of 1921 and 1922, in which years he was examined by Littlewood, Taylor and Fowler, was Frank Ramsey of Trinity who became a fellow of King's in 1924. He died tragically young in 1930, having dazzled Cambridge with his brilliance in mathematical logic, economics and philosophy. His friend Richard Braithwaite collected various of his essays and fragments under the title *The Foundations of Mathematics*, about which Keynes, himself the author of a *Treatise on Probability* (1921), observed in an almost awe-struck manner – 'logic, like lyrical poetry, is no employment for the middle-aged'. Keynes tells us that Ramsey believed that conversation and argument had been more or less effectively destroyed by the nineteenth-century advance of science and the decay of religion, all the old general questions having thereby become either technical or ridiculous. This left nothing to talk about except shop and people's private lives, neither of which was suitable for general conversation. Hardy would not have subscribed to such a severe programme (any more than did Ramsey in his less cerebral moods). He once sent a postcard inscribed with the following New Year wishes: 'Prove the Riemann hypothesis, make 211 not out in the fourth innings of the last test at the Oval, find an argument that would convince the general public of the non-existence of God, be the first man to the top of Everest, be the first combined president of the USA, USSR and Germany and murder Mussolini.'

Writing in the early thirties, Max Newman described the birth of quantum mechanics in 1925 as bringing about a happy reunion between mathematics and physics after a hundred years of estrangement, during which pure mathematics had dwelt with pride on its security from utilization and even applied mathematics had found little of common interest with the dwellers in laboratories. The meeting place of mathematical and scientific minds was the Philosophical Society, founded in 1819. It was to the Philosophical Society that Dirac read his epoch-making paper on the quantum theory of the electron in 1928, the first indication of the existence of a particle other than the proton-electron pair. Among the earliest post-war presidents were C. T. R. Wilson and Seward, who as well as being Vice-Chancellor and Master of Downing was Professor of Botany, which he taught for forty-six years; and among the secretaries were H. F. Baker of St. John's, who produced four volumes of *The Principles of Geometry* in the twenties, Aston, the zoologist James Gray from King's, Fowler and Cockcroft. Yet the Philosophical Society was so poor that it had to sell off its original Audubon for £400 in 1924. At one of the society's dinners in St John's, Haldane demonstrated an efficient way of splitting walnuts without nutcrackers by employing the table as an anvil and his forehead as a hammer. In 1923 a former Professor of Chemistry G. D. Liveing read a paper on 'The Recuperation of Energy in the Universe' at the age of ninety-six.

The Regius Professor of Modern History at the end of the war was J. B. Bury, who had held the Chair from 1902 when he succeeded Lord Acton. Bury's academic respectability was impeccable by conservative standards in that he had once been a professor of Greek and had edited Pindar, as well as the standard text of Gibbon, and had produced much other work of great international celebrity. He was undoubtedly a strong formative influence on Cambridge History in the twenties and was still lecturing on the barbarian invasions. Other powerful influences were ghosts of the comparatively recent past – Acton himself, Maitland, Bishop Stubbs, S. R. Gardiner and Archdeacon Cunningham.

Acton's monument, *The Cambridge Modern History*, all fourteen volumes completed by 1912, sixteen years after its conception, was the precursor of many another collaborative Cambridge history, envisaging, as it did, some kind of definitive history, based on 'hard' facts and a more or less common view of what 'mattered most'. Acton's plan for the history tells us: 'The several countries may or may not contribute to feed the main stream, and the distribution of matter must be made accordingly. The history of nations that are off the line must not suffer; it must be told as accurately as if the whole was divided into annals. But attention ought not to be dispersed, by putting Portugal, Transylvania, Iceland, side by side with France and Germany. I wish to speak of them when they are important, and not, whether or not, according to date.' J. N. Figgis' article on Acton in the *Dictionary of National Biography* describes him as 'historian and moralist' and this affords us a clue as to exactly what was deemed to be important, for Figgis might just as well have written 'historian and Whig moralist'. The Acton tradition, however, was significant not only in the sphere of value judgements, but also in its approach to the learning and practice of history. G. M. Trevelyan, Bury's successor in 1927, spoke not only for his own generation but for all those taught in schools with an academic tradition between the wars: 'I was made to learn dates and poetry by heart, as all children ought to be while their memory is still good and retentive, instead of being stuffed with generalizations about history and criticisms of literature which mean nothing to their empty young minds.' Maitland said that he believed Acton could have written all twelve volumes of the Cambridge Modern History himself. When, as a young fellow of Trinity Hall, C. W. Crawley demurred about having to examine tripos questions in Ancient History, Laurence sternly rebuked him – 'any fellow elected in history should be prepared to lecture, supervise and examine on any subject in the Tripos'.

The medievalists with Bury at the helm had their own collaborative *magnum opus*, *The Cambridge Medieval History*. Originally planned by Bury, it grew to include many chapters by illustrious European scholars like Henri Pirenne, although more surprisingly drawing also on the services as contributors of H. J. Laski and the Communist apologist Prince Mirski, later to die in one of Stalin's purges. After twenty-six years the last volume, appropriately termed *The Close of the Middle Ages*, appeared in 1936. The editors of this volume were Z. N. Brooke of Caius and C. W. Previté Orton of St John's.

Zachary Brooke's outline lecture course on medieval European history continued term by term virtually without interruption from 1919 to 1942. At nine o'clock in the morning his lectures were to say the least educationally uncompromising. As his obituarist comments: 'No attempt was made to render them palatable by the adventitious aids to which other lecturers commonly resort.' Brooke had taken a first in classics in 1905. Previté Orton never left St John's between 1905, when he arrived as a twenty-eight-year-old freshman, and 1947. A prodigious worker, despite being blind in one eye and never particularly robust, he edited the *English Historical Review* from 1927 and was rewarded by becoming the first Professor of Medieval History ten years later. It was said of Previté Orton that History was to him a science, a technique, and medieval history the department of the historical Cavendish where he spent his days, a comment which reveals him as a true disciple of Bury, whose most celebrated doctrine was that history was 'a science, no less and no more'.

The most colourful figure among the Cambridge medievalists of the period was described by a French admirer as *ce savant Mr Coulton au visage couleur de brique, aux yeux bleu céleste*. After thirty years in the scholastic wilderness, he had come back to Cambridge in 1911, an experience so rapturous that we owe to him the most romantic description ever penned of college rowing – 'victor and loser were alike transformed; it seemed no human struggle; splendid young limbs swung splendidly through the bewildering flash of oars and the dazzle of the sun among the quicksilver eddies, while the spray splashed higher and faster as the fight became more desperate . . .' St John's made him a fellow when he was sixty-one in 1919 and the new English Tripos depended entirely on him for the period 1000 to 1500, since for a long time he held the only lectureship in that subject, as well as lecturing for the History Tripos. His erudition in all things medieval was prodigious. Apart from an unusually capacious memory, he amassed huge quantities of raw material, carefully indexed and stored in more than 300 notebooks, each of 200 quarto sheets. He was an Actonian in his belief in the importance of moral judgements in history, scorning the quest for impartiality. He allowed himself decidedly unorthodox comments such as – 'I am not greatly concerned whether . . . what I write is not, strictly speaking, history, so long as the stuff is reasonably true, and conveys to the public a reasonably clear impression of what men did and thought in the past.' In the twenties he was at work on his *Five Centuries of Religion*, the volumes of which started to appear in 1923, and *The Medieval Village* (1925). Apart from this, he missed no opportunity to engage in acrid controversy with Catholic historians as the self-appointed champion of the 'moderate Protestant position'. He probably cared relatively little if Mr Belloc's sins were scarlet, but was passionately concerned that his books should not be read. In his capacity as a lifelong advocate of compulsory national service, he regarded it as one of his main tasks to expose the pacifism of Sir Norman Angell and Lord Ponsonby.

The hereditary strain in Cambridge History, which derived from Archdeacon Cunningham, author of *The Growth of English Industry and Commerce*, came to full fruition during the inter-war years in the work of his pupil Clapham. Clapham was in a sense the intellectual progeny of a marriage of minds between Acton and Alfred Marshall, the economist. He attended Acton's lectures and until 1912, in which year he produced a book about Sieyès, he was not committed irrevocably to economic history. Professor Butterfield has recorded, however, that as far back as 1897 Marshall wrote to Acton: 'I feel that the absence of any tolerable account of the economic development of England in the last century and a half is a disgrace to the land and a grievous hindrance to the right understanding of the economic problems of our time. London and Cambridge are the only places where the work is likely to be done well; but till recently the man for the work has not appeared. But now I think the man is in sight. Clapham has more analytical faculty than any thorough historian whom I have ever taught . . . If he works at anything but recent economic history he will disobey Babbage's* canon that everyone should do that work for which all his best faculties are wanted and no other.' Marshall's prophetic vision was abundantly justified. Clapham followed *The Economic Development of France and Germany 1815–1914* (1921) with the first

---

* Charles Babbage, originator of the computer and an implacable opponent of organ-grinders.

volume of *An Economic History of Modern Britain* (1926), completed in 1938, and described by Sir George Clark as 'the most important book in the whole field of economic history'; it elicited from Trevelyan the comment: 'No more completely and characteristically Cambridge product was ever published by the University Press.' Clapham became Cambridge's first Professor of Economic History in 1928. His massive personality and imposing delivery made an unforgettable impression in the lecture room. He would enter majestically, lay his cap flat on the dais, blow his nose into a large red and white handkerchief and then place it ceremoniously inside the cap. This was the signal for the assembled undergraduates to stamp rhythmically with their feet for about forty seconds, a friendly process which would be stilled by Clapham almost imperceptibly raising his hand. What followed is described by a fellow Kingsman, John Saltmarsh: 'In his lectures, English economic history ranged from neolithic times to the twentieth century; from early man, his tools and weapons, to Roman roads and towns and villas; from British coins to fine Samian ware and tiles . . .; from Saxon conquerors with their British slaves, the "swarthy Welshmen", whose descendants had lived on, not only in Wales, to his Cambridge pupils. He would pause, glance round his audience and say: "Yes, just as I expected; every year the same; more dark heads than fair".' As a teacher he was a master of the calculated digression, whether in lecturing or supervision, sensing just when his pupils were overcome with weariness about the technicalities of villeinage or bills of exchange. Despite Benson's strictures, he was a highly cultured man, as well as an assiduous lay reader.

There was also a strong tradition of constitutional history in Cambridge, fathered by Maitland and the two great Oxonians Stubbs and Gardiner. 'Stubbs' Charters', in the form of small Latin 'gobbets', formed a compulsory *pons asinorum* for Part I candidates, much dreaded by those with only vestigial Latinity. A suggestion that early constitutional history should not be compulsory was greeted by Lapsley with the expostulation that the pillars of the house were falling. J. R. Tanner of St John's, who numbered both Previté Orton and Brooke among his pupils, left Cambridge in 1921, but his influence lived on through his books, especially his skilfully annotated collection of *Tudor Historical Documents*, in the preface of which he wrote that nearly forty years of preparing candidates for the tripos had convinced him that documents would never be properly studied if they were divorced from the history and printed in separate collections 'often only to be read up in a hurry on the eve of an examination'. That was quite certainly what tended to happen to Stubbs' charters.

We have a glimpse in 1923 of one of the most formidable of constitutional historians starting a course of supervisions with the outstanding scholar of that year in his own college, albeit not one destined to achieve conventional academic honours. 'But now here I was gowned, seated uneasily on the edge of the chair, reading my first essay aloud to my history tutor, the dreaded Mr Gorse. The subject of the essay was "Better England free than England sober" [Bishop Magee of Peterborough's comment on Gladstone's Licensing Act of 1872.] I had finished it with some pride: it exactly suited my idea of Mr Gorse's requirements – snappy, epigrammatic, a bit daring in language . . . only now, for some reason, all my effects seemed to have gone wrong; the verbal fireworks were damp; the epigrams weren't epigrams but platitudes, pompous, painfully naïve, inept and priggish . . . The last paragraph was particularly heavy going, because Mr Gorse had begun to drum with his fingers on the mantelpiece. "Yes, yes . . ." he kept muttering: "Yes, yes . . ." as though his impatience were increasing with every word. "Well", he told me when, at last, I had finished, "I'll say this for you – it's not the work of an entirely uneducated fool." '

Christopher Isherwood's experiences with Kenneth Pickthorn (Mr Gorse) of Corpus were only marginally more unnerving, though different in kind, than those undergone by the pupils of the Reverend F. A. Simpson of Trinity. Simpson's reputation as a historian was then at its height. The first two volumes of his projected trilogy on Louis Napoleon had appeared respectively in 1909 and 1923, though the world was still waiting in vain for the completion of the third volume by the time of his death in 1974. During a supervision his tall body would be elegantly draped over a sofa; and he might smoke a cigar with his eyes shut, while the pupil read his essay aloud. Once delivered, it was often greeted with not more than one comment, usually deflationary, followed by a statement of the subject matter for the following week's essay. It was widely believed that on one occasion Simpson absent-mindedly turned on the wireless while a man was reading a particularly boring essay. He always lectured on The Theory of the Modern State or The Eastern Question in the Nineteenth Century, lingering lovingly over the Turkish and Bulgarian atrocities.

Trinity in the twenties provided the history faculty with two particularly popular and stimulating teachers. D. A. Winstanley, one of the outstanding college tutors of the period, was a stentorian lecturer, who had one annual set-piece, which attained such celebrity that it was attended by crowds of under-graduates reading subjects other than history. The particular topic was the death of Charles Yorke, three days after he had pusillanimously accepted the Great Seal from George III. Amid rising excitement, the lecture always ended – 'the question is – who sent Charles Yorke to the levée on that morning of Wednesday, 17 January 1770? With that question I shall go on next time.' Much younger was George Kitson Clark, a legendary Cambridge figure for some fifty years. His great skill as a lecturer in constitutional history lay in his capacity to hold the interest of the more intelligent members of his class while making his subject matter entirely compre-hensible to the benighted and not over-zealous young men, who brought up the predominantly public school tail of the History Tripos. Something of the flavour of his personality was captured by an irreverent interviewer on behalf of *The Trinity Magazine*. 'Like all great men I was not altogether happy at school. I remember that Father Knox, then a master at Shrewsbury, said he found taking his form to be one long conversation with Kitson Clark. I took to history after a copy of verses with thirty false quantities in twenty lines . . . The most chastened day of my life, however, was that in which I was asked to become a member of the College Feast Committee, and, five minutes later, to take the part of Falstaff at a meeting of the Trinity Shakespeare Society . . . I distrust your timid eater. Breakfast is the best meal in the day, and my breakfast is always constructed round a couple of scrambled eggs. Perhaps I enjoy it most among a number of friends ready to take an interest in the bulletins of my progress which I issue from time to time. Lunch I have had to give up; I ate too much. I like dining in Hall, but as I have to make conversation for the whole High Table, I often find myself left behind.' The interviewer is then supposed to have asked whether Kitson was the centre of an intellectual circle and to have received the reply: 'I *am* an intellectual circle, shot through with a rich vein of idealism. Beneath a comparatively chill exterior I hide a warm heart.'

By the end of the thirties Peterhouse was a particularly strong college in history. In due course three of its history fellows in the twenties – Harold Temperley, Paul Vellacott and Herbert Butterfield – all became Masters of the College, Temperley succeeding Field Marshal Lord Birdwood in 1938, only to die in the following year. Temperley had written five chapters of *The Cambridge Modern History* between 1907 and 1909, was a member of the Paris Peace Delegation, edited with G. P. Gooch thirteen volumes of documents on the origins of the war, wrote a much acclaimed book on the foreign policy of Canning and was the founder and editor of *The Cambridge Historical Journal* in 1923. When his readership in Modern History was converted into a professorship in 1930, there was still no chair in Medieval History, so Temperley covered that as well. Much more a man of the world than most of his colleagues, he combined a generous disposition with an irascible temperament and could be seen at faculty meetings tearing up quarto sheets of paper into tiny pieces in order to control his rage. A more recent Peterhouse acquisition (Temperley had been made a fellow in 1905) was Ernest Barker. Barker had come to Cambridge in 1927 in his fifties, with a tremendous reputation, as the first Professor of Political Science, described at this period as 'a subject whose importance is more readily admitted than its nature defined, but in its pursuit the university may contribute effectively to the solution of the problems of the larger society' – which was certainly a large hope.

Barker was the son of a miner and an ambitious mother, who very deliberately had him christened Ernest. He was a product of Manchester Grammar School, to which institution he very properly attributed his rise from humble origins to fame and fortune, and Balliol, where he secured Firsts in Mods, Greats and History. Although he was generously appreciative of Cambridge and its scholarship, he described himself as an Oxford man through and through and said of his own lectures – 'they did not set the Cam on fire; it is less inflammable than the Isis'. The transplant was not in fact a great success. Barker recalled his disappointment when Sorley, Professor of Moral Philosophy, proposed the setting up of Social and Political Studies as a Part II Tripos subject. 'The scheme failed; neither historians, nor economists, nor lawyers, nor philosophers wanted a dubious competitor, which was all the more dubious because it might be attractive and seductive to the young.' Barker's hopes of becoming a Cambridge Aristotle, surrounded by a Lyceum of eager students, were dashed. It was his young Peterhouse colleague Butterfield, educated in the Trade and Grammar School at Keighley, who was to make a far greater impact on the manner in which historians look at politics.

Despite the esteem accorded it by the Royal Commission and its popularity with undergraduates (199 men and 29 women took Part I in 1929), history was not as yet so securely established as might be supposed. Temperley, on returning from the Serbian front and the Peace Conference, discovered that the annual grant from the university for the Seeley History Library fluctuated between £12 and £20 a year and Clare College apparently saw no need to elect a history fellow even in the thirties. The appointment to the Regius Professorship of Trevelyan in 1927 was undoubtedly of crucial importance in this respect. As a Trinity freshman in 1892 he had been told by Sir John Seeley, then Regius Professor, that history was a science and had nothing to do with literature and that Carlyle and Macaulay were charlatans. Accurately described by one of his research students, J. H. Plumb, as 'a poet at large in history', Trevelyan, during the twenty-five years which he had been away from Cambridge, had not only demonstrated that in his hands at any rate history could be great literature, but had also become a best seller and a national figure in the process. He now proclaimed in his inaugural that 'the appeal of history to us all is in the last analysis poetic.

But the poetry of history does not consist of imagination roaming at large, but of imagination pursuing the fact and fastening on it.' Seeley, Acton's predecessor, held that history was 'past politics'. Under the influence of Trevelyan (largely indirect, for he attended faculty meetings as seldom as possible) and of Barker and Clapham, the emphasis in Cambridge history would begin to move somewhat away from politics, war and diplomacy to institutional and social change. The old-fashioned 'factual' historian, even as conscientious a researcher as Holland Rose of Christ's, was becoming an anachronism. Still more so was Hadley, the Master of Pembroke, who used to summon all the history students in his college, including R. A. Butler, and subject them to a termly class on Napoleon under the impression that it was invariably vital for their prospects in the tripos.

The Modern and Medieval Languages Tripos was not one of Cambridge's showpieces in the twenties. There were indeed still to be found those who would echo Dr Mayo's view that as a 'genuine and patriotic Englishman' he thought the teaching of foreign languages futile and to be deprecated in the highest degree. Oliver Prior of St John's, Draper's Professor of French from 1919 and Chairman of the Faculty Board till his death in 1934, was immensely conscientious, as befitted somebody who had run physical education at Rugby during the war. He laid foundations on which subsequent generations have built. But he was not a literary man, his interests being essentially grammatical and historical. He was fond of quoting La Motte-Houdard – '*La prose dit blanc dès qu'elle veut; et voilà son avantage.*' At the beginning of the academic year, the freshmen, numbering some ninety, were set a prose composition. The best dozen or so were then selected for the professor's *Cours Pratique*, to which they brought their proses for criticism and dissection. Nobody was excluded, but unless you belonged to the chosen few, the professor did not look at your prose. It was wiser in that event to go to Mr de Glehn, who was *persona non grata* with the professor for recommending a dubious *Dictionnaire du Style*. In the field of French literature, the professor was hard at work on his *Morceaux Choisis*, published in 1930. There was always a good attendance in the

Great Hall of Trinity, when the Reverend H. F. Stewart lectured through a megaphone. He allowed himself, as befitted the cloth, some more than Actonian moral judgements, as for instance that to peruse the works of Rostand was a degrading experience.* However, his devotion to French literature and to France was never in doubt (at the age of seventy-seven in 1940 he dedicated a book on Pascal '*à la France quand même*'), and he was a great faculty man. A keen Mozart lover, he was for many years a much respected president of the CUMS, and once rebuked a loquacious member, who claimed that he only wished to be helpful, with the rejoinder 'there are occasions when nothing helps so much as silence'.

The most popular German lecturer and the most effective modern languages teacher was Edward Bullough of Caius, who took Dante as well as Schiller in his stride and became Professor of Italian in 1933. The Professor of German in the twenties, Dr Karl Breul of King's, was much concerned to find an academic niche for his son, a young man with a black beard and a truly remarkable capacity for reducing the regular number of those attending his lectures. This proved unsuccessful. There was no Professor of Spanish till 1933, but the first Serena Professor of Italian (1919), Thomas Okey of Jesus, was a true Samuel Smiles hero. After leaving school at twelve, he worked for many years as a basket-maker for eighteen pence a week for a twelve-hour day. Mr Pettoello's lectures on *Orlando Furioso* were said to consist entirely of his reading the text aloud. E. D. Chaytor of St Catharine's, although possessed of an atrocious French accent, had been a headmaster and something of a realist. He would commonly advise his abler pupils to sign on for most lectures in the faculty at the first session but to leave it at that.

Undoubtedly the most colourful figure in this somewhat sombre barnyard was Donald Beves, a tutor of King's for sixteen years and one of Cambridge's leading actors, described by Rylands as 'a supreme Shakespearean comic'. Perhaps his greatest performance was his Falstaff, alongside the economist Dennis Robertson's Shallow and Redgrave's Prince Hal. In spite of, or perhaps because of, the fact that he had once com-

* Rather out of character, he had earlier in life sponsored Lytton Strachey for membership of the Savile Club.

manded the Army drill school, he was notorious for what Cambridge calls *incuria*, a lack of attention to administrative detail, but was a great connoisseur, possessing what was believed at the time to be the best private collection of Stuart and Georgian glass, and a commendably assiduous entertainer of all the undergraduates whom he supervised. Mrs Prior, the professor's wife, was greatly addicted to pageants during the Long Vacation and Donald Beves did very well as Henry VIII.

The redoubtable, if diminutive, Stewart, Chairman of the Special Board for Medieval and Modern Languages during the Great War, had become uneasily aware that the existence within his tripos of a limited study of English literature might soon become a cuckoo in his linguistic nest. His fears were shared by W. W. Skeat's successor in 1912 to the Chair of Anglo-Saxon, H. M. Chadwick, who thought that things might soon develop in such a way that Anglo-Saxon tied to English literature would resemble a dinghy towed in the wake of a great galleon. He was an unusually versatile scholar, whose first publication in 1894 had been *The Origin of the Latin Perfect Formation in -ui*, followed shortly after by a work on *Ablaut Problems in the Indo-Germanic Verb*. But he had enough on his hands, since he taught, in addition to philology, the Anglo-Saxon, Norse and Welsh languages and Teutonic and Viking history and mythology. Over-pressure may have impelled him to suggest as a tripos question: 'What were the recreations in the Viking Age of (a) men and (b) women?', which prompted A. B. Cook to enquire whether a candidate might earn full marks by answering (a) women and (b) men. He hankered after detaching his particular concerns from Modern and Medieval Languages and joining forces with Archaeology and Anthropology, which he eventually achieved in 1928. It was in the garden of Chadwick's house in Gresham Road during the Easter Term of 1916 that he, Stewart and Quiller-Couch conspired effectively to create the English Tripos.

There had naturally been antecedents. By 1905 Benson was lecturing on Milton in the hall of Magdalene and his collection of English books became in due course the nucleus of the faculty library. Ridgeway, since he hated Germans, hated philology and suggested that it be replaced by the 'content' of great literature. In 1909 it was even proposed to make it possible to acquire a degree in English alone, but Henry Jackson would have none of it. The decisive advance occurred when the future Lord Rothermere endowed the King Edward VII Professorship of English Literature in 1910, stipulating that the subject be 'treated on literary and critical rather than on philological and linguistic lines'. Dr Mayo felt constrained to point out that in his view: 'It would be a professorship of English fiction, and that of a light and comic character, and for that reason the Professorship of English was a professorship unworthy of this University.' McTaggart, who read about four novels a day, thought that the chair would be 'not only useless, but positively harmful'. Conservative fears were somewhat allayed by the appointment of the classical scholar Verrall. However, he soon died and Asquith appointed 'Q', whose impeccable Liberal sentiments aroused dark suspicions in Ridgeway's mind that the appointment was political. Benson, on the other hand, wrote to the new professor in welcoming vein – 'It is really a great opportunity. What we want is a man who will really found and organize a *school* . . . Everything is ready for this, and what is needed is a strong personality, to do for us what Raleigh has done at Oxford . . . You will be much welcomed here . . .'

The 1917 reforms achieved by Stewart, Chadwick and 'Q', though partial, enabled the first examination in the new English Tripos to take place in the Easter Term of 1919. What was now required for a degree was Section A (English literature, medieval and modern) together with Section B (early literature and history, but no compulsory philology). However, relatively few undergraduates struggled with Section B, since Section A, together with part of another tripos, sufficed. Thus, F. R. Leavis of Emmanuel, after war service as a stretcher bearer, followed a II.ii in history with a first in English, and Basil Willey of Peterhouse, wounded and taken prisoner as a Lieutenant in the West Yorkshires, had firsts in both history and English. The tripos lists for 1920 and 1921 contained the names of G. B. Harrison, J. B. Priestley, Frank Kendon, Gerald Bullett and Rosamond Lehmann, as well as those of Leavis and Willey. It was no use

Dr Mayo telling people that 'the Englishman is English all his life; he needs no teaching of English'. Teaching would be necessary. The available staff were two professorships, held by Chadwick and 'Q', and one unfilled lectureship, which soon devolved, as we have seen, on Coulton, since someone had to manage the Middle Ages.

'Q' was, however, a most unusual professor and in him the man matched the hour. To begin with, he was by now the best known figure in Cambridge. The editorial of *New Cambridge* for 31 January 1920, begins: 'In these days we have become accustomed to Girton and Newnham. They seem as much part and parcel of this University as the Senate House or "Q".' In addition, he was a national figure – as a prolific novelist; as an influential critic; as the compiler in 1900 of an anthology, the *Oxford Book of English Verse*, which was to be found on the shelves of almost every cultivated house in the land and in a good many others as well; and as a celebrated wit, who once described Augustine Birrell as representing Fife as it ought to be represented – by wind. As an administrator, his methods were cavalier. E. M. W. Tillyard, having marked a large number of tripos scripts, was once summoned to Jesus College for what he assumed would be in the nature of an examiners' meeting. He found 'Q', unmistakably dressed for an imminent departure to his home at Fowey (where he was usually Mayor). Tillyard was offered a glass of sherry and a large pile of 'Q's' unmarked scripts, with the encouraging comment: 'Eustace, my boy, I have every confidence in your judgement', and asked if he could lend a hand with the luggage. However, 'Q' not only lectured to large and appreciative audiences, but also taught a few undergraduates who might take his fancy, the dramatic critic W. A. Darlington testifying that: 'he read everything I wrote and mostly made me write it again'. Writing of the early twenties, Basil Willey, who held the same chair in 1946, considered that 'in those days he was a spell-binder, who by sheer force of style and prestige brought réclame and faith to the new school'. A verbatim report of 'Q' lecturing on *Antony and Cleopatra* in the Lent Term of 1920 conveys an atmosphere as close to that of modern academic English as an Edwardian country house weekend to a *New Statesman* office party – 'She is the woman

Pater saw in the depths of La Gioconda's smile. She is older than the rocks . . . Indeed the theme itself is overpoweringly too much for our poor commentator, as it has ever been too strong for all but the elect; for it is of love; not the pretty amorous ritual played on a time by troubadours and courtiers in France and Navarre; not the delicate sighing languishment which the Elizabethans called Fancy; not the business as understood by eighteenth-century sentimentalists; but Love, the invincible destroyer . . .' That was in February. In March, 'The Professor concluded his lecture with a brilliant rendering of Charmian's death scene.' But he could also be engagingly earthy, as when in 1925 he compared the love making of Lorenzo and Jessica with the occasion on which he inadvertently overheard in a Cornish hedgerow a love-sick maiden telling her swain: 'Oh, Albert, ain't the moon lovely – it does *add* so.' Discussing the declining prestige of *Longinus on the Sublime*, he said: 'Still, and thank Heaven, and if I may put it so, the mischief with the final word is precisely that it is final; and the more it seems or affects to be final the less it can be true.' 'Q', at any rate, would never seek to put the Muse in chains. As Willey wrote of Tillyard's supervision classes: 'We felt ourselves to be a happy band of pioneers, united by a common faith, despised perhaps by the older academics, but sure of triumph in a glorious future.'

One of the happiest of the pioneers was Mansfield Forbes of Clare, whom Chadwick of the same college, had brought over from history, in which he had secured a first with distinction in 1911. A Scotsman of independent means and markedly independent thought and habits, he aroused deep admiration and affection among his colleagues. His close friend I. A. Richards wrote of him retrospectively in 1973: 'Forbes gave its original character to the tripos. No one saw, as he did, its unique invitations and hazards or feared more realistically what it might become'; for Willey, Mansfield Forbes had 'a truly seminal mind, an imagination from which ours caught fire, and an extraordinary sureness of taste and rightness of judgement'. A pupil, Professor L. C. Knights, records that 'the moment of awakening was in the classroom of Mansfield Forbes, that teacher of genius at Clare College . . . One day, I can remember now, he took Wordsworth's lovely poem on his dead daughter: "Surprised by joy, impatient as the wind", and I suddenly found the poem wasn't out there any more, it was inside me and working. This was a revelation. If it didn't sound complacent, I should say I never looked back.' Forbes' advice to his pupils was to read the originals, to stay with the best critics and to read slowly, aloud and tolerantly. They would pass their examinations if they were 'to collect facts with discrimination, and adopt a brooding and ruminating mode of work made possible by serenity of mind'. So equipped, they would be able to answer 'large general questions from a sudden point of view'.

Although nobody could think harder and deeper about poetry, Manny Forbes' method of discourse and personal habits were in the highest degree idiosyncratic. In a course of lectures on Shakespeare and Tolstoy he spent two hours on Moby Dick, since he could never resist discoursing on the whiteness of the whale. Whenever a new book took his fancy, he bought large numbers of copies and distributed them to his friends and pupils. He was quite incapable of moving about Cambridge unless he was carrying huge quantities of books and papers. An offer of help from a kind lady, who observed him staggering along with a pile of books higher than his head, was met with the remonstrance: 'Pray do not disturb me, I have the stability of a pregnant kangaroo.'

In the Long Vacation of 1919 Chadwick said to Tillyard: 'There is a man called Richards. All I know about him is that he got a first in moral sciences and has a red nose. But Forbes says he's all right and I've put him on the lecture list.'

We left Ivor Richards on a gas-lit staircase on 11 November 1918, gestating with his friend Ogden *The Meaning of Meaning*, a work which they published jointly in 1923. In that Michaelmas Term of 1919, Richards began lecturing on the theory of criticism. But it was touch and go, and entirely due to Forbes, that this was to happen. Having successively abandoned history and medicine, Richards had almost succumbed to the potent spell of G. E. Moore's philosophy – 'I don't think I ever understood anything. But it was complete subjugation.' However, there remained something, which was to prove of the greatest importance to Cambridge English, which he knew he must one day get across to the world. 'Moore was vocally convinced that few indeed could possibly *mean* what they said. I was silently persuaded that they could not possibly *say* what they meant.' But where in 1919 was the pulpit from which he could preach the message which led Basil Willey to describe him as 'in many important senses, the Coleridge of our time' (a title subsequently claimed for F. R. Leavis by his supporters)? There being no obvious post available in Cambridge, Richards, a life-long mountaineer, asked Forbes to use his influence in Scotland to secure him a job as a mountain guide. Forbes immediately wrote letters to seven Highland lairds. Then they discovered that between them they had no stamps, so instead Forbes sent a note to Chadwick, and Richards began a career, which was to change the face of English literary criticism. Combining, as he did, a curiously benign personality with an exceptionally astringent mind, he would rapidly and almost painlessly eradicate the then fashionable sort of literary criticism exemplified by an article of Henry James in 1913, which claimed that 'Poetry may be best compared to the breeze that blows the trees. We are the trees; the leaves are our senses; and poetry is the unfettered word . . .' The Aeolian harp had been twanged too long. It was time to concentrate on the reader and his responses, about whom Richards was very practical: 'Sit by the fire [presumably open-hearthed], with eyes shut and fingers pressed firmly upon the eyeballs and consider with as full "realization" as possible:

1. Man's loneliness (the isolation of the human situation).
2. The facts of birth, and of death, in their inexplicable oddity.
3. The inconceivable immensity of the universe.
4. Man's place in the perspective of time.
5. The enormity of his ignorance.

Not as gloomy thoughts or as targets for doctrine, but as the most incomprehensible and inexhaustible objects for meditation there are . . .'

Then when the time came to read, the thing to do was to concentrate on the words on the page and work away at four kinds of meaning (a) sense (b) feeling (c) tone (d) intention. 'The arts are our storehouse of recorded values. They spring from and perpetuate hours in the lives of exceptional people, when their control and command of experience is at its highest, hours when habitual narrowness of interest or confused bewilderment are replaced by an intricately wrought composure.'

As history began to dispense with Actonian value judgements and philosophy was adopting a very wary attitude towards notions of the good and the beautiful, English began to concern itself more and more with moral values. 'Bad taste and crude responses', taught Richards, 'are not mere flaws in an otherwise admirable person. They are actually a root evil, from which other defects follow.' He proceeded to enrich the national vocabulary by the invention of terms like 'stock responses', 'bogus entities', 'emotive language', 'pseudo-statements'.

But, however serious his intent, he was always remarkably entertaining. Benson's diary for 13 October 1923 records: 'Richards next [at High Table], very interesting. He suggested as a good examination for English students to print five extracts of poetry and prose, with no clue as to author or date and containing one really *worthless* piece, and ask for comments and opinion.' A month later, we find them setting a test for an English prize at Magdalene. 'Richards and I have selected six pieces – de Quincey, Belloc, [Ella Wheeler] Willcox, Jeremy Taylor, etc. – some good, some bad, and we present these to a dozen candidates to comment as they like and say what they like (the result most curious and interesting) – no critical faculty, no taste, taken in by a shoddy sonnet. It shows how little our teaching trains discrimination.' These exercises were the beginnings of the famous 'protocols', essays by undergraduates in the criticism of unattributed poems, eventually enshrined in Richards' *Practical Criticism* (1929), in which one victim, criticizing Lawrence's famous poem 'Piano', commented: 'I don't see how a child could sit under the piano. He could sit under the keyboard but not under the piano.' Donne's sonnet 'At the round earth's imagined corners' even found a critic who described it as expressing 'the simple faith of a very simple man', and Hopkins' 'Margaret, are you grieving' was described as 'extraordinarily bad poetry, embodying the trite philosophy that the world is a vale of tears'.

Practical Criticism had been preceded in 1923 by *The Meaning of Meaning* by Richards and Ogden and *Principles of Literary Criticism* (1925) by Richards alone. Ogden and Richards managed to tabulate sixteen main definitions of the word 'meaning' itself and vigorously criticized Coleridge for talking of a 'willing suspension of disbelief', when what he should have said was 'an involuntary accession of conviction'. Richards summed up his earlier attitude to criticism perhaps most succinctly in an article he contributed in 1923 to Ogden's quarterly *Psyche* – 'the qualifications of a good critic are three. He must be an adept at experiencing, without eccentricities, the state of mind relative to the work he is judging. Secondly, he must be able to distinguish experiences from one another as regards their less superficial features. Thirdly, he must be a sound judge of values.' But by 1929 he was thoroughly aware of the dangers of too dogmatic an approach to literary values – 'it is less important to like "good" poetry and dislike "bad" than to be able to use both as a means of ordering our minds.' The last section of *Practical Criticism* is entitled *Humility* – 'the lesson of all criticism is that we have nothing to rely upon in making our choices but ourselves'. He was essentially in sympathy with F. L. Lucas's view that 'the more I see, in education, of criticism in its ordinary sense, of judging books – what the elect call "evaluation" – the more I doubt its use. And the vital difficulty, it seems to me, about all University courses in English is to prevent them becoming organized orgies of Opinion.'

Tillyard, a Milton scholar and, like Richards and Forbes, interested in the deeper layers of meaning, considered that Richards in the twenties provided both leadership and a policy – 'Richards was the main instrument in this country, and perhaps anywhere, of developing in literature the seminal ideas of Moore in philosophy.' But Freud's emphasis on subconscious motive reinforced an attitude to literature which played helpful havoc with the higher aestheticism, as instanced by the undergraduate who began an optional original contribution in the tripos with the words: 'I am the midwife of the Soul.'

As the twenties ended, the new tripos was quite firmly established and Richards' popularity was such that his most famous Magdalene pupil William Empson, whose *Seven*

Types of Ambiguity arose directly out of a supervision, records that at one stage Richards had to lecture in the street to accommodate his audience. Frequently to be seen at the back of Richards' lectures was Dr F. R. Leavis, about to become the first member of the faculty who had actually taken the English Tripos. The gifted amateurs without doctorates – 'Q', Forbes, Richards, Tillyard, Aubrey Attwater, whose lectures captured even Cecil Beaton's attention, Willey, Roberts, Lucas, B. W. Downs – were soon to find themselves very severely 'evaluated'.

On 8 November 1924 the Cambridge University Moral Sciences Club celebrated its jubilee. The President, W. E. Johnson of King's, was too unwell to attend, but Dr G. E. Moore of Trinity was in the chair. There was a dinner, followed by a symposium on 'the Philosophy of the late Mr Bradley'. Bradley, the author of *Appearance and Reality*, had only just died, three months after becoming the first philosopher to receive the OM. It is to be hoped (the minutes of the Club do not help on the point) that Moore, out of reverence for the bones, if not the soul, of the departed, was on this occasion less categorical in his condemnation of Bradley's metaphysical cast of mind than he had been when addressing the Club in 1916. On that occasion 'the bulk of his paper was taken up with a criticism of parts of Mr Bradley's *Appearance and Reality*. Dr Moore tried to find some consistency in Mr Bradley's use of such terms as "is, is a fact, exists and is real" or failing that, the variation in meaning of the above terms. Mr Bradley had arrived at certain blatantly erroneous conclusions. This was due to an illusion, fostered by language, that there is a concept "reality". There is no such concept and any proposition in which "reality" occurs as grammatical predicate is either meaningless or wrongly expressed. If the proposition "this lion is real" is to have meaning, it must be expressed "something has the property of being leonine". This last point formed the focus of the discussion which followed and which was maintained till eleven p.m.' The path of Cambridge philosophy in the post-war years had been clearly signposted.

In 1919 Moore was forty-six. His *Principia Ethica* (1903)

notoriously prompted Maynard Keynes at the end of the thirties to declaim to the assembled Bloomsberries: 'its effect on us and the talk which preceded it and followed it dominated and perhaps still dominate everything else'. From then on 'What *exactly* do you mean?' was the phrase most usually on the lips of the Keynesian circle, while their *mores* conveniently conformed to a rather widely interpreted acceptance of 'certain states of consciousness, which may be roughly described as the pleasures of human intercourse and the enjoyment of beautiful objects'. In the rigorous elucidation of meaning, Moore undoubtedly practised what he preached. Richards, who was taught by him in 1918–19, describes how 'he certainly expanded our notion of how much discussion a question can deserve. For example, he could take a single sentence from James Ward's *Encyclopaedia Britannica* article on psychology and stay with it for three weeks lecturing on: "What on earth could Ward possibly have meant by saying that 'the *standpoint of psychology* is *individual*' " – underlining the key words perhaps seventy times, gown flying, chalkdust rising in clouds, his intonations coruscating with apostrophes, and come out by the same door as in he went, looking up to heaven and shaking his head in despair.'

Moore succeeded James Ward as Professor of Mental Philosophy and Logic in 1925 when the latter died aged eighty-two. There were two other senior philosophers, however, still very much at large in the twenties – McTaggart and Johnson. Despite the fact that Moore read his celebrated programmatic paper 'A Defence of Common Sense' in 1924 (just before its publication) in McTaggart's rooms with R. B. Braithwaite in the chair, E. M. Forster was surely correct when he wrote that 'it would be too much to say that Moore dethroned McTaggart, who was essentially undethronable'. Apart from anything else, Moore was a relatively mild man, quite happy pushing a perambulator along the Backs, whilst McTaggart was decidedly formidable and afraid of no man, not even Bertrand Russell. In 1920 at a meeting of the Moral Sciences Club at St John's, Russell read a paper entitled 'Perception and Physics', the aim of which was 'to give an account of the objects of perception in accordance with the principles of realism and assuming that the results of physics are the nearest approximation to truth that we have yet obtained with the ultimate object of founding a materialistic philosophy'. McTaggart told the Club in 1923: 'it seems that Mr Russell wishes to assert that both the propositions and terms of philosophy are all *a priori*. For him, whether matter exists would be a problem belonging to one of the special sciences. But there are many problems discussed by philosophers and regarded as philosophical, which belong to none of the physical sciences and also fall outside the realm of pure logic'. McTaggart, although a conscientious atheist, believed in the immortality of the soul, and with prodigious ratiocination attempted to erect a vast structure of deductive metaphysics. His introduction to his metaphysical approach to the emotion of love was described by C. D. Broad as 'hitting his readers below the intellect'. McTaggart's death in 1925 left the field in Cambridge to the champions of common sense. 'No man is justified in a religious attitude', wrote McTaggart 'except as a result of metaphysical study.' Less ambitiously, it was suggested at the Moral Sciences Club in 1927 that 'the safest attitude for the theist was that expressed by saying "I am convinced by immediate experience that God exists and I offer you no arguments in support of this conviction".' In this connection, Moore as an undergraduate composed a paper, which began: 'In the beginning was Matter, and Matter begat the Devil, and the Devil begat God' and ended 'And then God died, and next the Devil died, and Matter remained.' However, for some years both he and Russell were considerably rattled by McTaggart's philosophical virtuosity, before they both recovered their celebrated common sense.

Keynes tells us that Moore had a nightmare once in which he was unable to distinguish propositions from tables. Such a disaster seems less likely to have befallen W. E. Johnson, from whom Keynes derived much of the material for his 1921 *Treatise on Probability*. For Johnson, a proposition 'is only a factor in the concrete act of judgement'. As far back as 1892, his work on 'The Logical Calculus' had been enormously influential, as had his subsequent teaching, in emphasizing the essentially analytical approach to philosophy which would progressively dominate the Cambridge scene. Now, in 1921,

1922, 1924 he published three volumes entitled *Logic*. H. W. B.
Joseph of Oxford claimed to be able to distinguish twenty
different senses in which Johnson employed the word 'proposition'. However, Johnson was held in the greatest respect
by his Cambridge colleagues. A rather heroic figure, who
battled for many years against asthma, he would lecture to
the small groups of moral scientists, wrapped in a red shawl,
latterly in his own house. In 1921 another Cambridge philosopher Susan Stebbing read a paper to the Moral Sciences
Club called 'Some Points in Mr Johnson's *Logic*'. The minutes
tell us that 'unfortunately Mr Johnson was unable to be
present, so the discussion was needlessly complicated in
several cases by an imperfect understanding of what the
author really meant'. Johnson was a hero not only to Keynes,
but also to Russell. On one occasion, he gave a heavily attended
lecture on the subject of possibility, which turned out to consist
of eight lines read from a postcard, followed by a heavy
silence, whereupon Russell diplomatically came forward and
suggested that the lecture might be repeated. Johnson died in
1931.

Charlie Dunbar Broad became a fellow of Trinity in 1923
and when he died in 1971 his Trinity obituarist wrote: 'Many
fellows of Trinity are knowledgeable but Broad came nearer
to omniscience than any of his generation.' He occupied
Newton's rooms, into which he incorporated a carpenter's
bench for the purposes of the large model railway which some
friends allowed him to operate in a garden in the Trumpington
Road. A modest man, though possessed of one of the most
trenchant wits in Cambridge, he had been trained as a scientist.
Very productive, he was nevertheless reluctant to commit
himself to conclusions, being a master of the art of setting out
the advantages and disadvantages of other people's theories –
what he called 'the humbler (yet useful) power of stating
difficult things clearly and not too superficially'. In his *The
Mind and Its Place in Nature* (1925), Broad not only analysed
seventeen possible theories of the relation between mind and
matter, but shocked the apostles of common sense (a quality
which he was markedly disinclined to venerate) by appearing
mildly sympathetic to psychical research. He observed characteristically that 'he would be more annoyed than surprised if

he found himself surviving the death of his physical organism'. It was Broad who perpetrated the disrespectful epigram '*si Moore savait, si Russell pouvait*' – pointing out that Russell produced a different system of philosophy every year in contrast to Moore, who never produced one at all.

Broad's preface to *The Mind and Its Place in Nature* prophetically anticipates the extraordinary excitement which would be engendered among Cambridge philosophers by what he irreverently described as 'the highly syncopated pipings of Herr Wittgenstein's flute'. The preface of the *Tractatus* (which, as we have seen, appeared in English in Frank Ramsey's translation in 1922) contains the daunting words: 'What can be said at all can be said clearly; and whereof one cannot speak, thereof one must be silent'. This confronts the lay commentator on the influence of Wittgenstein with a welcome about as encouraging as *lasciate ogni speranza voi ch'entrate*. Nor is it particularly consoling to read in a letter of Russell to Moore in May 1930: 'I find I can only understand Wittgenstein when I am in good health, which I am not at the moment.' Indeed, if we are to believe Russell (writing to Lady Ottoline Morrell in 1916), it appears that he found that Wittgenstein's criticism inhibited him from doing any further fundamental work in philosophy. Nevertheless, few books of so small a size as the *Tractatus* have resulted in such an enormous output of subsequent exegesis and commentary.

Alfred Marshall used sometimes to come down from his study observing: 'I have had such a happy time, there is no joy to be compared to constructive work.' Work for Wittgenstein was more like a form of torture – 'the measure of a man's greatness would be in terms of what his work *cost* him'. To adapt one of his most celebrated images, one can assume that the fly has a hell of a job to get out of the fly-bottle. 'The right method of philosophy would be this: to say nothing except what can be said, i.e. the propositions of natural science, i.e. something that has nothing to do with philosophy; and then, always, when someone else wishes to say something metaphysical, to demonstrate to him that he had given no meaning to certain signs in his propositions.' We must stop trying to explain and be content to describe and even then we must always remember that language disguises thought.

Although Cambridge knew of the *Tractatus* in the twenties it knew relatively little of Wittgenstein himself. Sebastian Sprott reviewed the *Tractatus* for *The Cambridge Review* in 1923, deeming it 'a criticism of the use of language which is one of the most important contributions to philosophy of recent years'. From 1920 to 1926 Wittgenstein was teaching in Austrian elementary schools, but visited Cambridge under Keynes' auspices in 1925; he then worked as an architect; established his contacts with the Vienna School; had his interest in philosophy revived by Brouwer; and returned permanently to Cambridge in 1929. In May of that year he told the Moral Sciences Club that no paper should last longer than seven minutes and that they should stop reading the minutes of the last meeting. One of his earliest pupils was a handsome undergraduate at Corpus called Desmond Lee, then reading the philosophy option in the Classical Tripos. Apart from finding Wittgenstein's logomachies remarkably fascinating, Lee found his strange teacher, as did other young men who came under his spell, curiously magnetic. 'He was already engaged on the work which was to lead in 1952 to *Philosophical Investigations*. He had abandoned or modified much of what he had written in the *Tractatus* and it was the desire to correct his former views which had driven him back to philosophy . . . He referred to his time as a primary school teacher, and said he had once considered going into a monastery. He also spoke of the house he had designed for his sister in Vienna, and once showed me a couple of photographs of it. He had clearly taken the job with immense and characteristic seriousness; the problem of design had worried him a great deal and he told me in illustration of this that once when he was ill with a fever during this period he thought he was a chair – the problem of designing a particular set of chairs being much on his mind at the time . . . He dominated discussion; he had a personal magnetism which once felt was irresistible; and yet his personal and intellectual force was so strong that it had a numbing effect on those who listened to him, certainly if they were young or comparatively young . . . This hypnotic influence was accounted for, largely, no doubt by L.W.'s extraordinary force of character and intellect which had to be experienced to be appreciated. He had also that more elusive capacity for attraction, which men of genius often have, and which we describe in a metaphor as personal magnetism. But I think that the peculiar nature of his influence may have been due to his not regarding himself as a *teacher*. He said to me once that there is something odd about all teachers, and that the old Greek myth that made Chiron the teacher of Achilles a centaur was a parable of the teacher not being like other men.' Wittgenstein told Desmord Lee that he admired St Augustine, Schopenhauer, and Kierkegaard; of his contemporaries, he found Broad's methods repugnant; thought Russell now past his prime and *The Conquest of Happiness* 'a vomitive'; liked Johnson personally, but thought nothing of his logic; and liked and respected Moore.

The reason for Wittgenstein's approbation of Moore is perhaps not far to seek. Richards tells us that Russell sent Wittgenstein to Moore, whom hardly anybody ever questioned, and who had till then a tendency to put his hands over his head and scream if anyone in his classes used imprecise language. 'Wittgenstein started asking Moore questions. For the first time in our many years' experience of Moore, Moore was submissive, gentle, doing his best to understand . . . From that moment came Wittgenstein's dominance over Moore and over Cambridge.' Had Frank Ramsey not died in 1930 at such a young age, it is legitimate to speculate just how absolute Wittgenstein's dominance might have been. Philosophers of the calibre of R. B. Braithwaite and John Wisdom were established on the Cambridge scene by the end of the twenties, but Ramsey had already indicated that he was thoroughly prepared to begin where Wittgenstein had left off. Controversies might have erupted in places more public than the columns of *Mind*.

Despite the arduousness of philosophical argument among Cambridge's leading practitioners, remarkably few undergraduates actually read the tripos. Between 1921 and 1930 the average number reading Part I was five, there being twelve in 1921 and three in 1930; the average figure for Part II was just over seven. Perhaps J. J. Thomson was not alone in regarding it as 'a subject in which you spend your time trying to find a shadow in an absolutely dark room'.

Another minority first degree course was Anthropology. Before it became linked, as we have seen, with Chadwick's Anglo-Saxon, Norse and Celtic empire as well as with Archaeology in 1928, Anthropology averaged four or five candidates a year. Yet the author of *The Golden Bough* was a fellow of Trinity from 1879 to 1941. Over two hundred of the most prominent figures in the world of learning subscribed their names to an address presented to Sir James George Frazer in 1921 on the occasion of the foundation of the Frazer Lectureship in Social Anthropology, founded at Oxford, Cambridge, Glasgow and Liverpool Universities. In this address, Housman wrote: 'The Golden Bough, compared by Virgil to the mistletoe but now revealing some affinity to the banyan, has not only waxed a great tree but has spread to a spacious and hospitable forest, whose king receives homage in many tongues from a multitude resorting thither for its fruit or timber or refreshing shade. There they find learning mated with literature, labour disguised in ease, and a museum of dark and uncouth superstitions invested with the charm of a truly sympathetic magic. There you have gathered together, for the admonition of a proud and oblivious race, the scattered and fading relics of its foolish childhood, whether withdrawn from our view among savage folk, or lying unnoticed at our doors. The forgotten milestones of the road which man has travelled, the mazes and blind alleys of his appointed progress through time, are illuminated by your art and genius . . .' If the best way to promote knowledge is to ask the right questions, then Frazer had proved himself particularly penetrative when he asked – 'Why had Diana's priest at Nemi, the King of the Wood, to slay his predecessor? And why, before doing so, had he to pluck the branch of a sacred tree?' If, in addition, genius is a matter of taking pains, Frazer was certainly painstaking. A standard working day, which he maintained for years, ran from 4 a.m. to 8 a.m., 9 to 12, 3 to 6, 7 to midnight.

Frazer went to Glasgow University in 1869 before he was sixteen. He successively edited Sallust, the *Fasti* of Ovid, and Pausanias, the second-century Greek traveller, 'without whom', he claimed, 'the rivers of Greece would for the most part be a labyrinth without a clue, a riddle without an answer'. After Frazer came to Cambridge in 1878, the philosopher James

Ward drew his attention to the work of Tylor, the founding father of anthropology. The disputatious heretic and orientalist Robertson Smith set Frazer to work on the *Encyclopaedia Britannica*, making him responsible for the articles on Pericles, Praefect, Praeneste, Praetor, Priapus, Proserpine and Province. In 1887 Frazer started sending out questionnaires to missionaries and explorers, who were in those days as thick on the ground as Coca-Cola representatives are today. The appearance of the first volume of *The Golden Bough* was in 1890, and that of the last supplementary volume of the twelve in 1936. Frazer was a lovable and essentially modest man and in reply to Housman's adulatory remarks in 1921 he wrote: 'As you know, I have never sought to formulate a system or to found a school, being too conscious of the narrow limits of my knowledge and abilities to attempt anything so ambitious. I have been content to investigate a few problems in the history of man; but I am well aware, and I have endeavoured to keep my readers constantly aware, of the extreme uncertainty of all the solutions which I have ventured to offer of these problems, always remembering that the study of man's mental evolution, like the study of the physical universe in which he appears to exist as an insignificant particle, is still only in its inception . . .'

Frazer never saw a genuine savage in his life, but Malinowski, who frequently did, described himself as 'a faithful disciple of *The Golden Bough*' and called its author 'the greatest anthropologist of our age'. The leading Cambridge field anthropologist A. C. Haddon, who planned and led the university expedition to the Torres Straits in 1898–9, owed much to Frazer's inspiration and encouragement. He became a fellow of Christ's in 1901. When he retired in 1925 (the year in which Frazer received the OM), the farewell dinner given on his birthday was the first occasion on which women ever dined in the hall of a men's college, since this intrepid investigator of head-hunters had long been an enthusiastic supporter of women's education.

The Disney Professorship of Archaeology, the oldest in the British Isles, was founded in 1851. It is of some interest that its present holder, Professor Glyn Daniel, in his *The Origin and Growth of Archaeology* makes no mention at all of two very well-known Cambridge scholars of the twenties, who, whatever the diversity of their interests, were certainly labelled archaeologists, as the term was then understood. The Disney Professor until his death in 1926, Sir William Ridgeway, we have already met in his role as the contumacious (if very happily married) opponent of female emancipation. R. S. Conway, his obituarist in the *Proceedings of the British Academy*, felt impelled to say of him – 'whatever may be the judgement of posterity upon others, it will assuredly rank Ridgeway with Darwin and Mommsen as a great master and maker of knowledge'. His published work certainly evinces a remarkable catholicity of interests, including the size of the Homeric horse, Pythagoras' concern with the prismatic qualities of precious stones, early Greek weapons, the origins of metallic currency and standard weights, Greek tragedy and the dramatic dances of non-European races. One of his pupils D. S. Robertson, a future professor of Greek, testified that Ridgeway 'did not like formal lecturing; but round a table with half a dozen students he was incomparable. His vivid imagination, his width of view, his unbroken contact with reality, kept one spellbound as gems, coins, axeheads, totem spoons tumbled on to the table from his inexhaustible pockets.'

Ridgeway had been President of the Classical Association, and A. B. Cook of Queens', Reader in Classical Archaeology in the twenties and first holder of the Lawrence Chair of Classical Archaeology in 1931, had been a professor of Greek in London in 1893 at the age of twenty-four. E. M. W. Tillyard described him as 'endlessly clever, the clearest and most persuasive lecturer in the university'. In middle life an Evangelical and Sunday School teacher, he became a prodigious expert on ancient religions and successive volumes of *Zeus, a Study in Ancient Religions* came out in 1914, 1925 and 1940. For a quarter of a century he was Curator of the Museum of Classical Archaeology, of which it was said, before he transformed it, that it would have been a disgrace to a backward borough council. As he lay dying in 1952, the Dean of Queens' read him the opening verses of the hundred and twenty-first psalm, and Cook took his last opportunity to point out that they were mistranslated. By then, we are told, his earlier missionary evangelicalism 'had been purified into a calm and considered deist philosophy'.

Fifty years after the Royal Geographical Society urged the university to take a serious interest in geography, a tripos leading to an honours degree was approved in 1921. That this was achieved was certainly not the fault of Dr Mayo, who contended that historical geography must involve the study of Strabo and Pausanias in the original language. 'Would they do this? Of course not. Well, then, where was the sincerity of those who proposed it?' Though there had been a board of geographical studies and a diploma course since 1903, there was no professorship in the twenties. The reader was Frank Debenham, an Australian who had originally taken an ordinary arts degree at Sydney. He survived both Scott's Antarctic expedition and being knocked out at Salonika by a 5·9 inch shell. He was to become the first professor in 1931. Another future Professor of Geography, H. C. Darby, came up to St Catharine's from Neath Grammar School at the age of sixteen and a half. He was supervised largely by B. L. Manning, who was an ecclesiastical historian by training. Darby, as we have seen, was to become the first PhD in Geography, just as St Catharine's was the first college to offer an open exhibition in the subject in 1928. Tripos questions still tended to be on a rather heroic scale, such as 'Explain the importance of Asia Minor for either the Eastern Empire, or Modern Europe' or 'Outline and account for the present position of Japanese activities on the continent of Asia'. When Darby explained to Sheppard the content of his thesis on the role of the Fenland in English history, the genesis of one of the great works of scholarship of our day, Sheppard commented: 'Very interesting, dear boy, very interesting. Just like those chapters in Scott's novels which nobody reads.' Darby went off to the University Library to see if he was right and on the whole found that he was.

Debenham was not the only Antarctic explorer in the Cambridge of the twenties. R. E. Priestley of Clare, a future Vice-Chancellor of Birmingham University, was another. In 1912 the two of them began to ponder the possibility of collecting and organizing the survey materials of the several expeditions while doing a geological survey on the slopes of Mount Erebus in the vicinity of an old hut of Shackleton's. In December of that year Debenham committed to paper the outlines of what was to become the Scott Polar Institute, while sheltering in the hut from a blizzard. In 1919 he enlisted the aid of Sir Arthur Shipley, the Master of Christ's and Vice-Chancellor, a keen zoologist and always a strenuous patron of science, described by his doctor as a kindly, corpulent bachelor who spoke in deep grunts and got so fat on College port that his butler had great difficulty getting him in and out of the bath. This was enough to ensure a flow of funds sufficient to get the Institute started in 1921 in a large attic room in the Sedgwick Museum of Geology. Cambridge interest in the Arctic, fostered particularly by J. M. Wordie of St John's, ensured that the interests of the Institute stretched from pole to pole. The vice-chancellorship of Seward, who had been to Greenland, assisted in a move to a house in Lensfield Road, where a spacious new building, opened in 1934, was the work of Sir Herbert Baker, with an inscription reading *Quaesivit Arcana Poli Videt Dei.**

Professor H. D. Hazeltine wrote in the foreword of the first volume of *The Cambridge Law Journal* in 1921: 'men now see that social and political justice, as well as legal justice, are in large measure in the keeping of trained lawyers' – a point of view perhaps more easily demonstrable in terms of Camden, Mansfield and Denning than of Robespierre, Vishinsky and Nixon. However, he quoted Pascal in the same article to the effect that '*le droit a ses époques*' and certainly the Cambridge Law School in the twenties made significant progress. In 1921 there were thirteen vigorous college law societies, all but one founded since the Armistice. The Law Faculty took a relatively long time after the war to emancipate itself wholly from the old-fashioned local 'coach' or crammer. Even by 1928 there were only eleven law supervisors in the whole University – two each at Trinity Hall, Trinity, Downing and St John's and one each at Caius, Jesus and Corpus. Yet in that year 74 men and one woman took Part I and 111 men and 3 women Part II. Part II expanded greatly during the inter-war years,

* 'In seeking to unveil the Pole, he found the hidden face of God.'

undoubtedly drawing considerable numbers from Part II
Classics. Such improvements as were made in the faculty
were predominantly due to Hollond's organizing ability. Until
1925 it was possible to obtain both a BA and LL.B on the
two parts of the Tripos. This was supposed ideally to be a
four-year course, but it could be crammed, and often was, into
three years in a very unscholarly fashion. A great deal of
Part I was devoted to Roman Law, the subject of increasingly
virulent criticism by the more vocationally minded. After
1925 Part II was much reduced in scope and a three-year
course became in consequence a more civilized affair educationally. The most popular lecturer was Percy Winfield of
St John's, who provided unusually good value for money by
generally offering two lectures – one neatly set out on the
blackboard and the other delivered orally. Nevertheless, Adcock
could never persuade Keynes that King's needed a law don –
'the breed was anathema' to him.

Alfred Marshall's tenure of the chair of Political Economy
ended in 1908, when he was succeeded by A. C. Pigou. This
was five years after the beginning of the Economics Tripos.
The Principles of Economics – 'it's all in Marshall', as many
generations of undergraduates were taught – had appeared as
long ago as 1890. In 1923, the year before his death, Marshall
published *Money, Credit and Commerce* at the age of eighty-one.
It was from the Moral Sciences faculty that he had wrested his
new empire and as far back as his inaugural of 1885 he had
expressed the hope that the study of economics would 'increase
the number of those that Cambridge, mother of strong men,
sends out into the world with cool heads but warm hearts,
willing to give some at least of their best powers to grappling
with the social suffering around them, resolved not to rest
content till they have done what in them lies to discover how
far it is possible to open up all the material means of a
refined and noble life'. Pigou, who had taken firsts in both
history and moral sciences at the turn of the century, felt
that these aims would be best achieved by a return to the gold
standard and a general tidying-up of the loose ends in Marshall.
For the trouble with Marshall was that he was inclined to
disturb the models of classical economics – Say's Law and

perfect equilibrium and *laissez-faire*. As Keynes put it 'some of the most important work of Alfred Marshall was directed to the leading cases in which private interest and social interest were *not* harmonious'. Marshall would point out in his awkward way that supply doesn't create the demand it properly should if there is a failure of confidence, with the result that investment declines and markets contract. He even said that he would be a Socialist if he had nothing better to do.

The problems which confronted the post World War I economists were inflation, the need to find some workable standard of value, the erosion of British assets and an uncertain productive capacity – much the same witches' brew as confronted their successors after World War II. By the thirties was to be added what seemed to be massive unemployment. Until the end of the twenties there was little tendency in Cambridge to disturb the orthodoxies or approach these difficulties from a macro-economic view. You had the equilibrium model and you demonstrated its workings with an abundance of clarificatory algebra. Keynes, very much a monetary economist at this stage, although of course also a particularly shrewd political observer, was in no doubt at all about the consequences of inflating the currency, prophetically observing in 1919 that 'Lenin was certainly right. There is no subtler, no surer means of overturning the existing basis of society than to debauch the currency. The process engages all the hidden forces of economic law on the side of destruction ...' Increasingly, Keynes began to wonder about the universal validity of the theory of a stable equilibrium of supply and demand, given that such a stable equilibrium seemed to exist below the level of full employment in normal, as opposed to crisis, conditions. Perhaps it was not enough to envisage the British economy as a Rolls-Royce purring along smoothly until there was a crater in the middle of the road. You might also have to fine tune the engine as it went along. His friend Dennis Robertson of Trinity opened a series of lectures on unemployment in February 1921 by proclaiming himself very sympathetic to human misery, as he undoubtedly was, but went on to point out that 'by the practice of working short time, general distress may be to some extent diminished, but the volume of unemployment remains unaltered . . . The unemployables, the "born tireds" are not peculiar to the lower grades of labour; they are to be found in all stages of society. In the higher grades they have chosen their parents more successfully and may become county potentates and members of the best clubs.' In the end, 'the remedy in a word is this; if an industry is decaying, drive people out of it. If it is merely fluctuating, interference is unnecessary; labour will sooner or later be required . . . Any scheme for the alleviation of unemployment by tariffs is based on a faulty diagnosis of the trouble and will never solve it.' One can see Liberal *laissez-faire* still well entrenched there, but just beginning to feel the need to put a good face on itself. Robertson wrote a very well received, but highly traditional, book called *Money* in 1922 with quotations from *Alice in Wonderland* as chapter headings; Pigou wrote *The Economics of Welfare* (1920), employing the techniques of marginal analysis in an appropriately orthodox manner but suggesting clearly enough that there could be a significant gap between self-interest and the interests of society as a whole which could appropriately be filled by certain types of state intervention. Later on, in 1926, Robertson wrote *Banking Policy and the Price Level.* The ice was now beginning to melt, for in this work, the result of much discussion with Keynes, really fundamental questions were asked about the function of saving, how it is generated and how it is affected by the money supply. Even the percipient Clapham, straying out of his confines, wrote an article in *The Economic Journal* in 1922 called 'Of Empty Economic Boxes', in which he politely enquired just how much content there was in the economists' boxes labelled 'Diminishing Returns', 'Increasing Returns' and so on.

The great fame of Keynes has consigned Pigou and Robertson to comparative oblivion. The fact that they entertained in their different ways reservations about certain aspects of what came to be called the Keynesian revolution does not make them appear totally benighted fifty years later. Pigou, after all, wrote that in the real world 'transition rules always; stationariness never; the long run never comes'. The 'Prof', as he was widely known, was eventually a fellow of King's for fifty-seven years and in the immediate post-war period something of a national figure, serving on the Royal Commission on

Income Tax (1919) and on two committees on the currency. His college memorialist describes him as being addicted to a peculiar personal jargon 'often accompanied by an indefinable foreign accent'. It was a moot point whether he or J. J. Thomson was the worst dressed man in Cambridge, Pigou for instance affecting white gym shoes with black laces. He liked to go mountain climbing with undergraduates, many of whom became greatly attached to him. 'To the end of his life he would regularly attend the admission of scholars to study the form and from time to time he would "pick a winner". He liked them to be intelligent or amusing or athletic or handsome, though he was suspicious of what he continued to call "aesthetes" and viewed with disfavour Gaselee's wearing of a hair-net when playing tennis.'* Keynes once went out of his way to describe Dennis Robertson as the possessor of an absolutely first-class mind, despite the latter's modest disclaimer that he was no good at algebra. Certainly, his undergraduate career had been astonishing – firsts in classics and economics; the Craven Scholarship and the Chancellor's Medal for English Verse (also won by Pigou); President not only of the Union but of the ADC as well. An active pacifist till the last possible moment, he joined up on 4 August 1914 and was decorated in 1916. A life-long bachelor, like Pigou, he walked strenuously with his pupils, preferring hill walking to mountain climbing. The depth of his emotional attachment to Rylands makes some of the most poignant reading in Benson. The story of his relations with Keynes has been variously interpreted; Austin Robinson, one of the up-and-coming young economists of the twenties, concluded that the sensitive Robertson eventually found the strain of acting as a sort of sounding board and intellectual conscience to the brilliant and mercurial Keynes rather too much for flesh and blood to bear.

* Sir Stephen Gaselee, a colourful figure who was for a short time during the period a fellow of Magdalene. Librarian to the Foreign Office. Benson has an entry: 'Gaselee sometimes brings down experienced topers to Magdalene. I was sitting with them in the Combination Room when some old port came in. Bower sipped and said to Lord Kintore, a merry chatty man: "What do you make of that, Kintore? Pretty firm, isn't it?" K. tasted, rolled his eyes, tasted again, and said in a tone of deep conviction "Fat!" '

In 1922 a clever 'fresher' in Girton, Joan Maurice, asked her supervisor in economics what was the objection to employing men on publicly financed schemes and received the reply that, the dole being less than the wage, it was more economical to leave them unemployed. By the time she came back to teach in the faculty seven years later as Joan Robinson, matters were very different. A vigorous debate was going on about the basic principles of classical economics, into which she hurled herself with what she described in a letter to Keynes as 'my rough manners in controversy'. An Italian Communist Piero Sraffa, who had understandably left Mussolini's Italy, and became a fellow of Trinity in 1939, had written an article in the December 1926 number of *The Economic Journal* attacking the orthodox theory of competitive value based on the symmetry of supply and demand, which he described as 'essentially a pedagogic instrument, somewhat like the study of classics'. It was no good teaching economics as a form of mind training remote from the realities of the world, in which instead of perfect competition there were often conditions of near monopoly or consumer preference for one product rather than another, regardless of the appropriate market price. It was no use blinking at economic realities which did not fit the model, describing them as 'fictions', which the working of competition would soon overcome.

The equilibrium model had been fragmented precisely at the moment when, as the twenties were drawing to a close, capitalism and the structure of international relations were to come under almost intolerable strains. In May 1929 Keynes and Hubert Henderson wrote a pamphlet 'Can Lloyd George do it?', supporting that statesman's campaign for public works and sketching out the theory that a budget deficit can reduce unemployment without causing inflation. A new era in economics, as in much else, was about to begin.

———◆◆◆———

CHAPTER THREE

Politics

At the height of the General Strike on 9 May 1926, Parry, Vice-Master of Trinity, collected the signatures of some senior members of the University urging Baldwin to take the initiative at once in reopening negotiations with the TUC. This provoked a counter-manifesto. The doves numbered 104 and included Forbes, Blackett, Keynes, Lucas, Willey, Adrian, Broad, Burnaby, Cornford, Hollond, Littlewood, D. H. Robertson, D. S. Robertson and Winstanley. There were 215 hawks, including Spens, Gray, Cockerell of the Fitzwilliam, 'Q', Temperley, Housman, Laurence, Beves, Sorley, Attwater and Hadley.

There were many Cambridge dons who had been bred and nurtured in the traditions of the now old-fashioned Liberalism. As Bishop Barnes told the Union nostalgically in the centenary debate of 1921 'one Victorian Chartist is worth a thousand Glasgow Bolsheviks'. Of B. L. Manning it was said that his personal philosophy was based on the Glorious Revolution, Mr Gladstone's platform in 1886, and the Dissenting interest. Of a similar type were men like Glover and F. R. Salter of Magdalene. History was still Whig history and economics *laissez-faire* economics. Keynes's 1925 pamphlet 'Am I a Liberal?' found an echo in many Cambridge hearts and minds. 'How could I bring myself to be a Conservative? They offer me neither food nor drink – neither intellectual nor spiritual consolation.' As to Labour: 'I do not believe that the intellectual elements in the party will ever exercise adequate control.' The extreme Left is 'the party of catastrophe . . . In Great Britain it is, in its extreme form, numerically very weak. Nevertheless, its philosophy in a diluted form permeates, in my opinion, the whole Labour party . . . It is necessary for a successful Labour leader to be, or at least to appear, a little savage. It is not enough that he must love his fellow-men; he must hate them too.' In that same year Ramsay MacDonald, whose acquaintance with duchesses was not yet as extensive as it became, exemplified this dictum in an address to the town and gown Labour organizations (an affair described by D. R. Hardman as 'the greatest event in the history of Cambridge Labour') by telling them that 'gentility is the greatest curse that ever fell on a virile intelligence'.

However, throughout the twenties the prevalent majority in the university was undoubtedly Conservative in outlook. Their main political enthusiasms were hostility to Bolshevism, suspicion of the motives of trade unions and Labour politicians and a belief in the continuing utility and virtues of the British Empire. Professor Paul Milyukoff, leader of the Cadets in the Duma, told them in February 1919 something of Bolshevik methods and aims at first hand. Dean Inge two years later took part in a debate, in which he said that 'in 1906 when the trade unions were exempted from the law of conspiracy, democratic government virtually committed suicide'. McTaggart, on learning that certain trade unionists had been complaining that a well-known Labour leader had done no manual work, observed: 'Nothing could be more unjust; his hands are horny with wire-pulling.' Benson in July 1924 went to Gresham's School speech day, where the new Labour Minister of Education was giving away the prizes. 'Charles Trevelyan . . . spoke at Holt yesterday. He is a handsome man with the pale eyes of a fanatic. He made a vulgar attack on the old public schools – and rejoiced that the blue-blooded land-owning aristocratic product was down in the market. He thanked God that for the first time for two hundred years there was no Etonian in the Cabinet. But as he is a blue-blooded aristocratic landowner, and a Harrovian, and as Chelmsford is a Wykehamist etc, it ended by being only a jealous attack on Eton. He spoke idealistically and with some passion and impressed the boys – but it was sickeningly egotistical – I'm afraid he is a fake as a Labour man. I disliked him heartily.' On Empire Day 1925, the Archbishop of Armagh's sermon included the following passage: 'Yes, the British Empire is in the main the splendid monument of men who sought, not empire, but space for great endeavour and ampler labours. And they built far better than they knew; for they not only won new territories from the wilderness, but incidentally they opened the way for the spread of education and the liberation of the enslaved. Gradually too, as the Empire develops, we can trace the emergence of higher principles and better methods. Slavery is abolished; sympathy for the oppressed extends; the Christian missionary comes, bringing with him the message of Christ, the highest medical skill and establishing schools and colleges. Savage people are transformed. I could quote instance after instance of such developments from every part of the Empire. It is a glorious record. Yes. Let us keep Empire Day with a good conscience . . .' Less felicitously, from the University pulpit, the Right Reverend T. C. Fisher, Bishop of Nyasaland, told his congregation that some years previously a writer had been a good deal criticized for saying he wished to try to train the African native as he trained his dog, but that he himself did not feel inclined to criticize the sentence so sharply as he knew both the writer and the dog. In 1927 there were just over a hundred Indian students in residence. R. B. Whitehead, their Cambridge adviser, told the Tutorial Representatives next year that a friend of his in the ICS had received a Christmas card addressed to his wife and himself from a Punjabi on which was written 'to my respected father and dearly loved mother'. This, he observed, was intended quite seriously, as the Indian claims not only the privileged position of a child, but the treatment which a spoiled child receives from indulgent parents. To him, the Adviser's agency was not a front entrance through which only those properly accredited could pass, but a back door through which they could slip in spite of rules and regulations.

The Union in the twenties provided the nursery battle ground for some prominent Conservative politicians of the future. *The Cambridge Review*'s reporter in May 1922 said that Mr R. A. Butler of Pembroke 'should go far'. In 1924, *Granta* with its lighter touch described him, now President of the Union, as 'a Tory, if ever there was one, though *on dit* . . . with progressive leanings'. He was described as living very hospitably in '*une mansarde pittoresquement meublée*', as befitted the General Secretary of the French Society. A rather more irreverent reporter wrote of him in November 1924 as speaking of 'the desirability of keeping the fulcrum of the balance, the via-media-ah, a compromise. All the little boys and girls love Uncle R. A. B.' Geoffrey Lloyd and Selwyn Lloyd were both Presidents of the Union in the twenties, but whereas the former fought a South London constituency as a Conservative while Vice-President, Selwyn Lloyd figures frequently in debate as a militant Liberal. In 1924 we learn of him speaking 'as a Liberal who felt nearer Labour than Conservatism and spoke very well'. In the following year, whether from conviction or merely to argue a case, he inveighed epigrammatically against field sports – 'cruelty, corpulence and corruption are the characteristics of hunting men. Hunting is morally degrading and bestial.' In that same year, 1925, the year of the Archbishop of Armagh's sermon, he pointed out that dividends in Indian jute were 400 per cent and that there was exploitation on the one hand and the sending out of missionaries on the other, an observation which presumably swayed the Union to vote for immediate self-government for India within the Empire by 228 votes to 123. In 1927 he was adopted as Liberal candidate for Macclesfield.

Other prominent Union debaters of the period to achieve subsequent distinction in various spheres of public life were A. M. Ramsey (Magdalene), P. A. Devlin (Christ's), G. Crowther (Clare), Gilbert Harding (Queens'), D. R. Hardman (Christ's), and H. L. Elvin (Trinity Hall). The future Archbishop of Canterbury was President in 1926, in which year Asquith told a Cambridge gathering that 'in my opinion a future leader of my party is in your very midst'. While still an undergraduate Ramsey was adopted as a Liberal candidate. In a 1924 debate he was to be found on the same side as Dobb, viewing with pleasure the prospect of a Labour administration, a motion lost by only ten votes in a sizeable house. Despite what *Paradise Lost* has to say on the subject, he told the Union in 1926 that 'it is not authority but revolt against authority that produces creation'. He was enormously successful, but met his match in a debate in 1924 on a motion with a somewhat familiar ring about it, to the effect that 'Liberalism is moribund and futile'. Devlin, we are told, made on this occasion 'an exceptional first speech on the paper', and was described as having 'good red hair and a voice which carries', while Ramsey was urged to 'avoid sing-song rhetoric'. Devlin was impatient with strikers, observing, again in 1924, that 'a strike in the army would be called a mutiny and in the same way those occupied in important trades who strike should be treated as mutineers against the State'. Geoffrey Crowther, a future editor of *The Economist* and industrial magnate, was presciently described in 1928 as having selected for his chosen profession 'magnacy'. He carried a 1926 debate on trade unions against Selwyn Lloyd by 378 to 237, telling the house that 'trade unionism was born in and thrives on discontent; and if there is no discontent it manufactures it'. Gilbert Harding, one of the great characters of the early days of television, was even as an undergraduate too abrasive a personality to achieve the presidency. But we have an interesting glimpse of the child being father to the man in 1927, when he is described as tearing Lord Pentland limb from limb, spitting on the remains and performing a war dance. It was a pity that he did not in later life recall the warning given him by *The Cambridge Review* in 1927 that 'abuse is only tolerable when it is amusing'.

Hardman and Elvin were Socialists. The latter, from a trade union background and a fine scholar and athlete, who eventually became a prominent member of the English faculty and a professor of education, was a Fabian and a pacifist. He became President in 1927. He told the Liberals that they would never deal effectively with poverty, because they refused to conduct an onslaught on the private ownership of land and industrial capital. David Hardman, who for a short time after the Second World War was a junior Labour minister, was described by *Granta* as 'an immaculate apostle of the people's cause'. As President in 1925 he headed the signatories of a letter, which included Elvin, to the effect that: 'We, the undersigned, convinced that all disputes between nations are capable of settlement either by diplomatic negotiation or by some form of international arbitration, hereby solemnly declare that we shall refuse to support or render war service to any government which resorts to arms.' However, at a subsequent explanatory meeting it was conceded that 'pacifism is a dogma, subject to the interpretation of the individual conscience'. The Labour Club had between a hundred and a hundred and fifty undergraduate members in the early twenties. By 1926 Girton had twenty Labour Club members to thirty-four paid up Conservatives. The fact that in 1927 the Labour Club had its first May Week ball in fancy dress suggests that we are still some distance from the grimly committed Left of the thirties. As far as fancy dress was concerned, it was suggested by the relentlessly frivolous Right that one might be appropriately apparelled as a herald of the Red Dawn.

The only Communist to earn consistent publicity was Dobb, but there was a fair amount of party activity above ground. C. W. Guillebaud, Marshall's nephew, a knowledgeable tutor and teacher, wrote that the undergraduates of the twenties were much less conservatively minded than they had been. 'War, inflation, and deflation, with their devastating effect on the value of investments, have weakened the whole idea of property in people's minds . . . The Russian experiment has aroused very great interest inside the university. It is felt to be bold and constructive.' He noted the existence of a very small, though active and vocal, Communist society with perhaps thirty members. Slavish adulation of the USSR had not yet become the prevalent *trahison des clercs*. (Eliot, incidentally, reviewed Benda's book of that title for *The Cambridge Review* in 1928.) Russell and Keynes vied with each other in denouncing what they saw during characteristically short trips to Russia, of the sort which would later provoke an almost mystic exaltation among British middle-class worshippers at the shrine of Magnetogorsk. In 1920 Russell described himself as 'infinitely unhappy in Russia', 'stifled by its utilitarianism, its indifference to love and beauty and the life of impulse'. Twenty-one years later he had not changed his mind, writing to Gilbert Murray that he had no doubt 'that the Soviet Government is even worse than Hitler's'. Keynes' visit in 1925 prompted him to write: 'It is hard for an educated, decent, intelligent son of Western Europe to find his ideals here, unless he has suffered some strange and horrid process of conversion which has changed all his values.' And again – 'in Western industrial conditions the tactics of Red revolution would throw the whole population into a pit of poverty and death'. Dobb, however, knew how to strike just the right note. Debating at the Union in November 1925, he claimed that an aristocracy of intellect was more likely to rule Russia than any other country and that science and art were prospering as never before.

Earlier in that year the urgent desirability of class war was proposed by Mr C. W. Brown, described as an active young Communist from the Old Kent Road. His speech was greeted 'with a volume of applause that is seldom accorded by the house'. However, not only did Devlin tell him that class war meant revolution and revolution never had and never would benefit working people, but Mr C. L. Cartmell, a Tory ware-houseman from Walworth, declared roundly that class war was out of date, and Mr Brown only mustered 61 votes against 431.

There was never any shortage of politicians and pedlars of utopian nostrums converging on Cambridge by limousine or by the LNER from Liverpool Street. Most of them arrived unmolested, but an exception was S. Saklatvala, Communist MP for North Battersea, who was prevented from speaking in November 1924 by a gang called the British Fascisti. The undergraduates involved were publicly condemned in a joint letter signed by Butler and the officers of the other political clubs. A popular speaker was the future leader of the Labour Party, George Lansbury, who tended to be 'cheered to the echo' for his particular brand of radical pacifism and political soul searching. He aroused somewhat un-Christian sentiments in a future ecclesiastical dignitary, Charles Smyth, then at Corpus and a particularly voluminous Tory polemicist, who wrote in 1924: 'Mr Lansbury combines with his ostentatious and greasy piety a record of three imprisonments . . . an avowed admiration for Russian Bolshevism and a violent advocacy of direct action and republicanism. There is only one possible comment on his much advertised piety and it is the emphatic and comprehensive comment of Mr Scrooge: "Humbug!"' Sir Samuel Hoare's almost unique gift for inaccurate prophecy was exemplified when he declared himself in 1927 as being of the firm belief that we were not drifting into war but moving steadily and surely towards organized peace. Arthur Ponsonby tirelessly advocated Britain adopting a posture of total unpreparedness for war, although in 1928 the

Union was not in favour of 'peace at any price' by 304 votes to
222, G. K. Chesterton prevailing over Beverley Nichols.
Harold Laski in fine populist form told the Marshall Society
in 1928 that 'the validity of the law is based on common consent and in so far as law is not in accord with their will citizens
have every justification for disobedience . . . the truest citizen
must have in him the Athanasian element and all political
action should be surrounded with contingent anarchy.'
Perhaps all this twentieth century speaking with tongues was
at the back of the Bishop of Portsmouth's mind in his Commemoration sermon at Christ's in 1927 and so led him to
indulge in optimistic and suitably nautical metaphor – 'if we
do not yet see the City of God coming down from heaven we
do see hundreds of people manning ropes of varying calibre,
intended by united effort to bring it down.'

Actions spoke a good deal louder than words during the
General Strike in 1926, described in *The Dial* as the greatest
national crisis since the fall of the Stuarts. Rather less por-
tentously, the Christ's magazine observed that 'most men
regarded the strike as a gigantic and well-timed rag, and the
haste to volunteer was less from lack of sympathy with the
individual striker than anxiety not to be left out of the fun . . .
even the most hardened socialism was apt to break down before
the lure of realizing at last a latent but long-cherished desire to
drive a real train'. The strike lasted from the 3rd to 12th May.
On 10 May the Tutorial Representatives reported that 2650
undergraduates (i.e. over half) had registered for emergency
duty and 1450 had been called up and gone away. The original
embargo on the release of men considered likely to obtain
firsts had been lifted and it had been agreed to postpone the
examinations if necessary.

Hull, Grimsby, Southampton and London were the important centres of undergraduate activity. The gentle Charles
Crawley of Trinity Hall and Owen Morshead of Magdalene, a
future librarian of Windsor Castle with a brilliant war record,
led a contingent to Hull docks where they directed proceedings
from a battleship guarded by soldiers with Lewis guns.
Berthed near by was another party commanded from a liner
by the intrepid Dean of King's, Milner White. A Queens'

contingent recorded: 'We started to unload the *Rother* at about tea-time and finished her at 1.45 the next morning. Ship unloaded in record time. Cargo – butter, dead pigs, condensed milk, pigs' offal in large barrels, one of which burst on our heads.' They reported that while several Hull men had their lives threatened and were forced to leave their trams, undergraduates seemed to amuse the strikers too much for them to be more than passively hostile as a rule. The general population felt rather differently – 'never shall I forget the moment when an old lady came up to us in the streets of Hull, where we were being somewhat of a nuisance, and said: "God bless you boys, you have saved Hull by your cheery spirits." ' The Port Master of Grimsby Docks gave it as his opinion that 'while other volunteer labour was procured, there is no doubt whatever that the stiffening of the morale of the volunteers was achieved by the splendid example of courageous and untiring energy set by the splendid young men from Cambridge University'.

W. H. Powell, the captain of the Cambridge lawn tennis team, drove a Metropolitan Electric from Whitechapel to Ealing and Joseph Needham a steam engine from Cambridge to London. An undergraduate on being given a tip at Liverpool Street by an old lady for driving the train successfully from Cambridge told her that he had only discovered how the brakes worked at Bethnal Green. Portway was naturally in the thick of things in command of an Officer Training Corps party in London docks, with his HQ on a New Zealand liner. Since the strikers had cut off the electricity there were no cranes, but Royal Navy submarines were on hand to provide the necessary current for the refrigerators. A group of Queens' men who had hoped to drive the London tubes were headed off to Chiswick to drive buses, an experience described with a certain retrospective archness by one of them as follows: 'This, to a being that moves in predestinate grooves, was something more than a shock, it was a derailment. All sense of inevitability was gone. One would dive about anywhere, skidding and bumping into things. Besides, up till now my life had not been haphazard; it had been run on the best lines; and if I sometimes wondered whether I wasn't after all a tube, I knew I wasn't a bus.'

At the end, Admiral Royds wrote to Seward, the Vice-

Chancellor: 'You have need to be proud of your young chaps; healthy, strong, keen, and entirely the right stuff', and hoped that the examiners would remember the mental and physical strain they had endured. A less exalted personage, the chairman of the Hull Tramways Committee, wrote: 'It is impossible for me to express adequately the moral effect which the undergraduates produced; their exuberance, pluck, and, above all, their willingness and ability to carry out work which does not in an ordinary way fall to their lot was a revelation to the people of Hull.' He thought he would improve the shining hour by asking them to break a strike which had started before the General Strike and was nothing to do with it, but this they very properly refused to do. The Southampton authorities wrote to the Proctors thanking the volunteers, who had kept the port going. Two conspicuous Cambridge figures who stayed behind were Gilbert Harding, who had been brought up in an orphanage and emphatically didn't hold with strikebreaking, and Steven Runciman, who is said to have claimed that the interruption in his normal studies had just given him time to read the whole of *The Cambridge Modern History*. Volunteers from Caius were mostly special constables in Whitechapel. They recorded on their return that the fury of those who had never been sent off was a pleasant sight to see. By 21 May, *Granta* felt able to announce that 'despite the strike, despite the cold, despite the rain, some sort of a May Week seems to be coming'.

Outwardly, everything seemed to be returning to normal in Cambridge. But it is possible to detect an accumulation of small indications of increased social concern and anxiety before the second Labour government and the slump were to usher in a different political atmosphere. In March 1927 the Conservative Association reached a record membership of over seven hundred, over twice what it had been in 1923, and dined Stanley Baldwin at the Lion with much singing of 'For he's a jolly good fellow'. But that same year the Marshall Society was launched with P. A. Sloan, a left-wing socialist, as secretary, its promotional credo running: 'Have you ever thought of taking an interest in the lives of other people? In all of us as a community? Of the boons of some and of the sorrows and difficulties of others? Oh, no, not a political society; nor a religious society – but a society unmoved by such prejudices.' By the end of the year it had recruited 150 members and had organized a visit to the Gas, Light and Coke Company. In February 1928 under the Society's auspices a party of London dockers visited Cambridge; in 1929 thirty dockers and fifteen wives were similarly entertained. In November 1928 an appeal for distressed miners was launched under the signatures of C. D. Aarvold of Caius, Captain of the Rugby XV (a future Recorder of London), E. S. Abbot of Jesus, Chairman of the Student Christian Movement (a future Dean of Westminster) and Crowther, then President of the Union. The letter stated that 'the approaching winter will mean starvation and misery to many thousands in this country . . . unemployment insurance benefits are totally inadequate to cope with a catastrophe of such dimensions'. Arthur Greenwood told the Marshall Society that while he admitted the possibility that twenty per cent of council tenants might keep coal in the bath, he nevertheless considered that housing was more important than education as a factor in producing quality in the people. In a well attended confidence debate in October Keynes pitched into the Government, defended by Leo Amery – 'their one definite idea, that of insisting on economy at all costs, has become with them an obsession so disproportionate as to exclude all others . . . all schemes which would cause more employment are indiscriminately turned down by the Government on the ground of expense'. This speech carried the day by 292 to 207.

On 30 May the following year the General Election entailed the formation of the second Labour government. For once, Sir Samuel Hoare would be vindicated by subsequent events when he asked the Conservative Association just before the election to consider what unity there could be among revolutionaries, trade union leaders and sentimentalists. But for the moment matters looked very different. Maurice Dobb had just revisited Russia; Bernal published *The World, The Flesh and The Devil*, advancing the view that Marxism and Communism are not ends in themselves, but the best available means of achieving the transfer of power to the scientist; George Lansbury had told the Union that if you rule out the working classes nobody worth while is left; Jennie Lee aroused great enthusiasm when addressing the Labour Club in Matthews's Cafe; and the Union voted for women to have full University status. Lord Pentland, now President, felt it necessary to write to the Conservatives asking them to try to improve the quality of their speakers to match 'the wealth of Progressive talent'. Even Captain Anthony Eden, described the year before in the Conservative Association's programme as 'a marked man among the younger back-benchers', was unable to rally much support for his proposed cure for unemployment – imperial preference, rate relief, rationalization of industry and rigid economy. *The Eagle* indeed went so far as to define a Cambridge Conservative as the proud possessor of a certain tie, obtained by signifying with a subscription his refusal or his inability to think out any social question.

The editorial of *The Cambridge Review* on 22 November put to its readers what it evidently saw as a rhetorical question: 'Can it be that Cambridge is more serious-minded than had been expected?'

Part II

—◆◇◆—

THE THIRTIES

'I would rather have the Communists than the Fascists' said Mrs Maclintick, compressing her lips.

'Only because you think it is the done thing to be on the Left' said Maclintick, with an enraging smile. 'There isn't a middle-brow in the country who isn't expressing the same sentiment. They should try a little practical Communism and see how they like it.'

(Anthony Powell –
Casanova's Chinese Restaurant)

CHAPTER FOUR

Men, Women and Manners II

Evidently something had gone wrong. Unemployment after the General Election in May was at a figure of 1,164,000. By January 1930 it had reached 1,520,000; by the end of the year 2,500,000. Early in 1931 the Education Minister Sir Charles Trevelyan, once the object of Benson's animosity, resigned because of the government's inactivity, as Sir Oswald Mosley had before him. By June unemployment was approaching three million and next month the Macmillan Report on Finance and Industry, largely drafted by Keynes, highlighted the lack of balance between supply and demand and the decline in British exports. By August the financial and political crisis had led to the formation of the National Government.

To some extent Cambridge opinion reflected the impact of all this. In the University sermon on 7 March 1930, the Reverend F. Homes Dudden, Master of Pembroke, Oxford, preached on the theme of signs of the times, using phrases like 'widespread dissatisfaction with the general conditions of life . . . all seem more or less unhappy . . . we have been woefully let down . . . our hopes have not been realized . . .' Later in the year, the Bishop of Wakefield on the same topic referred to 'a wave of pessimism which is attacking all alike'. The Union debated a startlingly chosen motion to the effect that the British Empire was moribund. A reviewer of *Portraits in Miniature* gently chided an author hitherto above fashionable criticism – 'Mr Strachey's values seem bland and banal. It is less easy these days to do without a conscience.'

Many, dons and undergraduates alike, politicized their consciences. So many in fact that one of the most celebrated undergraduates of the late twenties, Julian Bell, whom we have already encountered lampooning Wittgenstein, wrote a famous letter to the *New Statesman* in December 1933, which was to form the basis of a decidedly misleading – indeed almost hackneyed – mythology about Cambridge in the thirties. 'In the Cambridge that I first knew, in 1929 and 1930, the central subject of ordinary intelligent conversation was poetry. As far as I can remember we hardly ever talked or thought about politics. For one thing, we almost all of us had implicit confidence in Maynard Keynes' rosy prophecies of continually increasing capitalist prosperity. Only the secondary problems, such as birth control, seemed to need the intervention of the intellectuals. By the end of 1933, we have arrived at a situation in which almost the only subject of discussion is contemporary politics, and in which a very large majority of the more intelligent undergraduates are Communists or almost Communists . . . If Communism makes many of its converts among the "emotionals", it appeals almost as strongly to minds a great deal harder. It is not so much that we are all Socialists now as that we are all Marxists now . . . It would be difficult to find anyone of any intellectual pretensions who would not accept the general Marxist analysis of the present crisis.' In 1933 this was nonsense. It would be 1937 or 1938 before it even approximated to the truth. Bell was writing as a true son of Bloomsbury, one of the *illuminati*, for whom their truth is all truth. To do him justice, he was soon to bemoan publicly the extent to which all free discussion among the Apostles was stultified by Marxist dialectical rigidity. In fact, the collectivist fervour of the thirties left the university as such remarkably unaffected, the twenties with the new statutes and the influx of grant-aided students being a much more significant era of change. As to the undergraduates, there were plenty with intellectual pretensions and no Marxist predilections, such as Enoch Powell, Iain Macleod, Alastair Cooke, F. H. Lawton, Anthony Blackwell, J. H. Plumb, Michael Grant, J. R. Colville. During the General Election of 1935 a concurrent undergraduate poll produced the following result:

> Hesketh (national Conservative) 650
> Charles Fletcher Cooke (Socialist)* 275
> Layton (Liberal) 171

Attitudes in fact changed comparatively slowly with the

* A Conservative MP since 1951.

majority of traditionally minded dons and undergraduates. In some Colleges – Clare, Corpus, Pembroke, Peterhouse, Selwyn – the prevalent ethos altered only imperceptibly between 1924 and the outbreak of war. In Magdalene under A. B. Ramsay there was a positive (or perhaps more properly negative) reaction against the heady intellectual excitements of the era of Empson and Redgrave. The entry in October 1925 comprised sixty public schoolboys (ten Etonians), two from overseas and two from maintained schools; in October 1938 sixty-five public schoolboys (nineteen Etonians), five from overseas and two from maintained schools. In 1931 Clare had no fewer than eighty-five members of the Conservative Association and in a 1938 *Granta* article entitled 'Clare, the Public School College', the author complained that living in it he felt that the institution of staircase prefects was only a question of time. Invited to decline to wear the old school tie in 1935, the members of the Union decided that they proposed to go on doing so, although two years later they concluded that the public schools were a disgrace to twentieth-century England. When the *Daily Worker* printed the menu of a Trinity feast *in toto* in 1932, *Granta* suggested that the moral was to stop being one of the workers and become a Trinity don instead; in 1933 the Union voted against the opening of cinemas on Sundays; and in 1934 a serious article on American coeducation argued that no theory could present a case against coeducation so strong as the practice of it in most American colleges. On the death of George V in 1936 it was reported that 'there has been no false emotion, but everywhere the mourning dress, the black boarded shop windows and a sort of subdued atmosphere have borne witness to the real awe and sorrow in our hearts'. True, there were a few who chose ostentatiously to wear red ties to mark the occasion, but it seemed to *The Cambridge Review* that anyone doing so revealed himself as one of nature's prunes.

Julian Symons in his brilliant short study called *The Thirties* sees the middle-class, Left Wing cult, which is usually labelled with the name of the decade, as resembling a pyramid. At the apex was a very small and highly influential group of poets, journalists, makers of documentary films, novelists of social realism, theatre directors, politically active scientists, 'mass observers' and other opinion formers; in the middle some 50,000 concerned and potentially active sympathizers; and a base comprising the general intelligentsia of the nation, a million or so of them, more or less responsive to the new intellectual fashions and providing an audience. This useful image is to some extent transferable to Cambridge under- graduates. At the apex the small, tightly knit groups – Guest, Cornforth, Burgess, Cornford, Klugmann, Maclean, Kiernan, Hobsbawm, Keuneman, Kettle, Nahum, with a strong but small group of directing and supporting dons; in the middle those who at least joined political clubs and the occasional procession; and a base of vaguely interested sympathizers, of uncertain or no political allegiance, becoming increasingly concerned and anxious about unemployment and the growth of Fascism. Till at the earliest 1933, the whole of the pyramid constituted no more than a small fraction of the undergraduate population. But by 1938 the Socialist Club claimed a member- ship of 1000 out of rather less than 5000 undergraduates.

However, the analogy can be pushed too far. The University Camps for the Unemployed, through which many under- graduates saw unemployment in Jarrow at first hand and made friends personally with men who had been out of work for years, were Christian in inspiration, and not Marxist. Although the Marxist David Guest saw briefly the inside of a prison in Germany, he was by no means the only Cambridge man to visit that country and so able to form his own con- clusions at first hand as to how things were going. A. G. K. Brown, an outstanding track runner, was probably at least as effective an anti-Nazi propagandist as a result of competing in the Berlin Olympics. And in particular, in the general emotional ferment after 1936 the Moral Rearmament movement made rapid progress among those whom Julian Bell called 'the emotionals'.

For the large body of undergraduates, politics was something that could wait, since there seemed little they could sensibly do, and Moral Rearmament something with no relish of salvation in it. Meanwhile, many of them felt a certain amount of anxiety about their future, while being aware of abundant opportunities to enjoy themselves, a mixture calculated to create, as it did, a rather heady *carpe diem* atmosphere. Job prospects were not quite so secure as they had been and after 1936 the possibility of war no longer merely a distant menace. To Oxford men the Cambridge of the twenties had seemed comparatively serious and dowdy. Now that began to change. The Festival, always in a state of near bankruptcy under Terence Gray and then Joseph Gordon Macleod, became more experimental than ever. In *The Merchant of Venice* the Doge disported himself with a yo-yo and Portia discoursed on the quality of mercy bolt upright on a swing; in *Twelfth Night* Sir Toby came on in roller-skates and one whole scene was enacted in Elizabethan pronunciation; *The Wild Duck* was presented with orange screens painted with black ducks; and the last impossible act of *Cymbeline* was unceremoniously despatched as if it were a game of ring a ring o'roses. In 1931 Rylands produced Redgrave at the ADC in *Captain Brass-bound's Conversion*, with scenery designed by Guy Burgess, the future defector, and he followed this in 1932 with a notable *Othello* in which he himself played Emilia. The theatre was burnt down in 1933. Dennis Arundell and Mrs Prior brought *The Fairy Queen* out of her wraps again, Rootham staged *Samson* in the Guildhall and this was followed by *Jephtha* and *Saul*. The two major developments of the period were, however, the advance of the cinema and the opening of the Arts Theatre in 1936. In 1929 *The Cambridge Review* carried a very serious article purporting to demonstrate that the 'talkies' could never be a serious rival to the 'cinema proper', and another in 1931 stating that the ultimate test of any sound film arises when the sound-projecting apparatus breaks down. By the end of the thirties, the middle-brows at any rate would have complained loudly if the sound track had impeded their enjoyment of the Astaire-Rogers epics or the contrasted charms of Mae West or Greta Garbo. But for the high-brows, a weekly visit to Norman Higgins' excruciatingly uncomfortable Cosmopolitan Cinema, opened in 1933, was obligatory. It is indeed arguable that more young Englishmen of the period acquired their pacifism from *La Grande Illusion* than from Lord Ponsonby and their communism from Fritz Lang's *Metropolis* than from Marx. But there were also to be seen *Sous les Toits de Paris* and *A Nous la Liberté, The Testament of*

Dr Mabuse and '*M*'. By 1936 there were no fewer than ten cinemas. Keynes chose Higgins as the first General Manager of the Arts Theatre, his particular brain-child, which opened just off King's Parade in 1936 with a gala performance by the Vic-Wells ballet with Robert Helpmann in *The Rake's Progress* and Constant Lambert conducting. There was a notable season of Ibsen with Jean Forbes Robertson and Lydia Lopokova as an unforgettable Nora in *The Doll's House*.

Cambridge won the Boat Race year after year. Steve Fairbairn is alleged to have continued coaching the Jesus boat from his death-bed in 1938, a circumstance which no doubt occurred to his obituarist when he reminded his readers of the great man's dictum that you should face your stretcher as honestly as you should face your God. For the less dedicated, it was the heyday of poker and bridge and it was lamented that as the tripos approached in 1931 the voice of the croupier could no longer be heard from Trinity Street ringing out in Great Court.

In ball games, a theoretical competition between the heroes of the twenties and those of the thirties would be won by the twenties, although not by a great margin, except perhaps in cricket and lawn tennis. H. Ashton, A. E. R. Gilligan, A. P. F. Chapman, G. O. Allen, K. S. Duleepsinhji, who made 254 not out in four hours against Middlesex in 1927, in cricket, and H. W. Austin in lawn tennis were in their prime more or less *hors concours*. Lord Burghley as a hurdler and W. W. Wakefield and C. D. Aarvold as Rugby players were in the same class. Ashton, Wakefield and R. R. Stokes, a Rugby blue, became MPs and Aarvold and Rowe Harding, a Welsh Rugby international, judges. L. G. Crawley, a cricketer and golfer, and C. T. Ashton, a cricketer and Association footballer, were by any standards remarkable all-rounders. The Rugby players of the thirties were consistently formidable year after year, especially perhaps the Welshmen C. W. Jones and W. Wooller; N. W. D. Yardley was a particularly talented all-round games player and like Gilligan, Chapman and Allen a future England cricket captain; and an American D. N. Jones had the fastest service in the world at lawn tennis while a Cambridge undergraduate. There were also three interesting examples of outstanding games players of particularly high academic ability. J. G. W. Davies of St John's secured a double first in Classics, as well as bowling Bradman out for nought before lunch at Fenners in 1935, being rebuked by the treasurer of the cricket club for thereby impairing the club's finances. W. O. Chadwick of the same college, a future Master of Selwyn and Regius Professor, had firsts in History and theology, as well as a Rugby blue and an England trial. A particularly spectacular personality was K. C. Gandar Dower, whose career spanned the end of the one decade and the beginning of the next. A history scholar of Trinity, he just failed to secure the first classes expected of him, but was considered the outstanding Union debater of his time and was at one period editor of *Granta*, which wrote of him in the summer of 1931: 'there is no one who will be so universally missed when he goes down at the end of the term'. In the Freshmen's lawn tennis tournament he played two singles and a double and in the same afternoon made fifty-four not out in the Freshmen's cricket match. He had blues or half blues at lawn tennis (at which he won a set at Wimbledon as an undergraduate against Henri Cochet), real tennis, Rugby Fives, Eton Fives and billiards. He also found time for flying aeroplanes. After going down, he did some exploration in Kenya and tamed a team of cheetahs, which he brought back to England to race against greyhounds. At the outbreak of the war he was photographing gorillas in the Congo.

All in all, it was undoubtedly a period when athletic prowess was much valued, though without the grimness of dedication which today tends to turn games into a professional treadmill. Even as late as 1938 one could read in a column entitled 'the Cambridge Sportsman's Diary' a metaphorically rather unfortunate observation to the effect that boxing is the acid test of guts. However, many of the graduates of that particular year would emerge into a world where physical strength and agility would be prerequisites of survival.

Socially, the thirties were the high noon of King's. To say this is not to disparage the formidable intellectual quality of the college, but rather to emphasize the extent to which those who, like St Paul's Athenians, sought to hear some new thing, tended to gravitate there. Sheppard became Vice-Provost in

1929 and Provost in 1933. He had come a long way since Benson had written of him in 1923: 'Sheppard is very low, feeling that he is deliberately excluded by the classical people etc. – the reveries of the rather tattered butterfly! One can't go on being like Puck and Ariel and thinking everyone else pompous and absurd, and then suddenly hatch out into a serious and well-respected man.' His Greek plays continued to thrive – *Bacchae* (1930), *Oresteia* (1933), *Frogs* (1936) and *Antigone* (1939); he was in constant demand to give informal talks to college societies; he saw all his college scholarship candidates by groups, characteristically sitting with them on the floor asking them about themselves. Eric Hobsbawm described him lecturing in 1937 as follows: 'The Provost has risen slowly from his chair and is leaning over the desk looking slowly round the amphitheatre. He does not say a word, his mouth is frozen half-open and his eyes enjoy themselves. One could hear a pin drop if one was interested in pins at the moment, but one is busy admiring the beautiful management of the pause and the resonance of the whisper with which he ends it quite suddenly, with a jerk and a quotation from the Odyssey. And he goes on in short rhythmical phrases and beautiful suppleness of tone. He sways slightly to and fro in his high chair, his face a cross between Buddha and Mr Pickwick in its all-embracing benignity. He takes off his spectacles with slow deliberateness and lets the house watch him. "*Musa mihi causas*", he says in a mixture of the conversational and the rotund, and looks harmlessly at the puzzled Americans who do not know whether it is worth noting down, and the man in the Clare gown, who looks as though he had dropped in by mistake.'

With Sheppard, Beves, Rylands and Keynes, King's was the natural centre of Cambridge theatre. As for music, Boris Ord, who became organist of the College in 1929, succeeding Dr Mann who had held the post for over fifty years, was an unusually versatile musician, creator of the University Madrigal Society and the successor of Rootham in 1936 as the conductor of the CUMS. The prevalent ethos in the college was considerably more liberal, permissive and on the whole stylish than that which generally obtained in Cambridge.

Arguably the founding father of this attitude, Goldsworthy

Lowes Dickinson, the legendary Goldie, died in 1932. The posthumous publication of his autobiography, with its cloying repetitive accounts of rather gloomy *grandes passions* for a succession of young men, combined with a fetishistic fervour for highly polished boots, has done his memory no service at all. On the other hand, the affection he inspired in his life-time has probably led to his being posthumously over-valued. F. L. Lucas, for instance, considered him the only saint he had ever met, 'an ivory-yellow mandarin in his black-silk Chinese cap, whose despair would suddenly relieve itself in a smiling handshake, a little crackling laugh, and a wave of his hands at the diabolical irony of things.' Sheppard was wildly off the mark when he wrote that Lowes Dickinson's most celebrated book *The International Anarchy* might come to be recognized by future generations as the greatest contribution Cambridge ever made to historical research. If we can believe Kingsley Martin, the first edition sold only a thousand copies. Lowes Dickinson liked to imagine that he was a reincarnated China-man. Shelley and especially Plato were his heroes and Lucas described him as one of the few idealists who do not raise one's opinion of materialism. E. M. Forster, whose *Passage to India* (1924) was pretty generally praised in the thirties as almost the greatest of modern novels (except by some who had lived a long time in India) wrote a sensitive, if highly laudatory, biography of Goldie in 1934, in which he went so far as to claim that the truest words said about him were those of his former bedmaker: 'He was the best man who ever lived.' Goldie was an occasional, if not particularly felicitous, poet. From one of his pieces, we learn that the attitude of the Cambridge don should be that of one 'not wholly from the world withdrawn nor wholly to its service drawn'. For his part, he was a great League of Nations man. Indeed, according to Forster he virtually invented the idea. Lowes Dickinson and Forster, elected a fellow in 1927, had much in common. Forster's posthumous novel *Maurice* would have been better left unpublished in the bottom drawer along with Lowes Dickinson's autobiography. When Forster described his friend Goldie as a tortured humanitarian he could equally well have applied the phrase to himself in the thirties. They were both, of course, prominent leaders of the enlightened *bien pensants* of their day. Stephen Spender, in *Forward from Liberalism*, quoted Forster to the effect that no political creed except Communism offered the intelligent man any hope, an observation made at the height of Stalin's purges. However, if all that glittered in King's in the thirties was not pure gold, it was certainly a college where the *beau monde* of Cambridge enjoyed itself prodigiously.

A pre-war Kingsman, Will Spens, had transferred his allegiance in 1906 to Corpus Christi, where at the age of twenty-four he became the college's first director of studies in natural sciences and thereafter tutor and finally master in 1927. Spens was by origin a Scottish Episcopalian and a devout believer and, as such, not obviously destined for preferment at King's. His new college, after being at a very low ebb indeed early in the nineteenth century, was beginning to recover just before 1914 and by the end of the thirties had developed a distinctive ethos and reputation, which affords an interesting illustration of the extent to which conscious planning and unity of purpose can rapidly affect the fortunes of so apparently intractable a corporate institution as a Cambridge college. Before Spens took over the mastership from Pearce certain significant decisions had already been taken. The college would be kept small, so that all undergraduates could dine together at one sitting; only candidates for honours degrees would be admitted; all freshmen would be housed in college; dons and undergraduates would lunch together at the same table; compulsory chapel was abandoned but much was made of a sung eucharist every Sunday. Spens operated on the principle that if you looked after the High Table the college would look after itself. The Fellowship in the twenties was only just over a dozen. A successful candidate was not only expected to be very good academically but must also be adjudged likely to 'fit in'. For this the criteria were sincere churchmanship; intelligent Conservative politics; conversational skill; a willingness to dine in college at least three times a week including Sundays; and preferably a tacitly understood agreement not to marry under the age of thirty. A policy of entertaining the famous and influential was sedulously and successfully pursued; two of the fellows Sir Geoffrey

Butler and Pickthorn sat in the Commons as burgesses for the university; and Baldwin summoned Spens privately to No. 10 to sound him out on public opinion at the height of the abdication crisis. The Chaplain Sir Edwyn Clement Hoskyns translated Barth's *Commentary on Romans* in 1933 and with another Corpus don F. N. Davey wrote the best selling *Riddle of the New Testament* (1931). Pickthorn commented on the fact that Hoskyns must have been one of the very few eminent theologians who read the *Farmer and Stockbreeder* most weeks. There will be more to be said later on about his influence as a theologian on Cambridge at large. Other Fellows included R. A. Butler; Charles Smyth; A. L. Goodhart, an American by origin, an international lawyer and a future Master of University College, Oxford; A. E. Clark-Kennedy, director of studies in medicine, who was virtually appointed by Spens when the latter joined him one day in 1919 in the underground at Mornington Crescent; the modern historian J. P. T. Bury; and Wittgenstein's pupil Desmond Lee, a future headmaster of Clifton and Winchester. Spens became Vice-Chancellor in 1931 and gave his name to the 1938 Spens report on education. But despite a multiplicity of outside interests he maintained a remarkable personal influence with the undergraduates, facilitated of course by the smallness and unity of the college. They in their turn had a good record in terms of first classes and university prizes.

Literary and aesthetic tastes continued to be iconoclastic and in revolt against the staid and the conventional. Hugh Walpole's reputation plummeted and *The Forsyte Saga* lay on the shelf gathering dust, which was to lie undisturbed till the far off days of coloured television. Auden visited King's to read remarkably salacious extracts from the Mortmere saga. *Ulysses* was very much in vogue, no doubt genuinely appreciated by some, while others, according to temperament, were shocked or enthralled by Mrs Bloom's soliloquy. Forbes on one occasion entertained a friend for the week-end, who was apprehended by the Cambridge police for improper conduct. Perhaps fearing that he might suffer the indignity of being summoned before the Vice-Chancellor, as had happened to Leavis in 1925 when the latter had been in trouble for using a passage of Joyce in his lectures, he clandestinely dumped all the 'unsuitable' books in his library in the Cam with the assistance of Sykes Davies, lest the police should find them on his shelves. The standard reaction of the highbrow undergraduate to Eliot, as summed up by John Davenport in 1931, was that 'to dispute Mr Eliot's philosophy is reasonable; to dispute his supremacy as a poet is ridiculous'. On the other hand, T. R. Henn of St Catharine's, a much loved and prominent member of the English faculty, read a paper to a literary society at St John's in 1933, emphasizing 'the vulgarity of most of Eliot's work, all the more pernicious since cloaked by an austere and pseudo-learned style'. Lucas, as librarian at King's, would not even allow Eliot's works to be bought for the library. As to Housman, Bronowski saw fit to dismiss him magisterially after his death as being so thin and silly that he could hardly be called a poet. Another hero of the twenties, Aldous Huxley, declined somewhat in favour, though he would no doubt have been surprised at being described by G. M. Turnell of Corpus as a writer handicapped by a rather limited intelligence. But overwhelmingly the man of the hour was D. H. Lawrence. It was not always the grim realism of *Sons and Lovers* which led the young to reflect solemnly on 'the hour in the night when Lawrence died' [March 1930], a moment celebrated by Auden in *The Orators*, so much as the life and loves of Connie and Mellors, slipped through the customs at Dover in the paperback Tauchnitz edition, or the exaltation of the role in human affairs of the lumbar ganglion, so energetically hymned in *Fantasia of the Unconscious*.

A visible expression of *avant garde* aestheticism was Forbes' house on the Backs called Finella, 'the spirit of fountains', in one of which, in the garden, he was occasionally to be found immersed naked during the summer months. It was a Victorian house converted into a not particularly stately but polychromatic pleasure dome with lilac and pink walls, a great deal of glass and recurrent extravaganzas, such as the painting of a fully uniformed guardsman in the servants' bath, designed to keep them cheerful. Epstein's *Genesis*, which was calculated to evoke cataleptic reactions from the bourgeoisie, was exhibited in the garden during May Week 1931. Finella was

not always particularly comfortable, especially in winter;
Granta observed that 'Manny's young pupils would be well
advised to wear their winter woollies', adding cryptically that
people who live in glass houses should undress in the dark.
In the last years before Forbes' sudden death in 1936, his
main interest other than his work in the English faculty was
his sponsorship of Trystan Edwards, who had a master plan
to avoid the spoliation of the English countryside, and
especially that aspect of it then generally known as 'ribbon
development', by the creation of a hundred new towns. What
is now called the environmental lobby is not an invention of
our own day. In February 1927 the Union debated a motion
that rural and urban England had already been spoiled beyond
redemption. The next year the Cambridge Preservation
Society was formed. By 1931, with Lowes Dickinson and
A. B. Ramsay very much to the fore, they were opposing a
by-pass across Grantchester Meadows and by 1932, now with
the assistance of G. M. Trevelyan, they secured the preservation in perpetuity of 110 acres between the Grantchester
road and the river. By 1935 a successful fight was under way
to save the Gog Magog hills. At the annual general meeting
in 1937 Ramsay said: 'We must remember that Oxford and
Cambridge were the pioneers in the movement for the Green
Belt. This movement has now caught on in England and is
becoming the fashion.'

The Cambridge Preservation Society was pleased with the
new Guildhall, built in 1938–9, which they regarded as 'an
important contribution to the dignity of the town'. With one
exception, new building for the university and the colleges
in the thirties was not of exceptional interest. Sir Herbert
Baker was not at his most successful in Downing; Sir Edwyn
Lutyens' Benson Court (1931/2) in Magdalene is perhaps
fortunately only one massive third of a project for a whole
court; and Sir Edward Maufe's activities at St John's cannot
be said to have added to his reputation. Sir Giles Gilbert Scott
was comparatively successful in a conventional manner in the
North Court of Trinity Hall. Sir Nikolaus Pevsner, writing
in the nineteen-fifties, considered that the Caius building by
Murray Easton facing the Market Place was at that time the
best building at Cambridge in the style of the twentieth

century. The university acquired also in the period a new Anatomy School, the busy Mill Lane lecture rooms, big extensions to the Engineering Laboratories and Workshops and the Scott Polar Research Institute.

All other building, however, was dwarfed by the new University Library, opened in 1934, Sir Giles Gilbert Scott having sketched his first plans in 1931. By the end of the war the old University Library, an extension of the Old Schools, built by C. R. Cockerell, was wholly inadequate and the university administrators were overjoyed to be able to announce in 1928 a gift of £700,000 from the International Education Board, founded by John D. Rockefeller Jnr, to be devoted to teaching, research and building in agriculture and the physical and biological sciences, and also to a new University Library. £250,000 had already been raised for the Library; £500,000 was allocated from the Rockefeller endowment; and the remaining £229,000 was raised by the university. The books were moved with remarkable despatch in the Long Vacation of 1934, despite rumours that it would require a scenic railway along the Backs. At 4 p.m. on 31 May the last reader left and the following morning the task began of moving 1,142,000 books in 689 loads. The Library staff and a team of porters from Messrs Eaden Lilley worked daily from 8 a.m. to 6 p.m. The job was completed in exactly eight weeks. Horse-drawn vans were used, since it was felt that greater vehicular speed would have resulted in a congestion of filled boxes at one end and empty boxes at the other. The length of the building is 420 feet, the height of the tower 156 feet and it has 40 miles of shelves. It was and is a pleasant place in which to work, but Cambridge has never been fond of it as a piece of architecture. A rather stern contemporary judge from *The Gownsman* considered that, impressionistically speaking, and except for the campanile, its main lines strongly resembled those of the Klingenburg power works in Berlin. However that may be, the university was fortunate in its Librarian, A. F. Scholfield of King's, who presided over the development and expansion of the library from 1923 to 1949.

Another notably successful administrator was Sir Sidney Cockerell of Jesus, Director of the Fitzwilliam Museum from 1908 to 1937. He had started life as a coal merchant and was fond of propagating his belief that a committee should consist of two people with power to reduce their numbers. He collected a quarter of a million pounds during his directorship, largely by sheer force of personality, and had no hesitation in pronouncing that he found the museum a pigsty and turned it into a palace. The biggest extension, the Marlay Galleries, was opened in 1924. Cockerell's biographer, Wilfrid Blunt, wrote of the new décor and arrangement of the Fitzwilliam – 'even after the passage of forty years, during which the humanizing of museums has become a commonplace, the shock of its beauty and fitness has not staled'. Among notable benefactions during the inter-war years were £104,000 from Miss Sydney Renée Courtauld, which enabled eight new galleries to be built to house paintings, pottery and porcelain, and the gift of over four hundred drawings and water colours by two Royal Academicians C. W. Shannon and Charles Ricketts, including works by Titian, Tintoretto, Tiepolo, Rubens, Van Dyck, Rembrandt, Goya, Watteau, Rowlandson and Hokusai. In 1933 the Marquess of Crewe presented Keats' manuscript of *The Ode to a Nightingale*.

The cause of female equality had still some way to run in a Cambridge in which a music critic could describe Myra Hess in October 1934 as playing Brahms with a virility which broke down the barriers between womanhood and greatness. Just before the war, however, Dorothy Garrod, who had discovered a Neanderthal child in Gibraltar, succeeded E. H. Minns as Disney Professor of Archaeology, thus becoming the first woman professor in either Oxford or Cambridge. The ADC under the presidency of R. B. Duff belatedly followed the Mummers in 1935 by allowing girls from Girton and Newnham to act in one production out of four, provided they did not use the club rooms, described in 1926 by *New Cambridge* as the only place of the sort where it was possible to feel at home without first ordering a whisky and soda. The Union, however, refused to grant women full membership in 1935, Colin Mann of King's declaring that women didn't want to become members and if they did they wouldn't be the sort of women whom the existing members wanted.

Life in the women's colleges became steadily less stifled by convention and hierarchy and, towards the end of the period, markedly more political in orientation. But it was still much circumscribed by the anxious concern of the authorities for the moral well-being of their charges. Miss Wodehouse, the novelist's aunt, who succeeded Miss Major as Mistress of Girton in 1931, was a tall and handsome woman with a very red face, periodically afflicted with hiccoughs, which punctuated the chapel services in a manner unhelpful to the less strenuously devotional of the girls. She felt it sensible to write a letter in 1932, which *The Cambridge Review* printed, with the object of clearing up any doubts about visits to men's colleges: 'A woman student does not go alone to an undergraduate's rooms except with such special sanction as is given, for instance, to a sister visiting a brother.' The Principal of Newnham since 1923 had been Miss Joan Pernel Strachey, sister of the belletrist, who may well have felt in her bosom a certain tension between the theory and practice of Bloomsbury and the tutelary responsibilities of her exacting office. The month after Munich she circularized the Senior Tutors of the men's colleges, pointing out that 'it would be a great assistance if one of our tutors could be informed when a Newnham student seems to be too much in college . . . If a student has to visit a man's room after 7 p.m. we require her to leave by 10 p.m.' Reciprocally, so to speak, men had to be out of Newnham by seven. The ground rules at St Catharine's in 1934 read as follows: 'Gentlemen may entertain ladies in their rooms in college between the hours of 1 p.m. and 6 p.m. provided that they have signed a book which will be kept in the Porter's Lodge, and provided that at least one other gentleman or lady is to be present besides the host and his guest.' As a sop to the spirit of romance 'in exceptional cases permission to entertain a lady alone, or to entertain more than one lady after 6 p.m. may be obtained from the Junior Dean'. The Porter had, we are told, strict orders to report any breach of the rules, which would incur severe penalties. At Fitzwilliam it was necessary to obtain a written permit from the Censor every time you wished to entertain a lady. One way and another, it was a great deal simpler for the gentlemen, if not for the ladies, to go to London.

In 1931, the Fire Brigade was still hard at it in Girton, with

Mansfield Forbes in the early twenties

Lord Rutherford

A group of Apostles in 1932. Left to Right – Richard Llewellyn Davies, Hugh Sykes Davies, Alastair Watson, Anthony Blunt, Julian Bell, Andrew Cohen

A BEAUTIFUL PHOTOGRAVURE PLATE ILLUSTRATING LIFE AT THIS FAMOUS OLD COLLEGE FOR LADIES.
INSET: THE MISTRESS.

1932 *Granta* cartoons by Alistair Cooke. His impressions of Girton include *top left* the Fire Brigade in action and *bottom left* Girtonians eagerly anticipating a

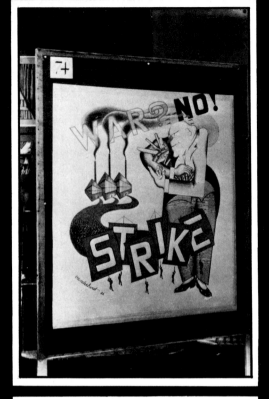

The Cambridge Anti-War
Exhibition of 1935

fire alarms twice a term and a wet practice at the end of the Easter Term. There is a note of exasperation in the report for the Michaelmas Term – 'Whoever took the rattle from Boots during the Long Vacation Term has caused the Brigade both inconvenience and expense.' Hierarchical attitudes lingered on. Margaret Masterman, the second Mrs Richard Braithwaite, wrote of Newnham in June 1933: 'We elect officers. Senior Students, Hall Senior Student, Senior Freshers, Hall Secretaries, Newspaper Secretaries, Flower Monitresses, Mistress of the Electric Iron, and others. Nearly all these elections are made for moral qualities, some are taken incredibly seriously. And then the meetings, and the notices on the notice boards – "Any student discarding her wash-stand must speak to me before taking such a step"; "buttercups must not be left in the bathroom".' But femininity was beginning to win through. Rooms would be furnished in the taste of the day with royal blue and orange cushions and royal blue bowls of orange flowers, and decorated with brass rubbings or reproductions from some of the brilliant Burlington House exhibitions which were a feature of the thirties. Of one Newnhamite we learn – 'Even now when the spirit moves her and when she can get an intimate to play for her, Serita will express herself and her music by dancing extempore and barefoot in her "digs" or in the fields.' The living was plain – huge vegetable dishes full of grey boiled potatoes, accompanying liver of an almost metal texture; but there was plenty of high thinking – at Girton, Muriel Bradbrook, a future Mistress of the College, had firsts in English in 1929 and 1930; at Newnham, Gowland Hopkins' daughter Jacquetta, future wife of Christopher Hawkes and then of J. B. Priestley, was a notable recruit in 1929 to the Archaeology and Anthropology Tripos. As elsewhere in Cambridge, a slight change of emphasis is discernible around 1933. A very learned medieval history don, Helen Cam, addressed the former Labour Club in Girton, now renamed the Socialist Group, on why she was a Socialist. The next year a small Marxist library and bookstall was set up in the college and in the Lent Term Bernal lectured the Socialist Group on that hardy perennial 'The Crisis of Capitalism'. The pervasive mythology of the period is pungently evoked by an article in *The Girton Review* of 1937 by Angela Linley who had spent three months the previous summer as a mother's help in Berlin: 'Daily, I became more ashamed I was British; the growth of Hitlerism lies at our door. The Treaty of Versailles and the sufferings of the Germans after the war were rarely mentioned, but every type of person said: "You are rich, you English; you have your colonies, we have nothing." '

Administration in Cambridge is invariably, and teaching often, described as a load. The number of undergraduates who required teaching remained almost static in the thirties, 1711 matriculating in October 1930 and 1731 in October 1937, and the number of research students rose only from 258 in 1933 to 384 in 1938. Nor was there of course anything like the complexity of administration to which universities have been subjected, or have subjected themselves, in the years since the Second World War. In 1931 Ramsay handed over the vice-chancellorship to Spens after two years in which not a single vote had been required of the Regent House, a situation which he attributed to 'harmony of interests and excellence of machinery' rather than to apathy or indifference. However, thirty new chairs were founded between the wars (ten in 1931 alone), as well as twenty-one new readerships (eight in 1931). The administrative 'load' was undoubtedly increasing and the academic lotus-eater more of a rarity.

The despatch of business in a university is characterized by idiosyncratic methods immortalized by F. M. Cornford in *Microcosmographia Academica* (1908). A master of the art was the Trinity zoologist C. F. A. Pantin. His method of ensuring that his own chosen candidate was duly appointed to a college committee combined the linear persistence of the tortoise with the circuitous locomotion of the hare. He would begin by saying that Dr A seemed the obvious choice, reciting his merits and qualifications. As soon as he saw signs of ingenious and obstinate objection, he would begin to express doubts himself. It would not be right to be stampeded or hustled. Apart from anything else, this would be grossly unfair to Dr B and Mr C, which led him to dilate on their meagre qualifications for the post. Or possibly Dr D? He was a bit old for the job and there were people who didn't like him, but such considerations should not in themselves be a sufficient bar to his appointment. Then there was young E, brash and immature admittedly, but he might learn wisdom on the job. By this time some member of the committee was bound to say that for his part he couldn't see why the claims of Dr A had been so summarily dismissed in the first place. At which point Pantin would observe that perhaps before they arrived at a final decision, it might just be wise to go back for a moment and reconsider A. Merely to test opinion, he would propose that Dr A be recommended for the appointment. This resulted in Dr A being unanimously recommended.

A startling glimpse of the difficulties academic administrators impose on themselves is afforded by G. H. Hardy's aphorism that it is never worth a first-class man's time to express a majority opinion. By definition, there are plenty of others to do that. Hardy's return to Cambridge as Sadleirian Professor in 1931 added considerable zest to life in Trinity, not least as a result of his zeal in the relatively rare capacity of a proselytizing atheist. This was a militant posture markedly different from what Bishop Barnes called 'wistful agnosticism', satirized by Glover in the lines:

> We know Thee not, nor guess Thee
> O vague beyond our dreams:
> We praise Thee not nor bless Thee
> Dim source of all that seems;
> Unconscious of our witness,
> The music of our heart,
> O It beyond all Itness
> If aught indeed Thou art.

Required to make his fellowship declaration in Trinity chapel, Hardy protested, not because there was any specifically religious connotation about the declaration, but because he had to make it in chapel. Eventually, he mumbled his way through it, which was not at all sufficient for Parry, the redoubtable Vice-Master, who was a great martinet with the dons, though very popular with undergraduates. 'That was quite inaudible, Professor Hardy. Please make the declaration again,' said Parry, and Hardy had to comply. Hardy enjoyed playing an elaborate game with Simpson based on the apparent capriciousness of the providential order, Simpson playing God and Hardy the devil. Thus a good harvest would be a point to Simpson, but a church struck by lightning five points to Hardy.

Simpson was now the possessor of a private aeroplane and found it very useful, since he was much in demand as a preacher at various public schools. Housman, who described himself as a Cyrenaic or egoistic hedonist, and claimed that the only form of Christianity which he professed was anti-Protestantism, was nevertheless in the habit of creeping surreptitiously into the organ loft when Simpson was preaching. Simpson's own catholicity, or at any rate his curiosity about the vagaries of Cambridge churchmanship, was exemplified by his habit at one time of attending half the sermon at St Clement's, which was very High Church indeed, and the other half at the Round Church, which was correspondingly Low.

Henry Sidgwick, who died in 1900, considered that in the universities of his day nothing was so fertile as a good semi-theological row. After the First World War, theology continued to command considerable general interest, but it was far from being a burning issue and generated few if any rows. In the thirties, however, the contrasting Christian attitudes and personalities of two Cambridge divines, Charles Raven and Sir Edwyn Clement Hoskyns, stimulated, if not a row, at least a comparatively fertile Christian controversy. Raven had indeed started his Cambridge career in 1909 in the thick of a real old-fashioned row as dean and lecturer in theology at Emmanuel. The Master, William Chawner, who had all his life been a regular communicant in the college chapel, suddenly read a paper entitled *Prove All Things* to a religious discussion group, which he published as a highly tendentious pamphlet. He also decided that he would attend chapel no longer. Chawner died just as Emmanuel's regular flow of admission candidates from Evangelical backgrounds was beginning to dry up alarmingly. As an army chaplain with the Royal Berkshires, Raven was sniped at and gassed at La Bassée. He came back to Cambridge in 1919 and became a proctor that year. He was a convinced Socialist and argued at the Union in 1920 against co-partnership and in favour of nationalization. Co-partnership would simply shore up the same old competitive firms, sheer undiluted greed and a continuance of the profits which they acquire from the unfortunate consumers. Real nationalization 'from the best ideals' could save the country. A sermon in 1921, later printed, contained the characteristic phrase 'the new physical sciences have rendered untenable the traditional ideas of authority, of the supernatural, of miracles, and in fact of the whole method of God's operation'. Not surprisingly, Raven belonged to the Modern Churchman's Union. He was a notable and passionately enthusiastic naturalist, often declaring that he would be content to spend eternity with a working-class moth collector. In his zeal to reform the world he was at times remarkably inept, but he had a fine mind and was an irrestistibly magnetic and winning preacher and lecturer. He became a Canon of Liverpool in 1924, but maintained frequent contact with Cambridge. Thus, during a typical visit in 1925 he preached the University sermon and two others on Sunday, as well as talking to undergraduates till midnight, then lectured on trade unions on Monday and on pulpit presentation to theological students on Tuesday. Raven's modernism, as explained in the preface of his book *The Creator Spirit*, set out 'to formulate and defend a Christ-centred view of the universe in such ways as to heal the breach between science and religion'. J. M. Creed, the Ely Professor, also examined this dilemma, which at that time much exercised theologians struggling with the atomization of Western culture, in his Commemoration sermon at St John's in 1930: 'it is essential to our health that we should never lose our hold upon the idea of knowledge as one inter-connected whole, relative in all its parts to the mind of man'.

As the agonizing political disappointments and difficulties proliferated on the national and international scene in the thirties, the links between liberal theology, socialism, unrealistic international idealism and pacifism strengthened. Thus Bishop Barnes, preaching in Cambridge in 1934, affirmed that 'Christ lives; it is well nigh impossible to go to a meeting of the League of Nations Union and not feel his presence'. 1934 was the very year in which Von Schleicher, Röhm, Dollfuss and Kirov were murdered and in which the

Italians and Abyssinians started fighting on the Somaliland frontier; the year of the abortive Naval Disarmament conference. Despite all this, the Bishop in the same sermon attacked excessive credulity. Charles Raven became a committed and proselytizing pacifist in 1930. In 1932 he was elected Regius Professor of Divinity and a fellow of Christ's. The Master, Norman McLean, died in 1936 and Raven found himself one of two almost equally supported internal candidates in a situation fictionally immortalized by C. P. Snow. Sir Charles Galton Darwin was elected from outside the College, but Raven in due course became Master in 1939. In 1934 he gave a series of singularly unprophetic lectures entitled 'Is war obsolete?' and in March 1936, the very month in which the Nazis occupied the Rhineland, he was taken to task by *The Times* for saying in a speech in Birmingham that it was almost certainly true that nine out of ten of the most virile young men at Cambridge would go to prison rather than go into the army.

Raven's theology, emphasizing evolution and psychology, differed significantly from that of Hoskyns, with its emphasis on revelation, tradition, atonement and eschatology. Hoskyns had studied under Harnack in Berlin, knew Schweitzer personally and had lectured in Tübingen; he too had been an army chaplain, very much on active service. As early as 1926 he wrote a celebrated essay, demonstrating to the very complete satisfaction of those who thought like him, that 'the Jesus of History' (the actual title of a book of Glover's) was not the Jesus of history at all. He contributed to a volume of essays called *Mysterium Christi* (1930) in which the emphasis was not so much on understanding the world as on overcoming it by listening to the language of the Bible. Hoskyns's translation of Barth's *Commentary on Romans* was a vitally important landmark in Cambridge theology, in that once again the subject became an uncompromising and uncomfortable one. It was in its own way perhaps as influential in effecting the demise of natural theology in our own time as was Moore's philosophical methodology. The early thirties was a period in which Pelagius was the favourite heretic in Christian circles and Hoskyns was a thoroughgoing anti-Pelagian. When he died, comparatively young, in 1937,

Pickthorn wrote of him: 'He had far too deep a heart to be a humanitarian, and far too free a mind to be a Liberal. He was far too generous to be other-worldly. He was every inch a priest, without any pretension.' It is pleasant to record, though not in the least surprising, that Raven composed a deeply sympathetic obituary in *The Times*.

Just before Hoskyns died, he wrote a letter to Karl Barth in which he referred to 'the characteristic English substitution of piety for theology'. As the thirties developed, Cambridge was increasingly permeated by the undoctrinal and often rather mindless evangelism which came to be known as Moral Rearmament. One does not have to be an admirer of the earthly founder of the movement to concede that many good and deserving people became adherents of Buchmanism, often perhaps unconsciously so impelled by the evident degradation of international morality. The conversion of a prominent games player was always esteemed a great capture. F. L. Lucas in his book *Style* records reading in a Moral Rearmament publication the phrase 'the university atmosphere is stabbed with praying giants'. The language of conversion had a directness which tended to disconcert the academic mind. C. W. Crawley, while visiting a nephew in Jesus, inadvertently found himself being entertained by a group of devotees consuming tea and crumpets and was startled at being asked: 'How many of your fellows are all out for God?' However, the side effects were often beneficial in unexpected ways. In 1934 *Granta* published a letter, in which the author wrote: 'About six months ago, there was a meeting of the Group in the Dorothy café where members were sharing their religious experiences. A lady from one of the women's colleges, after properly introducing herself, said she had felt great difficulty in comprehending Dr Richards' *The Meaning of Meaning*. Thanks, however, to the Group inspiration, she found sufficient will-power to wrestle with that difficult work and eventually to master it.'

In March 1937 Bertrand Russell, opposed by the Dean of St Paul's, advocated in the Union the disappearance of organized religion and was defeated by 314 votes to 176. Five years before, Haldane had argued that organized religion made its appeal only through fear and shame and was only necessary

for emotional and defective people. He claimed that the
theological colleges were filled with what he called the dregs
of the universities. This was never true of Westcott House in
Cambridge, where out of thirty men in residence under B. K.
Cunningham in the Long Vacation Term of 1929 five had
first-class degrees from Oxford or Cambridge. It was a group
of volunteers from Westcott who ran the first Cambridge
camp for the unemployed in 1933. Early efforts by the university in this field had not been strikingly successful. Sir
Arthur Steel-Maitland, the Minister of Labour, had written to
the Vice-Chancellor in 1929, suggesting that each college
should employ one unemployed miner. King's, Trinity Hall
and Christ's were unable to help. St John's telephoned to say
that they might possibly employ a boy. Corpus had employed
a miner as a kitchen porter but he had thrown up the job as the
work was too hard for his feet. Trinity took on a Welsh miner
as an extra gardener. But by 1934 six universities were represented on the Universities' Council for Unemployed Camps,
under Raven's chairmanship and the patronage of the Prince
of Wales. In 1934 there were six camps in operation, with an
average number of unemployed per camp of one hundred,
matched by an equivalent number of undergraduates. Each tent
had a staff leader with an unemployed second-in-command. The
mornings were spent 'in work of a kind that did not encroach
upon the proper spheres of paid labour'; the afternoons in
recreation or in visits by the undergraduates to the families
of the men on the dole. Initially, there was strong opposition
from the Cumberland and Durham trade unions. A rumour
circulated in Durham that the camps were being secretly
run by the War Office to test out new types of poison gas on
the unemployed. Once the trade union leaders had actually
seen the camps in operation, they gave the idea their blessing.

Nobody entertained any sort of illusion about the scale and
scope of the operation. Reporting on the 1935 camp at Helmsley,
a minute affair with only ten tents, a St John's undergraduate
wrote: 'No one will deny that the camps are mere palliatives.
They could not be anything else. It may well be asked whether
they are worthwhile and whether they are appreciated. If any
of us were expecting bouquets to be thrown at us, we were
disappointed. North country folk do not wear their hearts on

their sleeves. Some grumbled continuously, almost all took everything for granted, but . . . it was worthwhile for the friendships that were created.' The next year the tone of the St John's report altered significantly. 'Whether it was the beer or the sausages or just the consciousness that a well spent month was reaching its conclusion it would be hard to say, but whatever the reason the fact remains that everyone present was overwhelmed by an intense feeling of well-being and universal benevolence. Speech after speech was called for and made amid roars of applause and thumping of tables and when at last we left the marquee and dispersed to our tents, it was with the happy consciousness that the camp had proved itself a complete success.' One Durham miner wrote: 'Your camps are doing more than anything else to break down the spirit of class-hatred and misunderstanding.' At any rate, it cost a number of undergraduates a good deal more in time and money than it cost Guy Burgess to join the Hunger Marchers a mile or two outside Cambridge and drop out an equivalent distance the other side of the city.

Raffaello Piccoli, who succeeded Okey as Professor of Italian in 1929, wrote a poem printed just after his death in 1933, called 'A Song for the Coming War', of which one verse reads:

> Rumours of war are spreading
> over the country
> Black wings in the sky
> Curtains of fire by night.

At much the same time, in a by now highly unfashionable vein and with an obvious reference to the celebrated Oxford King and Country vote, the editor of *The Gownsman*, I. W. Danby of Jesus, wrote: 'Let us not follow the example of our feeble-hearted brethren in another city. Let us attend OTC parades, gain pilots' certificates, prepare deadly gases in our laboratories. Germany will arm. In three years France will declare war on Germany.' His forecast was wrong by three years, though had his advice been generally adopted France could well have contested the occupation of the Rhineland.

However, some undergraduates were in fact attending

parades and acquiring pilots' licences and as events transpired they could hardly have been better occupied. The Officers' Training Corps, which traces its origins to 1803, had suffered in the twenties to some extent from the post-war reaction and in terms especially of infantry recruitment from the lassitude often engendered by memories of school-based military training. Even by 1938 the infantry element consisted of only three platoons, two of which were machine-gun platoons. The cavalry had four troops in that year, two mechanized (with a total of two very light tanks) and two horsed. It was decidedly popular in a Cambridge which still bristled with livery stables in the twenties. Firing eighteen pounder guns also had its attractions, and since Portway commanded the engineers from 1919 to 1933 there was considerable purposeful activity in that field. Amongst the signals officers were R. E. Priestley and the Nobel prize-winning physicist E. V. Appleton.

The history of the University Air Squadron began in 1925 when an idea of Lord Trenchard was taken up by Sir Geoffrey Butler of Corpus, MP at the time for the University, and C. E. Inglis. Flying began officially at Duxford with one Bristol fighter with a maximum speed of 125 mph and two Avros, whose engines were lubricated disagreeably with castor oil. One of the first members was the explorer H. G. Watkins, who led the first and second Arctic Air Route expeditions in Greenland, where he died in 1932. By 1935 the squadron possessed seven aircraft and its members became increasingly well versed in formation flying and aerobatics. One hundred and twenty-eight members of the squadron were killed in the war and four won Victoria Crosses.

A perennial complaint about the careers which Cambridge graduates choose for themselves was voiced in *The Cambridge Review* early in 1939 – 'one of the weakest features of the universities is that they do not produce a large enough pro-portion of industrial and commercial workers'. Commerce and industry claimed 272 to education's 214 among those graduates placed by the Appointments Board in the year ending December 1937; the figures for 1938 were 247 in education, 95 in government service, 240 in commerce and industry. As a small, if unusually well-documented, sample we can follow the Peterhouse entry for 1934. Fifty-five under-graduates came into residence in that October, of whom 41 were from public schools (7 from Wellington alone), 2 from overseas, 2 Royal Engineers from the then Royal Military Academy at Woolwich, and one from Cranwell. Nine went into schoolteaching, 9 into industry and commerce, 7 into the peace-time armed forces (including Frank Whittle, inventor of the jet engine), 5 into the Civil Service, 5 into medicine, 4 into law and 4 into engineering. Only one went directly into the Colonial Service, an interesting statistic in relation to the still prevalent mythology about the public schools in this period being primarily designed to produce empire builders. Most of those who survived the war at least had something of a job to which they could return. In that sense they were the lucky ones.

CHAPTER FIVE

The Advancement of Learning II

B. L. Hallward of Peterhouse, a future headmaster of Clifton and Vice-Chancellor of Nottingham, long remembered by the theatrical *cognoscenti* of the twenties as a perfectly type-cast Apollo, wrote in 1933 that the prospects for the study of classics in the University had perhaps never been brighter for thirty years. Calculated in terms of those reading the Classical Tripos, the peak year between the wars was 1929 with 145 taking Part I and 66 Part II, but the comparative figures for 1932 were still 136 and 68 and for 1937 132 and 73. It seems probable that a big increase in the numbers reading Part II Law in the thirties represented something of a gain in that subject from Classics, but the position calculated purely on numbers was a very healthy one as compared with that obtaining in the twenties. Hallward went on to claim, with much justice, that undergraduates reading classics in the period included 'a high proportion of the best boys from the schools'. He attributed this in part to an increasing recognition 'in the confusion of a disillusioned and mechanized world' of 'the stabilizing wisdom of the past'. For what it was worth, fifteen headmasters of the leading public and grammar schools were eventually recruited from the ranks of those placed in the first class of the Classical Tripos in the thirties. Yet Henry Jackson, a fellow of Trinity for fifty-six years and described by Hallward as providing by his life and example an unsurpassable ideal of the life of a great college teacher, told D. S. Robertson in 1920 not long before his death that it was strange that he should have lived 'to see the end of Greek studies in Cambridge'. Had that been the case, Lowes Dickinson, whose 'modern' Platonic dialogues and *The Greek View of Life* made him a very significant popularizer of classical Greece, would hardly have lectured as confidently as he did during his last illness in the summer of 1932 to the Local Lectures Summer Meeting, choosing as his subject the contribution of Ancient Greece to modern life. Perhaps, however, the old idealist knew that he was posing, to say the least, a still unresolved question in these, his last few words uttered in public – 'can the Greek spirit, rising again more splendid and more potent than before, accomplish the salvation of mankind, in the greatest crisis with which it has yet been confronted?'

Robertson, who became Regius Professor of Greek in 1929, was unkindly described by Housman as a safe choice. It was always hoped that he would produce a definitive work on Pindar but in the event that was not forthcoming. However, his inaugural lecture was an elegant piece of writing and repays perusal. 'To me personally the supreme attraction of Greece as a field of study lies first in the extraordinary interest of every manifestation of the spiritual activity of the Greeks. The quality of their best work, whether in poetry or philosophy, in sculpture, painting or architecture is so undeniably excellent, so infinitely rich and subtle, that the student's worst doubts in his blackest moods of depression can never touch the intrinsic value of the thing studied.'

Thus the portents early in the thirties seemed distinctly promising. In 1931 two new chairs were founded, one in Ancient Philosophy secured by Cornford, considered by many the most brilliant lecturer in the faculty, provided that you did not expect to be spoon-fed, and the other in Classical Archaeology, which incontestably went to A. B. Cook. Cook in his inaugural engagingly quoted Sir Thomas Browne – 'time which antiquates Antiquities, and hath an art to make dust of all things, hath yet spared these *minor* Monuments. In vain we hope to be known by open and visible conservatories, when to be unknown was the means of their continuation and obscurity their protection'.

Every Cambridge generation throws up one or two truly outstanding scholars, or at least certainly should do so, but J. Enoch Powell, who came up as a scholar of Trinity from King Edward's School, Birmingham in 1930, was something of a prodigy. As a freshman he was Craven Scholar and won the Members' Latin Essay Prize; in 1932 he was Porson Prizeman and won the Chancellor's Classical Medal and a Browne Medal; in 1933 he won a Craven Studentship. There followed a Trinity prize fellowship, secured at his first attempt

in 1934. At this point in his academic career he made it generally known that he would accept no post other than a professorship. This he duly secured at Sydney in 1937. However,
after only just over a year of immersion in Antipodean Classics,
he applied for and was appointed to a chair at Durham, which
he was never able to take up owing to the outbreak of the
war. Starting as a private soldier in 1939, he became a Brigadier
by 1944. Achievements of this sort require, of course, not only
brilliance, but painfully hard work as well. His supervisor at
Trinity, Walter Hamilton, had not previously met him when
he arrived for the discussion of his first piece of written work.
At this first encounter, Enoch Powell said nothing whatever
except to point out (erroneously as it happened) that his
supervisor had made a mistake about a Greek accent. Thereafter his industry was all consuming. As with his hero Housman, the drier the subject matter the more satisfaction he
appeared to find in it. Presumably aware of the dangers of
expelling nature with a pitchfork, he allowed himself a slight
measure of daily relaxation by walking to the station and back
after dinner, winter and summer alike. It constitutes just
about the least agreeable walk in Cambridge. He produced a
lexicon to Herodotus in 1938 and two other works on that
subject in 1939. He told T. C. Nicholas of Trinity one day
while queuing for lunch that if all the text of Herodotus were
to disappear he could reproduce it by heart. It was therefore
not surprising that when he read a paper to the St John's
Classical Society on 'Herodotus in the making' it was recorded
that the theories advanced were so convincing that the discussion which followed produced confirmation rather than
criticism of what had been read. As a teacher he was described
as strongly interested in his pupils' progress (not merely as
scholars) and prepared to take infinite trouble even with the
least able. Whether out of conscious imitation of Housman or
not, he also published verses – *First Poems* (1937) and *Casting-
off and other poems* (1939). But poetry was not to prove his
métier:

> The autumn leaves that strew the grass,
> The flocks of migrant birds,

They all are poems; but alas,
I cannot find the words.

(First Poems XX)

Housman died in 1936. On Boxing Day 1930, he wrote to his friend Percy Withers – 'between a Feast last night and a dinner-party this evening, I sit me down to thank you and your wife and family for their Christmas greetings and wish you all a happy New Year. Rutherford's daughter, married to another fellow of Trinity, died suddenly a day or two ago; the wife of the Emeritus Professor of Greek, who himself is paralysed, has cut her throat with a razor which she had bought to give her son-in-law; I have a brother and a brother-in-law both seriously ill and liable to drop dead any moment; and in short Providence has given itself up to the festivities of the season. A more cheerful piece of news is that I have just published the last book I shall ever write (*Manilius* Vol. V) and that I now mean to do nothing for ever and ever.' He was, however, prevailed upon to deliver his remarkable Leslie Stephen lecture, *The Name and Nature of Poetry*, in 1933 with its affirmation that poetry is more physical than intellectual. He claimed that in the twenty-two years since he had delivered his inaugural lecture as Kennedy Professor he had not improved enough to become a literary critic (a genus which he believed appeared, properly speaking, only once in a hundred or two hundred years), nor so much deteriorated as to fancy he had become one. He wrote about the lecture and its reception to his brother Laurence – 'I am not proud of this, which I wrote against my will, and am not sending copies outside the family. But its success has taken me aback. The leader of our doctrinaire teachers of youth* is reported to say that it will take more than twelve years to undo the harm I have done in an hour . . .' In March 1936 he wrote to an American admirer that while George Eliot described herself as a meliorist he was a pejorist. He dined with the Family for the last time just over a month later, but could only manage a piece of toast and a glass of Burgundy, and died six days afterwards.

Some indication of the confident advance of the natural

---

* A reference presumably to Leavis.

sciences and medicine in the thirties can be gauged by the record of newly created professorships and readerships. There were new chairs in Colloidal Physics (1930) for E. K. Rideal; in Mathematical Physics (1931) for Fowler; in Metallurgy and in Mineralogy and Petrology, also in 1931. Readers were appointed in 1931 in Experimental Zoology (James Gray), Entomology, Geology, Geophysics, Mycology and Stereochemistry; in 1932 in Vertebrate Zoology; in 1933 in Physiology; in 1934 in Pharmacology; in 1937 in Invertebrate Zoology (Pantin), Plant Morphology and Plant Physiology. And in 1934 Eddington's professorship of Astronomy was appropriately renamed Astronomy and Experimental Philosophy.

In one of his last public lectures, Rutherford ended by reminding his listeners that it is not in the nature of things for any one man to make a sudden violent discovery; 'science goes step by step, and every man depends on the work of his predecessors'. That was in 1936. He died in October 1937, by which time the combined achievements of the Cavendish in the twenties had been crowned by even more spectacular success. 1932 was the *annus mirabilis*. James Chadwick had never lost sight of the hint thrown out by Rutherford in a Royal Society lecture in 1920 of the possible existence of an atom of mass 1 with zero nucleus charge. By 1931 a report of the work of the Joliot-Curie ménage in Paris gave him the final clue and by 1932 he had the answer. In his own characteristically modest words 'the neutron postulated by Rutherford in 1920 had at last revealed itself' – a revelation in effect of the vital new weapon for atomic disintegration and the release of atomic energy.

We left Cockcroft and Walton in the twenties as yet unsuccessful with their complicated machinery designed to promote Rutherford's frequently stated ambition 'to have available for study a copious supply of atoms and electrons which have an individual energy far transcending that of the alpha and beta particles from radioactive bodies'. In mid-1931 they had to dismantle their apparatus, as their semi-basement laboratory had been allotted to the physical chemists. So they had to start again from scratch. By April 1932 they were successful in disintegrating the nucleus of the lithium atom by bombarding it with artificially accelerated protons, effecting in the process a transmutation of lithium into helium. The age of particle accelerations in nuclear physics was now properly under way. Eddington later observed that splitting the once indivisible atom had become the ordinary occupation of the physicist since 1932 and that the social unsettlement of the age had extended to the world of atoms.

There was a considerable measure of social unsettlement among Cambridge scientists themselves in the thirties. Kapitsa had been working away on his magnetic fields and helium liquefier for eight years by 1930 without much security of tenure or remuneration. So in 1931 he was made a Royal Society Professor and a new laboratory was built for him alongside the Cavendish and formally opened in 1933 at a ceremony with speeches by Rutherford, Stanley Baldwin, then Chancellor of the University and J. J. Thomson. On twelve previous occasions he had taken a holiday in the USSR. On the thirteenth occasion in 1934 he did not return, as the Soviet authorities refused to let him do so. According to Charlotte Haldane, who saw him when she was a war correspondent in Russia in 1941, he sulked for several months and refused initially to co-operate. Catherine Carswell, writing to the *New Statesman* in 1940, claimed that she met him in Leningrad just after the authorities had refused him his passport. 'My object in seeing Kapitsa was to ascertain if he would object to my asking a certain Soviet minister with whom I stayed while in Russia (he is no longer in the limelight) whether the ban might not be removed in deference to the wishes of Cambridge colleagues and Kapitsa's own solemn pledge to return to Russia. If ever a man wanted to go from Russia to Cambridge at that date, that man was Kapitsa. He was, however, far too nervous and too loyal to associate himself with my request, which was accordingly made without involving him, though with his consent on this condition. My old and valued friend, the Minister, smiled his shrewd smile as he refused. "All very fine" he said, "but *we* do not believe that Kapitsa, once he got back to Cambridge, would ever want to come back here, or anyhow if he didn't we couldn't compel him. We badly need our good scientists just now. Why not send us a few good English scientists instead of asking us to take any chance of losing one of our own to England? . . ." No doubt Kapitsa is honoured and useful in Russia today. Possibly, after more than five years, he prefers permanent residence there to permanent residence in England. This does not mean that he relished the cancellation of his passport or the disbelief in his word. "Kidnapping" and forcible detention are not identical terms, but on occasion they may have similar effects. Friends of the Soviet Union must accept the fact that freedom of movement and confidence in a man's integrity are not there regarded as considerable when policy is in question.' As a contribution to the correspondence columns of the *New Statesman* (in which a month later Maurice Dobb was blandly denying a suggestion of Evan Durbin's that police torture ever occurred in Russia), Miss Carswell's account has a certain ring of authenticity. In 1935 it was agreed that Kapitsa's laboratory should be sold to the Russians for £30,000 and Cockcroft packed it up and despatched it. Kapitsa is recorded as having told English visitors that he felt like a woman who had been raped when she would have given herself for love.*

Despite the friendly relations which have persisted between Cambridge University and Kapitsa for the subsequent forty years, it remains legitimate for the layman to wonder just who had the best of the bargain. But 1935 was, after all, the year of the Webbs' *Soviet Communism. A New Civilisation?*; the year in which *Granta* commended Harold Laski's *Law and Justice in Soviet Russia*, which asserted that the law there is not tied to private property or the judgement of the past but has developed a real social conscience; and the year in which Joseph Needham, visiting the fifteenth international congress of physiology, wrote that 'when the congress as a whole travelled out to Peterhof in a procession of motor-cars, the soldiers of the Red Army at the gate of our barracks waved handkerchiefs and threw their caps in the air. Such behaviour on the part of an English regiment *vis-à-vis* a group of scientific workers would indeed be remarkable', [though, presumably, not if they were ordered so to behave]. Science appeared to be transcending national frontiers and uniting hitherto irreconcilable ideologies. In the process even the most eminent English

* See *Moscow Winter*, 1934, by Margaret Gardiner (*New Left Review* No. 98).

scientists were losing something of the detachment and scepticism which have traditionally been such valuable elements in their make-up. The warning note sounded sufficiently clearly, it might be thought, in the introduction to the Soviet translation in 1932 of Dirac's *Principles of Quantum Mechanics* – 'the publishers are well aware that there is contained in this work a whole series of opinions, both explicit and implicit, which are totally incompatible with Dialectical Materialism. But it is precisely the necessity for a smashing attack on the theoretical front against idealism, against mechanism, and against a whole series of eclectic doctrines, that makes it the duty of the publisher to provide Soviet scientists with the concrete material that plays a crucial part in the foundation of these theories in order that, critically assimilated, their material may be employed on the front for the fight for Dialectical Materialism.' One begins to see why it would be so necessary for J. D. Bernal to look up from his microscope from time to time in order to enter the philosophical lists in positive support of Dialectical Materialism and all things Marxist. Dirac, despite his own vaguely left-wing sympathies, was providing ammunition by the middle forties for Arthur Koestler's disturbing reflections on yogis and commissars by his assumption that all phenomena in space and time derive from a sub-stratum which is not in space and time and entirely beyond measurable grasp. We shall return to Bernal.

Haldane left Cambridge in 1933 for University College, London, which he was heard to say 'was as full of bloody Communists as Cambridge'. Before leaving, he had written his *Philosophy of a Biologist*, in which he claimed that it was inconceivable that a chemical compound could have the properties which DNA is now known to have. His readership in Gowland Hopkins' department went to Needham; he was not slow to criticize his predecessor, whose address to the Institution of Mining Engineers drew from Needham a stinging and magisterial rebuke – 'with the characteristic blindness of old-fashioned philosophic liberalism, he did not in his address envisage the necessity of any radical change in the class-basis of industry and could only picture progress within the framework of the existing order. But no word is

more protean than materialism and Professor Haldane's own
love of social justice might find its fulfilment where, owing to
the Materialism of the past, he might least expect to look for
it, namely, in the Materialism of the future.' Haldane duly
embraced the Materialism of the future by joining the Communist Party in 1942, although this eventually proved too
much for Charlotte, who left him twenty years after their
joint triumph over the Sex Viri.

Whatever may be thought of Needham's attitudes to the
amelioration of the human lot – to which we shall have occasion to return – his brilliance and energy as a scientist in the
thirties is not in question. His *Chemical Embryology* (1931),
in three volumes, summarized what had already been achieved
in that field in terms of biochemistry. Needham would now
be in the van of research into the problems of morphogenesis,
working especially on the nerve tube inducing agent. His
lectures, published as *Order and Life*, aroused great interest and
excitement. In 1936 he master-minded a Cambridge History
of Science Committee which arranged a course of lectures
called *Background to Modern Science*, in which Rutherford, W. L.
Bragg, Aston, Eddington and Haldane, amongst others,
participated. He combined his prodigious scientific activity
with the relentless propagation of left-wing doctrine and his
own highly distinctive brand of Christianity, much inspired
by Conrad Noel, the so-called Red Vicar of Thaxted, a great
zealot of the Social Gospel. Needham in the thirties often
wrote with a sort of millenarian fervour. In an essay called
Cambridge Summer 1932, otherwise concerned with the spiritual
significance of nude bathing and Bishop Lancelot Andrewes,
we read – 'a classless society of unascetic, uninhibited men and
women in equal comradeship based on universal mechan-
ization and control over the forces of Nature would be in a
sense a dialectical synthesis of the Greek and the Christian
ethos. Hence the interest of the following passage: "William
Liebknecht says that Marx, excited and flushed over an electric
locomotive that he had seen on exhibition in Regent Street
in London exclaimed: 'Now, the problem is solved! The consequences are incalculable. In the wake of the economic
revolution the political must necessarily follow, for the latter
is only the expression of the former.' And we remember

Lenin's watchword: 'Electrification! Electrification!' " '

Blackett, another eminent scientist very much to the Left politically, was lost to Cambridge in 1933, after ten years in the Cavendish. His strong and authoritarian temperament had always been prone to clash with that of Rutherford. Bernal stayed until 1937, when an essay of his appeared, in which he argued that if science were applied for human welfare and not for profit [assumed to be opposites in the orthodoxy of the day], society would itself choose how much work it was worth doing to secure any particular standard of living and 'science itself would see to it that none of the work done was unnecessary'. This particular approach prompted an Oxford biologist Dr John Baker to define Bernalism as the doctrine of those who believe that the only proper objects of scientific research are to feed people and protect them from the elements, that research workers should be organized in gangs and told what to discover, and that the pursuit of knowledge for its own sake has the same value as the solution of crossword puzzles.

A crystallographer of an earlier generation and a great admirer of Bernal's work was W. L. Bragg, who with his father had won a Nobel Prize as long ago as 1915. He succeeded Rutherford as Cavendish Professor in the last year before the war. C. T. R. Wilson's successor as Jacksonian Professor in 1936, E. V. Appleton, was like Bragg already a scientist of world-wide distinction. A native of Bradford, like many other Johnians, he had been a member of the Cavendish between 1920 and 1924. His work on the ionosphere was of vital importance, not only for the rapid development of broadcasting, but also for radar. He was to become a leading Cambridge contributor to war-winning technology, both in the perfecting of radar and in work on the atomic bomb. The same was true of the versatile G. I. Taylor, who provided expert advice on matters as various as underwater explosions, fog dispersal on runways, the fragmentation of bomb casings, armour-piercing ammunition and rocketry.

G. H. Hardy, on the other hand, preferred like Housman to keep his formidable scholarship pure from the slightest taint of any such practical application. 'I have never done anything useful. No discovery of mine has made, or is likely to make,

directly or indirectly, for good or for bad, the least difference
to the amenity of the world . . . Judged by all practical standards
the value of my mathematical life is nil, and outside maths it is
trivial anyway. That I have created something is undeniable;
the question is about its value.' However, with Hardy it is
permissible to reflect that the wish was often father to the
thought.

A brisk debate on the value of practical utility in undergraduate
education enlivened the pages of *The Cambridge Review* in the
Easter Term of 1931, centring rather surprisingly on Law,
one of the more evidently vocational disciplines. A self-
appointed spokesman of the two hundred and fifty students,
alleged to be spending almost half their working life in
Cambridge on the study of Roman Law, urged a drastic
diminution in what he described as drudgery, boring and
irritating to the last degree, and of no practical significance.
P. W. Duff of Trinity, a future Regius Professor of Civil Law,
sprang eloquently to the defence of what he disarmingly
called his bread and butter. Although advocating the re-
tention of Roman Law in the tripos on grounds of utility,
his main line of defence was the educational merit of the
subject, deriving from its inherent difficulty. In language
which would not have been out of place in an educational
argument forty years later he wrote: 'Mental discipline has
been out of fashion for some decades: the play way devised
by Dr Montessori for young and backward children, to whom
it was no doubt admirably suited, has spread far beyond all
reasonable bounds; and there has been a deplorable tendency
to regard as the ideal form of education the effortless ingestion
of such miscellaneous scraps of information as come floating
on the stream of experience . . . Undergraduates are nearly all
capable, under pressure, of following a train of argument, and
this pressure the university ought to apply.' His defence of his
subject clearly failed to convince some of his critics, either in
point of utility or of mental therapy, but the correspondence
concluded with a strong letter of support from his Trinity
colleague, Lapsley, who was evidently confronted with much
the same trouble in medieval constitutional history and argued
that most people in the course of their lives have to master

subjects which are complicated, obscure, uncongenial and indispensable, training for which, he felt, was an additional merit attached to the study of Bishop Stubbs' charters.

The future of English in the university seemed peculiarly bright at the opening of the decade. Although English as an academic study still had its conservative critics, both the faculty and the tripos were firmly established; a much acclaimed anthology called *Cambridge Poetry* appeared in 1929 and 1930 with contributions from Empson, Richard Eberhardt, Bronowski, T. H. White, Ronald Bottrall, Malcolm Lowry and Michael Redgrave; and Empson had published his *Seven Types of Ambiguity* at the age of twenty-four. However, a new act of the drama was about to begin, as some of the leading actors of the twenties left the stage altogether or withdrew into the wings.

'Q', though by no means senile, had become increasingly anachronistic in style and method. It was no longer fashionable of him to describe Gerard Manley Hopkins as a precious, priestly, hot-house darling with no ear but a thumb. In 1934, at the age of seventy-one, he was roused to vigorous polemic by Eliot's far from untenable description of the England of the thirties as 'a society like ours, worm-eaten with Liberalism'. What Eliot meant by Liberalism, 'Q' concluded, was 'anything which questions dogma; which dogma, to be right dogma, is the priestly utterance of a particular offset of a particular branch of a historically fissiparous Church'. His celebrated 'spontaneous' lecture 'in front of the fire' to fifty under-graduates lost its reputation for spontaneity by being repeated word for word two Saturdays running. He began increasingly to develop a tendency not to turn up at his well publicized lectures.

Forbes, though his reputation as a superbly stimulating, if bizarre, lecturer persisted till his sudden death in 1936, was wholly unconcerned with faculty politics and increasingly devoted to Finella and the Hundred New Towns. His nine o'clock lectures in Clare were sometimes interrupted early in the proceedings by the appearance of his breakfast, brought in from the college kitchens, as was then the mode, on a wooden tray covered with green baize with each succulent dish under a metal cover. It remained untouched till he had extracted the last ounce of meaning from:

> The war of swords and spears
> Melted by dewy tears
> Exhales on high . . .

Richards, after the publication of 1929 of *Practical Criticism*, went first to China as visiting professor at Tsing Hua University of Peking and thence to Harvard. Although he continued on his return to lecture on criticism, he became more and more interested in collaborating with Ogden in the enterprise which the latter described as Debabelization, that is Basic English. This new universal language would have 600 nouns and 150 adjectives. Another 100 words could do the rest, except when the subject matter was scientific, when you might need 1000 words all told. Ogden and Richards, from the early days of the *Cambridge Magazine*, had invented a mythical character called Adelyne More, putative authoress of articles by one or other of them, when outside contributions sagged. She was still at work in the magazine *Psyche* in 1935, contributing an article on how not to make a dictionary, in which were recorded fifteen different meanings of the word 'definite'.

Tillyard, built up as an arch-intriguer by the hagiographers of Leavis, disliked sectarian controversy and anyway was busy producing in the thirties three books on Milton and one on Shakespeare; Willey's energies were primarily devoted to his lecture courses on the English Moralists, which he worked up into two notable books; and Rylands, whose highly acclaimed lectures drew almost as many outsiders as members of the English Faculty, was still in his heyday as a theatrical producer.

So it was that the spotlight centred increasingly on Leavis and the name of the play changed, as John Gross has epigrammatically put it, from the meaning of meaning to the value of values. Leavis was (and still is) a controversialist to the very core of his being. In that respect the only foeman worthy of his steel was Lucas – immensely well read in classical and modern European literature, a traditionalist in literary taste and a radical in politics, stylish and witty both verbally and on paper and afraid of no one, least of all Dr and Mrs Leavis.

In 1927 Leavis was appointed a probationary lecturer and in 1929 married Queenie Roth, whose PhD thesis, begun under Richards' tutelage, emerged as *Fiction and the Reading Public* in 1932. Lucas's critical demolition of it was devastating, e.g.: 'Hardy is allowed merits, but in *The Return of the Native* "the staple of his prose is abominable" (bold language for a writer to use, whose own style plunges, on her opening page, into such an elegance of imagery as – "a tangle of pregnant issues is involved").' Q. D. Leavis by way of emphasizing her stern condemnation of contemporary culture (except for that enjoyed by what she unhappily called 'the high-level reader' and 'the sensitive minority') exaggerated the refinements of Elizabethan civilization and the critical acumen of eighteenth- and nineteenth-century journalists. This enabled Lucas to observe that 'it is surely a great deal better to like the trashiest fiction than to enjoy seeing a witch burn, to go to the silliest cinema than to soak in an eighteenth-century gin shop'. He also had much fun over her evaluation of H. G. Wells as useful for 'keeping the lower levels posted with news of what is stirring higher up'.

Lucas regarded the Leavises and their followers as latter-day Puritans, intent on imposing exclusive and salvationist beliefs and values on the impressionable young, and he took every opportunity to say so. Thus: 'I shall not soon forget the ineffable remark of a girl undergraduate, who, being asked by her supervisor if she had enjoyed some book, replied: "I don't read to enjoy, I read to evaluate". Far better be a healthy farm-wench on a milking-stool.' Or again, – 'Tight-lipped Calvins of Art, teaching the young to love literature by first loathing nine-tenths of it, and carrying their white and lofty foreheads with the self-important anguish of waiters staggering under towers of exquisitely brittle crockery.' Himself knowledgeable and at ease in Classical culture, Icelandic saga, French and German, Lucas found Leavis narrow, insular and the very reverse of life-enhancing.

But it would be Leavis, not Lucas, who won the day and this for two reasons; the first was the great hold he exercised on generations of undergraduates, who propagated his views in schools and universities throughout the country; and the second the solid platform he provided for himself by the publication of *Scrutiny*, which first appeared in 1932, the year in which he became director of studies at Downing and four years before he at last became an assistant lecturer and published his immensely influential *Revaluation*.

T. C. Worsley, later literary editor of the *New Statesman*, found him a very stimulating supervisor. 'He would arrive dressed in an open shirt which shocked us to the depth of our conventional souls, his bald head brown with nature-culture; he would fling down the small common-or-garden sack which he carried slung over his shoulder, extract from it a battered copy of *The Oxford Book of English Verse* and launch himself into his attack on Quiller-Couch and all his works.' Worsley during his short career as a schoolmaster at Wellington recalls that he kept copies of *The Meaning of Meaning* and *Practical Criticism* on his shelves as a tribute to 'Dr Leavis's scathing denunciation of them when I was reading English at Cambridge.'

Towards the end of the thirties, Ronald Duncan, whose *Abelard and Héloïse* was described by Eliot as 'probably the best love poem written this century', deliberately chose to come to Downing because of Leavis's reputation. He was not disappointed, describing Leavis as reading poetry far more sensitively than Gielgud or Olivier, never missing an ambiguity, nor a shade of meaning. But the master would brook no rival for his disciples. 'Somebody asked him what lectures we should attend. Leavis studied the questioner with a mixture of tolerance and contempt. "I suppose you had better look in on Dr Richards, and I dare say the Bennetts are still murdering Milton, Potts piffling around on Byron, and then there's old Henn [a great authority on Yeats] getting his lecture-notes muddled with his expletives on the tow-path. Basil Willey on the seventeenth century isn't bad at all. But avoid Q; he's supposed to lecture on Aristotle's *Poetics*, but he never gets nearer than his bottle of Cockburn".' According to Duncan, Leavis always claimed that Richards' *Principles of Literary Criticism* had purloined ideas which Leavis had first articulated. In consequence, he carried a snapshot of Richards leaving what looked like a seaside bungalow. 'Dr Caligari leaving the scene of his crime'* he would say, as he put the photograph back in his wallet. Richards recalls the occasion when he was finally banished from the charmed circle. On his return from China and India, he was invited to discuss his travels with a group of the Leavises' friends at their house. During the discussion Richards launched into an honest but wholly unfashionable paean of praise for the magnificent work being done by young British Indian Civil Servants. The subsequent silence was chilling.

Apart from the Leavises, *Scrutiny* had some distinguished contributors. Richards himself, for one, before he fell out of favour; L. C. Knights; D. W. Harding, who 'discovered' Isaac Rosenberg; and L. H. Myers and Muriel Bradbrook, who in a contributory essay described Yeats' poetry with marvellous felicity as having 'the maximum of concreteness with the minimum of particularity'. *Scrutiny* was designed in part as a successor to Edgell Rickword's short-lived *Calendar of Letters* and the first number in May 1932 contained a quite uncompromising manifesto – '*Scrutiny* will be seriously pre-occupied with the movement of modern civilization'; 'analysis and interpretation will be with a view to judgement'. Judgement was occasionally explicit and oracular, e.g. of Edith Sitwell: 'for criticism she does not exist, either as a poet or a critic'; 'in so far as reading means ability to read A. L. Rowse is illiterate'; 'No. Mr Churchill cannot candidly be said to know anything, but he has his talent' (this last not by Leavis, but in a contribution by Auden). Leavis wrote in September 1933 on one of his favourite subjects, Milton's verse – 'Milton's dislodgement, in the past decade, after his two centuries of predominance, was effected with remarkably little fuss.' By 1935, Richards, much lauded in earlier issues, was consigned to the guillotine, despite which he remained imperturbably magnanimous. Classical culture was buried under huge spadefuls of earth by H. A. Mason in the summer of 1939. 'Too much stress has been laid on the "timeless" quality of the Classics. They can only be of quickening service in so far as they can appear modern . . . All the textbooks and critical appreciation of Classical literature current in schools (and in

* A reference to a highbrow horror film of the period, *The Cabinet of Dr Caligari*.

universities for that matter) are open to the same objection. They are based on critical values which are not held by those competent to judge.'

Something of the same tone informed Dr Q. D. Leavis's assault in June of 1939 on critics such as Cyril Connolly, Desmond McCarthy, Lord David Cecil and Logan Pearsall Smith – 'contemplating the literary reviewing we cannot help wondering how it is that the reviewers, who know all the literary figures of their world, have had the most expensive education, and are not so overworked that they have no time to think if they wanted to, are not only unable to make first-hand judgements but are also completely ignorant of informed opinion.' Dr F. R. Leavis's informed opinion about the award of an Oxford doctorate to P. G. Wodehouse, as set out in the September 1939 number of *Scrutiny*, is equally uncompromising – 'there may, of course, be an excessive lack of sympathy in the view that his humour is a cross of prep school and *Punch*, his invention puerile, the brightness of his style the inane, mechanical and monotonous brightness of the worst school-boy slang.'*

Dr Leavis in a long life has frequently boasted, and on the whole rightly, of his imperviousness to the infection of Marxism. Yet in *Scrutiny* (December 1932) he wrote: 'Let me say, then, that I agree with the Marxist to the extent of believing some form of economic communism to be inevitable and desirable, in the sense that it is to this that a power-economy of its very nature points, and only by a deliberate and intelligent working towards it, can civilization be saved from disaster.' Some of the Scrutineers' most cherished values have not particularly thrived under that form of economic organization.

Marxist apologetics in the History faculty were largely confined to a brilliant group of undergraduates, who were just about to embark on distinguished academic careers as the war approached. They planned yet another collaborative history – this time Marxist in interpretation – under the editorship of Roy Pascal, a fellow of Pembroke, in which the principal

---

* J. B. Priestley, a combative character, once advanced the view that Dr Leavis might have been frightened by a librarian in his youth.

contributors were to be Eric Hobsbawm, H. J. Habakkuk (a future Vice-Chancellor of Oxford) and Edward Miller (a future Master of Fitzwilliam). However, a faculty in which Pickthorn, Temperley, Kitson Clark, Winstanley, Simpson and Lapsley were still prominent figures was not easily given over to fashionable radicalism. Temperley, writing to the *New Statesman* in 1933, observed that history may be chiefly of use to prove that we do *not* understand the present, and went on to advance the view that no one could assert that the growth of representative government was necessarily a sign of the times or an index of progress. In his inaugural as the first Professor of Modern History in 1930 he poured scorn on many of the cherished assumptions on which Cambridge history had been originally nurtured – 'not only do we repudiate the ideal of Ranke that history should be colourless, new and impartial. We do not even suggest that it is desirable.'

In 1930 the great tradition of Whig history seemed safe in the hands of Macaulay's descendant, the Regius Professor. Trevelyan's output during the thirties was impressive, comprising as it did the three volumes of *England under Queen Anne* and *Grey of Fallodon*. When war broke out he was hard at work on *English Social History*. As Simpson put it felicitously, Trevelyan's great skill as a writer was to join together what pedants had put asunder. As a lecturer he was much less impressive. Hobsbawm described him in action in 1937 as being very nervous and talking in long sentences with an old voice. 'His hair is thin and white and his eyes are sunk; from a distance you hardly see that he has spectacles. He has a close-cropped moustache cut like a Turk's, corners drooping, and deep lines, and he talks about the Glorious Revolution and the constitution and liberty, which is out of fashion nowadays.' From his research students, on the other hand, like J. H. Plumb, who was working under his direction in 1934 on the social structure of the Commons under William III, he commanded the greatest respect and veneration.

The comforting assumptions of Whig history and the gloriousness of the Glorious Revolution were never to recover from the shock administered by an iconoclastic little book of Herbert Butterfield's, *The Whig Interpretation of History*, published in 1931. It would never be so easy again to be uncritical about Protestants and Whigs; to praise revolutions, provided they had proved 'successful'; to sort the progressive wheat from the reactionary chaff. History, like theology, would henceforth have to come to terms with the dimension of the catastrophic, unless it were prepared merely to substitute Marxist determinism for Liberal determinism. The lesson which Butterfield taught was that 'the study of the past with one eye, so to speak, upon the present is the source of all sins and sophistries in history'. History cannot prove that any man was 'right' in the long run. 'She is a harlot and a hireling, and for this reason she best serves those who suspect her most.'

The imposing and ponderous Clapham was succeeded by a very different figure in 1938. M. M. Postan of Peterhouse had been born in Bessarabia and served in the Russian army, before avoiding the unwelcome attentions of the Cheka by escaping to London. Still under forty when he became Professor of Economic History, his countenance was described as being of the orange-red hue of a Left Book Club cover and the vehemence of his lectures as reminiscent of a Seventh Day Adventist in full spate at Hyde Park Corner. He had 15,000 card indexes, inscribed with the detail of medieval economic and social history, and married Eileen Power, another expert in that field. He did not endear himself to the cnmmitted Marxists among his students by observing: 'I was a Communist myself when I was seventeen, but I grew out of it.' By general acclaim the mantle of Bury had fallen on Steven Runciman, whose *Byzantine Civilization* appeared in 1933. Behind the elegant but uncompromising demeanour of this stern academic such undergraduates as were privileged to attend his select dinner parties were able to detect the lineaments of the twenties aesthete who had so dazzled Beaton and his contemporaries.

There was certainly no shortage of promising young historians in Cambridge by the end of the thirties. In 1937 in St John's alone the History Society included, as well as Miller and Habakkuk, Brian Wormald, Peter Laslett and F. H. Hinsley. Geoffrey Barraclough, a young fellow, read them a paper in that year on the erudite topic of 'Litigation in Bremen in 1326'. At a lesser level of historical sophistication was the undergraduate (not from St John's) who described Dante in a tripos paper as 'standing with one foot in the Middle Ages, while with the other he saluted the rising star of the Renaissance'.

The Moral Sciences Club was off to a good start in January 1930 with a paper from Dr Wittgenstein on the congenial subject of 'Evidence for the Existence of other Minds'. After war had broken out and the Germans and Russians were over-running Poland, Moore chose for his topic 'Proof of an External World'. In between, the range of subjects discussed maintained for the most part a comparably high degree of technical rigour. In 1931, the year in which Moore succeeded Johnson as President, controversy centred on the question whether the proposition 'I saw a red patch' had the same meaning as 'I remember seeing a red patch', and in the following year whether the proposition 'Drury has toothache' has or has not a purely behaviouristic meaning. One of two visits by A. J. Ayer led to a motion deploring the excessive speed at which papers were being read. He seems indeed to have disturbed the Cambridge philosophical dovecotes to a considerable extent, judging by the title of a paper delivered by G. A. Paul in November 1936 – 'The Sinful Lust for Verification or the Ayerian Philosophy – an Infantile Disorder'. Moore protested his inability to understand anything that anyone could possibly mean who asserted 'the verifiability hypothesis'. Dialectical Materialism appeared twice on the menu. Maurice Cornforth attracted an unusually large gathering when he addressed the club in 1933 on the philosophy of communism. He told them that there was a priority of matter to mind and that the denial of this led to a negation of philosophy which he called Fideism. Though it could not be proved, physical objects did have an existence independent of mind. In 1936 it was Bernal's turn. He cited as instances of the dialectical process the emergence of life, civilization and the family, all of which contain the seeds of their own decay. The strangest meeting of the club in the thirties must, however, have been that which took place in November 1938, when Eddington maintained against Susan Stebbing that exact thought can be conveyed in inexact language.

In May 1935, John Wisdom, an engaging lecturer, who

endeared himself to his pupils by his habit of tethering his horse to a lamp-post during his lectures, surveyed the moral sciences teaching scene in Cambridge with some candour. 'People might say that Wittgenstein in his lectures spends an unconscionable time saying nothing definite, that Broad deals out dope and that Moore pursues a will o' the wisp, but he [Mr Wisdom] has observed that each produces a change in those who go to their lectures which, although it is different in each case, is in each case a change of a kind philosophers have sought.' Those who sat at the feet of Wittgenstein found him engaged in the throes of a massive recantation, induced by the rack and thumbscrews of his own remorseless intellect. Some verses from I. A. Richards' poem *The Strayed Poet* describe what it felt like to be an onlooker at what Richards called these 'non-lectures':

Few could long withstand your haggard beauty
Disdainful lips, wide eyes bright-lit with scorn,
Furrowed brow, square smile, sorrow-born
World-abandoning devotion to your duty.

Such the torment felt, the spell-bound listeners
Watched and waited for the words to come
Held and bit their breath while you were dumb
Anguished, helpless, for the hidden prisoners.

Poke the fire again! Open the window!
Shut it! – patient pacing unavailing,
Barren the revelations on the ceiling –
Dash back again to agitate a cinder.

'O it's so clear! It's absolutely clear!'
Tense nerves crisp tenser then throughout the school;
Pencils are poised: *'Oh, I'm a bloody fool!*
A damn'd fool' – So: however it appear.

The philosopher's furrowed brows reflected the need he felt to rethink what he had written in the *Tractatus* in the light of conversations he had had with Frank Ramsey and later with Piero Sraffa. We are told that discussions with Sraffa made

Wittgenstein feel like a tree from which all branches had been cut. Considering the havoc Sraffa had already caused in the academic groves of classical economic theory, he must have claims to be considered the greatest intellectual woodcutter of his day. Various unpublished articles and the notes dictated to his pupils, known as the *Blue and Brown Books*, eventually led after the war to Wittgenstein's posthumous *Philosophical Investigations*. His former view that there should be in principle a perfect scientific language which could describe the world is abandoned. The right proposition cannot be taken literally as a 'picture' of the reality which it purports to describe. Instead there would be much discussion of whether the phrase 'I know that I am in pain' is or is not meaningless. For Wittgenstein it only made sense if contrasted with 'I rather think I am in pain' or 'I strongly believe I am in pain'. This problem became, by ordinary standards at least, rather obsessive with him; Sykes Davies recalling an occasion when Wittgenstein summoned him to cross Trinity Street to ask him, presumably as a prelude to a philosophical investigation – 'Have you got a pain, Hugh?' In the 1939 Preliminary Examination candidates were asked: 'If someone says "This room is hot" does he mean that people feel hot in it, or that thermometers rise in it, or what?' An essay subject that year was 'Philosophy is syntax'.

The Modern and Medieval Languages Tripos expanded in the thirties and became notably more academic in content and approach. French continued to dominate the scene. It was a tribute to Prior's groundwork that there were 80 undergraduates reading the subject when he took over the department in 1919 and 500 in 1935 when he was succeeded by F. C. Green of Magdalene. A chair of Spanish was established in 1933, in which year there were thirty-four Part I candidates. The first professor was J. B. Trend of Christ's. Despite an unpromising start to his academic career with a third in natural sciences in 1905, Trend had long established himself as a leading scholar in his field as well as an effective popularizer. Italian studies suffered from some discontinuity as a result of the deaths of two Serena Professors in rapid succession. Piccoli, who died aged forty-six of tuberculosis in 1933, was a very popular Cambridge figure. Originally Professor of English at Naples, he translated several Shakespeare plays, some Shelley, *Urn Burial, Ash Wednesday* and *Pomes Pennyeach*. Bullough, who succeeded him, died eighteen months later.

In 1929 there were forty-three candidates in Part I Geography, a figure which had risen to seventy-four in 1938. It was still something of a soft option with no quantification and nothing of the later emphasis on town and country planning. Where other universities tended to treat the subject under regional groupings (e.g. the Geography of Great Britain or that of South America), Cambridge from the beginning dealt in categories – physical, economic, historical, survey and so on. In the academic year 1935–6 the department was at last reasonably well housed in Downing Place, a translation assisted by the demise of forestry as a subject of Cambridge study.

Archaeology and Anthropology was a relatively small tripos and the department was notably chary of awarding firsts, though Glyn Daniel of St John's succeeded in 1934 and 1935. The indefatigable Frazer was more of Cambridge than in it. His personal library of over 20,000 books, which was un-catalogued, was housed in a large room behind Trinity Chapel. The Head Porter frequently received scrawled messages from Lady Frazer such as: 'Send immediately *Handbuch der Chron-ologie Bd III*. Sir James says it is brown, and is on the left hand side of the case near the lavatory, top shelf (back row).' This formidable old French lady had a hooked nose and long hairs issuing from her chin and used a battery hearing aid which seldom worked and often emitted weird and strident noises. If we are to believe F. W. Filby, employed when the Frazers were in their eighties to try to bring some order into the anthropologist's library and to read to him from time to time, she could be cruelly tyrannical. Filby tells us that on one occasion Frazer asked him to read from Pausanias. Lady Frazer countermanded this and ordered a reading from a recent commentary on *The Golden Bough* – 'Pausanias is a long way away, Jimmy. You wrote that many years ago. Listen to comments on your great work.' Confusion and misunderstanding then arose, as a result of which Lady Frazer 'clenched her teeth and struck him with the back of her heavily ringed hand, drawing blood from his ear'. Nevertheless, Frazer produced in the thirties three volumes on *The Fear of the Dead in Primitive Religion* and four volumes of gleanings from his notebooks called *Anthologia Anthropologica*. The preface to the final supplementary volume of *The Golden Bough* contains the valediction: 'The priest of Nemi . . . for all the quaint garb he wears and the gravity with which he walks across the stage is merely a puppet, and it is time to unmask him before laying him up in the box.' Of the Bible, Frazer wrote in a manner that would have pleased Glover 'it strengthens in us the blind conviction, or the trembling hope, that somewhere, beyond these earthly shadows, there is a world of light eternal, where the obstinate questionings of the mind will be answered and the heart find rest'. He died in 1941. Less than twelve hours later Lady Frazer followed him, an event described by those who knew them in Trinity as the only tactful action of her life.

Frazer had always resolutely refused to read Freud and psychology was not a field of study in which inter-war Cambridge could be in any way regarded as prominent, although a chair of Experimental Psychology was set up in 1931. Sixteen years after the recommendations of the Royal Commission a Department of Education was created. The first Professor, G. R. Owst, was so notoriously and understandably sceptical about the utility of what he was supposed to be doing that even his obituarist in *The Times* many years later was unable to avoid mentioning the fact.

The Economics Faculty in the thirties was beset by no such doubts and uncertainties. Except for the ultra-sensitive Dennis Robertson, it was bliss to be alive and to be young was very heaven. In that confident age, few could have predicted that within half a century academic economists would be quite so vulnerable to the charge that by their fruits ye shall know them, or that what had once been called a dismal science would be so widely, if perhaps unfairly, believed to have converted itself into an elaborate exercise in cabbalistic necromancy.

We have it on Keynes' authority that 'good or even

competent economists are the rarest of birds', but the aviary that surrounded him – Austin and Joan Robinson, Sraffa, Richard Kahn, James Meade – was a very brilliant one. On the ruins of classical economics, they saw a golden opportunity to build a new and practical structure of economic theory, excitingly relevant to the evident needs of a society in which issues of national income and employment seemed incomparably more important than money and banking, the leading economic preoccupations of the twenties. As Austin Robinson recalls: 'We learnt something quite different from Keynes – that we had got to think about the world . . . that if we were not going to think about the world nobody else was.' They worked away busily drafting economic heresies, which Keynes discussed with them at weekends. In the summer of 1934 for Joan Robinson 'everything clicked'. In that year she mocked an eminent professor of economics at Chicago, Frank H. Wright, for believing in perfect competition with its concomitant absurdities of 'rational conduct on the part of buyers and sellers, full knowledge, absence of friction, perfect mobility and perfect divisibility of factors of production and completely static conditions'. Kahn worked out the details of 'the multiplier' – the attempt to define the ultimate increase in national income derived from such and such an increase in expenditure. Aggregate demand was what would help and not Treasury-led parsimony. *Epater le bourgeois* was the technique required to convert the uninitiated. Thus, in a famous broadcast in January 1931, entitled 'Saving and Spending', Keynes said that the best guess he could make was that whenever you save five shillings you put a man out of work for a day. 'Therefore, O patriotic housewives, sally out tomorrow early in the streets and go to the wonderful sales which are everywhere advertised.' With a rhetorical flourish which would have delighted Le Corbusier, he added: 'Why not pull down the whole of South London from Westminster to Greenwich and make a good job of it?' Criticizing the 1931 Budget in the *New Statesman*, he rightly pointed out that cutting the schoolteachers' salaries by 10 per cent would not help us to recapture the markets of the world.

All this was to culminate in 1936 in the most celebrated book emanating from Cambridge in the inter-war years, Keynes'

The General Theory of Employment, Interest and Money, with its central argument that the case for the 'crisis of capitalism' was the opposite to that normally adopted, since it was not the amount saved from consumption that settled the level of investment but investment that fixed the level of incomes at that point where the amount of saving needed to cover it is forthcoming. The thing to do was for the government to promote public works in order to generate the expenditure necessary to remove unemployment altogether. *The General Theory* did not at first commend itself universally in Cambridge. Clapham decided not to read it, being convinced from conversations with Keynes that he would not understand it. Robertson believed that the truth about the cure of depressions lay somewhere between the standpoint of the boosters, 'who believe that cheap and abundant money and the generation of a spirit of optimism can lift us out of them and that of the "penguins", who believe that high cost and inefficient concerns must be eliminated before business can revive'. Pigou wrote a highly critical review pointing out with some prescience that 'even if Mr Keynes' full employment were established, wage earners would still have a choice between policies that promote respectively higher real wage rates plus less employment and lower real wage rates plus more employment'. But as Austin Robinson sadly observed in a letter to Keynes in 1937: 'I find an almost insuperable difficulty in balancing one's affection for Pigou against one's love of truth.'

Keynes felt that Pigou had reacted like a sixth-form boy who had been cheeked, but no hostility developed between them. The fact was that even Pigou was far from being a purblind opponent of state intervention in the economy, which gained ever increasing momentum as the thirties drew to a close. In his *Socialism Versus Capitalism* (1937), he proclaimed that as a means of coping with unemployment 'a socialist system, with central planning, has definite advantages over a capitalist one'. The book is hardly distinguishable from a moderate Fabian pamphlet – 'if then it were in the writer's power to direct his country's destiny, he would accept, for the time being, the general structure of capitalism, but would modify it gradually'. He went on to argue for increased, if cautious, nationalization and fiscal policies to reduce inequalities. But both Pigou and Keynes issued warnings against headlong collectivism. Pigou quoted Marshall – 'Every new extension of governmental work in branches of production which need ceaseless creation and initiative is to be regarded as *prima facie* anti-social, because it retards the growth of that knowledge and those ideas which are incomparably the most important form of collective wealth.' Keynes' view was that 'the important thing for government is not to do things which individuals are doing already, and to do them a little better or a little worse, but to do those things which at present are not done at all e.g. sensible co-ordination of currency and credit, dissemination of data, savings policy, population'. In the last chapter of *The General Theory*, while conceding that 'a somewhat comprehensive socialization of investment' would be necessary, he stressed that it was quite unimportant for the State to own the instruments of production. 'Individualism . . . is the best safeguard of the variety of life, which emerges precisely from the extended field of personal choice, and the loss of which is the greatest of all losses of the homogeneous or totalitarian state.' It is also important to remember his earlier warnings against the evil social consequences of inflation. Nor was he in the least imperceptive about the possibility of another economic problem of the long run (in which, as he reminded us, we are all dead) when he referred to the trade unionists as 'once the oppressed, now the tyrants, whose selfish and sectional interests need to be bravely opposed'.

With hindsight, it is interesting to reflect that none of these increasingly politically minded economists seems to have considered the desirability of suggesting a massive rearmament programme from at least the late summer and autumn of 1933. This would have got the multiplier off to a flying start, rapidly mopped up unemployment, and stopped Hitler dead in his tracks. However, the British intelligentsia of the time, with Cambridge very much in the van, was suffering from collective delusions of an almost unprecedented unreality, the origins and nature of which we should now examine.

CHAPTER SIX

Politics II

The Leftward movement of Cambridge politics in the thirties has been extensively recorded by writers seeking the social and intellectual origins of the treasonable activities of Philby, Burgess and Maclean or the deaths in battle in Spain of John Cornford, David Haden Guest and Julian Bell. The two most intriguing questions for the social historian – or for that matter the psychologist – are how and why quite so many intellectually gifted people acquired what can only be described as a salvationist belief in Stalin's Russia and consistently preached pacifism and disarmament, while at the same time urging resistance to armed Fascism. Much as the idea would have horrified them, they seem at times almost to exemplify Hume's dictum that the reason is, and ought only to be, the slave of the passions. Needham reviewed the Webbs' *Soviet Communism* in 1936 with an enthusiasm bordering on rapture – 'this magnificent work, planned in that comprehensive style which the Webbs have adopted throughout their remarkable conjoint life, provides such a mass of material for thought and study and yet may be read with such enjoyment that it is difficult to find sufficiently sober words with which to describe it'. In 1937 at the height of the Yezhov two-year terror, at the end of which perhaps five per cent of the population had been arrested (with a far higher proportion among the educated classes), he told the Modern Churchmen's Union in an address called 'History is on our side': 'The conception of the utmost cultural autonomy for different peoples, side by side with economic union, is a grand one and we owe it largely to the genius of no other than Joseph Vissarionovitch Stalin.' Bernal's enthusiasm for the bloodstained Soviet regime was even less restrained. Writing in the *Cambridge Left* in 1933, he explained that there was no 'way out' through political democracy. The end to strive for could only be the establishment of a classless socialist world state, the only state to which an intellectual could give unqualified allegiance – 'the USSR is alone among the nations moving on. And not only economically, but culturally. It is no accident that Russia provides the antithesis to the whole catalogue of cultural reaction represented by Fascism. In science, in education, in religion, in the family, in the prisons, the USSR gives practical embodiment to the progressive ideas of the nineteenth and twentieth centuries. The Communists are the piers and only defenders of the liberal tradition.' The last sentence at least makes one understand why, just before his death as an ambulance driver in Spain, Julian Bell felt impelled to write to E. M. Forster – 'Liberalism is indeed political romanticism; it has no innate sense of human baseness and can only move between illusion and disillusion.' But then Bell, like Orwell, understood before he died what Communist politics entailed. As he wrote to Cecil Day Lewis – 'either one has the smell of the committee-room, the intrigues, wrangles, bigotry of doctrine, and squabbles on points of fact, or the worse noise, unreason and enthusiasm of the public meeting and street demonstration . . . Revolution is the opium of the intellectuals – pseudo-revolution.' That lesson was, however, only slowly learnt. In a 1937 compilation of left-wing essays, characteristic of the times and ironically entitled *Mind in Chains*, edited by Day Lewis, we even find a future Keeper of the Queen's pictures, Anthony Blunt, then a fellow of Trinity, torturing his critical sensitivity to conform with the new orthodoxy. He quotes Lenin to Clara Zetkin: 'Every artist . . . has a right to create freely according to his ideals, independent of anything. Only, of course, we Communists cannot stand with our hands folded and let chaos develop in any direction it may. We must guide this process according to a plan and form its results.' The new Realists, painters like Rivera and Orozco, would be for Blunt the hope of the future. The summer number of *Cambridge Left* in 1934 achieved perhaps the ultimate in hallucination when it published a piece by Richard Goodman, fashionably entitled *Canto from Work in Progress*. This read:

> YOU
>
> AND YOU
>
> AND YOU

do you know
have you heard
what we have done
what we do
over there
in the USSR
where the bourgeois is overthrown
and the word
of the WORKERS is law
(SOVIET POWER!)
where
comrades with comrades go
without loss
free at last from the boss
singing each like a bird
with joy,
never again to fear
the sack and the spy
sneaking near

The last number in the autumn of 1934 approved the speeches
of Bukharin and Radek (as yet unliquidated) at the All-Union
Congress of Soviet Writers, where they were described by
Stalin as 'engineers of the soul', and even brought the Mechanical Sciences faculty under Marxist scrutiny, concluding that
the possession of an engineering department of a satisfactory
sort in Cambridge must 'wait upon the establishment of a
Soviet Republic'.

To old hands like Maurice Dobb the new fervour of the
thirties was understandably gratifying. His role appears
principally to have been that of the guardian of doctrinal
orthodoxy. You could, if you wished, enjoy a weekend with
him, Prince Mirsky and Barbara Wootton under the auspices
of the Society for Cultural Relations with the USSR, or study
the gospel cogently argued in his *Russia Today and Tomorrow*,
Marxism Today or *Soviet Russia and The World*. In the latter
work you could learn about the new potash mine at Solikamsk,
the agricultural machinery factory at Selmashtroy and of
course the blast furnaces at Magnetogorsk. It was in agriculture,
thought Dobb, that 'the policy of the Soviet government met

with its most striking success', although it was true that 'methods amounting to open compulsion were used'. However, 'pictures of universal conscription and "forced labour"', one should hardly need to add, are grotesque parodies of the truth'.

But now there were effective activists in Cambridge, as well as accredited theorists. David Haden Guest, son of a respectable Labour politician, was at Trinity from 1929 to 1933. After spending a fortnight in a Nazi cell in Brunswick in 1931 for joining in a Communist demonstration, he came back to Cambridge and marched into college hall wearing a hammer and sickle emblem. With impressive organizational support from Maurice Cornforth, Guest was the inspiration behind the rapid growth of small Communist cells in Cambridge. When he went down to go and teach in Moscow, the succession was originally to have passed to the Magdalene poet (and pioneer of 'Mass Observation') Charles Madge. In the event the new torch-bearer was the young Trinity historian John Cornford, son of F. M. Cornford, the Lawrence Professor of Ancient Philosophy, and his wife, the poetess Frances Cornford. Cornford was brilliant, fearless, farouche and monomaniac. Capable of writing the exquisitely tender lyric 'To Margot Heinemann' just before his death in battle, he could savagely excoriate the bourgeois culture, which he had taught himself to execrate, as in his famous poem 'Keep Culture out of Cambridge':

> Wind from the dead land, hollow men,
> Webster's skull and Eliot's pen,
> The important words that come between
> The unhappy eye and the difficult scene.
> All the obscure important names
> For silly griefs and silly shames
> All the tricks we once thought smart,
> The Kestrel* joy and the change of heart,

* The reference is to Day Lewis's lines to Auden beginning: 'Look West, Wystan, lone flyer, birdman, my bully boy', with the key line: 'No wing-room for Wystan, no joke for Kestrel joy.'

The dark mysterious urge of the blood
The donkeys shitting on Dali's food,
There's none of these fashions have come to stay
And there's nobody here got time to play
All we've brought are our party cards
Which are no bloody good for your bloody charades.

Though he would have spat contemptuously at the comparison, Cornford was the Rupert Brooke of the thirties, dead in his own corner of a foreign field on the Cordova front, commemorating the idealism of a cause, which matched him with his hour, already an anachronism, as Orwell and Koestler would soon discover. The last stanza of his poem 'Full Moon at Tierz; Before the Storming of Huesca' reads:

Freedom is an easily spoken word
But facts are stubborn things. Here, too, in Spain
Our fight's not won till the workers of all the world
Stand by our guard on Huesca's plain
Swear that our dead fought not in vain,
Raise the red flag triumphantly
For Communism and for liberty.

Cornford was killed on 28 December 1936, the day after his twenty-first birthday. In his three undergraduate years he was largely instrumental in boosting the numbers of the Socialist Society from 200 to 600 and ensuring that it was Marxist-dominated to such an extent that for a time the moderates withdrew, before the politics of the Popular Front tended to draw them together again. If any hostility was shown by right-wing undergraduates as occurred in Armistice Week 1933 – first outside the Tivoli Cinema after a showing of a patriotic film 'Our Fighting Navy' and then at an anti-war demonstration on Armistice Day itself – the orchestrated outcry was predictably clamorous. Only one side was of course expected to wear kid gloves. Victor Kiernan records that his friend Cornford related 'with genuine relish' a story of the Hungarian Communist leader Bela Kun machine-gunning 5000 prisoners during a forced retreat during the Russian Civil War.

Of the three subsequently celebrated undergraduates of the

period who eventually defected to Moscow, Kim Philby was much less socially prominent than Guy Burgess or Donald Maclean. During the anti-war march to lay a wreath on the Cambridge War Memorial on 11 November 1933, Burgess acted as navigator for Julian Bell's car, which was armoured with mattresses. He was a compulsive party goer, secured a first in Part I History and was an Apostle, 'fathered', interestingly, by Anthony Blunt, whom we have already encountered as an enthusiast for Soviet realism in painting. Maclean was the son of a former chairman of the Parliamentary Liberal party, who received an honorary degree with J. H. Thomas, Bergson and Frazer in 1920. The future defector bequeathed to posterity a remarkable blue-print for student 'activism', something which was hitherto unknown in British universities in the twentieth century. This is contained in a letter which he wrote to *Granta* in March 1934 from Trinity Hall. He pointed out that something had to be done in view of the 'capitalist, dictatorial character of the University'. There were rumours of political discrimination having occurred at the Appointments Board together with economic exploitation of undergraduates etc., etc. He advocated the setting up of a Student Council. This should be 'democratically elected on a college and faculty basis, backed by the crescent volume of student protest' and 'could put through its demands against any opposition from the authorities'. He outlined a ten point programme:

    (i) Complete freedom of speech and action.

    (ii) Student control of college magazines without interference by the authorities.

    (iii) The right to use college and university lecture rooms for all political meetings.

    (iv) The right to have public discussion on lectures.

    (v) The abolition of official supervision of Colonial Students.

    (vi) A share in the control of tutorial fees and of college and lodging-house charges.

    (vii) Representation on the Appointments Board.

    (viii) Complete equality for women students.

    (ix) The abolition of petty restrictions, such as gate times

and the wearing of cap and gown.
(x) The election of a Students' Council to put through these and all future student demands.

Cornford, writing in a student symposium entitled *Young Minds for Old*, edited by Lincoln Ralphs, a future chairman of the Schools Council, was able to assure the middle class readers, whom he was seeking to convert, that 'it is notable that the Central Committee of the Communist Party pays far more attention, gives far more criticism and more assistance to the work of its student members than any other political body'. And their technique was, as it still is, impressive. At least seven of Maclean's points have been achieved and the University is thought by most people to have gained rather than lost in the process. The sting lies in the head and the tail – points (i) and (x).

The world of A. C. Benson was clearly under considerable threat by early 1933 when Charles Madge was warning the Kingsley Club in Magdalene that, since Hegel thought that thinking and doing should be identical and Christ that men should be known by their fruits, members should beware of introversion, idealism and Rome and turn their gaze towards the objective world, materialism and Moscow. Madge contributed some lines to *New Country* later in that year, which he called 'Letter to the Intelligentsia':

> Lenin, would you were living at this hour:
> England has need of you, of the cold voice
> That spoke beyond Time's passions, that expelled
> All the half treasons of the mind in doubt.

Throughout the twenties, the 'mind in doubt' had been very much a Cambridge phenomenon. As a psychological condition, it was relatively acceptable to a gentle homosexual like Forster, who used to enjoy perpetrating mild epigrams like 'the sanctity of doubt', but to those of a more active and sanguine temperament it was intolerable. It seemed to many of them by the middle thirties that the sacrifices of the First War had been in vain; that a social and governmental structure which seemed powerless to alleviate the dole queue was flatly unacceptable; that the received interpretation of both history and economics had been undermined beyond recovery; and that neither theological disquisition in Great St Mary's nor Moral Rearmament in the Dorothy Café provided any sort of acceptable answer. The scientists through their own achievement had glimpsed prospects of limitless power, but, as Bernal and Blackett constantly emphasized, their prestige was not commensurably high and the irrational structure of capitalism denied the common people the social dividend which they believed a collectivized society alone could offer them. So a number of the young scientists became committed Communists or fellow-travellers, and even a veteran like Gowland Hopkins was reported to be prepared to put his pen to the draft of any 'progressive' letter to the press put under his nose.

It has additionally to be remembered how disillusioned erstwhile moderates were with the performance of the two minority Labour governments of the twenties. Increasingly the dividing line between Socialism and Communism became blurred. John Strachey told the Union in 1937 that Communists were Socialists who mean what they say and that there was no doctrinal divorce between the two movements. At a memorial meeting for Cornford, Aneurin Bevan evoked loud applause when he declared: 'John Cornford was a Communist and I am a member of the Labour Party. I believe that the sacrifice of Cornford, Maclaurin and the International Brigade will weld these two parties into one.' It was the age of the Popular Front and 'no enemies to the Left'. There was much talk of fraternity and solidarity, together with a potent admixture of sheer sentimentality, as when the Needhams, reviewing an Auden poem in *New Writing 2*, found it encouraging to think that the young men and women in the student swimming-pool were Labour League of Youth members. 'The beauty of these people is not strange, not irresponsible, but piquant with the beauty of the new world-order.' Hewlett Johnson, the Red Dean of Canterbury, was a frequent visitor to Cambridge, wafting clouds of incense from his collectivist aspergillum, explaining that any Spanish churches which had been destroyed by the Republicans had invariably been used by Franco as ammunition dumps. Miss Monica Whateley told the Socialist

Club that the government air-raids in Spain were 'the most humane you can imagine'. The Spanish Civil War was enormously influential in diverting attention from the judicial travesties and massacres perpetrated concurrently in the USSR. So that W. R. F. McCartney, who eventually did seven years as a Russian spy, was heard in respectful silence as he told the Union that Russia alone possessed a penal system which was not based on a barbaric tradition and one of the last pre-war Presidents Pieter Keuneman told the Union in November 1937 that in the USSR there was freedom of conscience for all, freedom of the press, of assembly and of street processions.

The stridency of the Cambridge Marxists was, as we have seen, out of all proportion to their numbers. Yet few voices were raised in opposition. Nobody had Malcolm Muggeridge's unusual opportunity to study the Webbs at close quarters; while it was legitimate to assert almost any half-truth or fantasy about the USSR, any hint of criticism led to accusations of bad faith and tainted evidence; and nobody relished being called a Fascist sympathizer, an accusation freely bandied about. A notable exception was Michael Oakeshott of Caius, who in 1934 reviewed *Aspects of Dialectic Materialism*, in which Bernal, who was a contributor, had observed that Marx 'in contrast to the founders of most philosophical systems' was not an ignorant man. Oakeshott observed that among its followers Dialectical Materialism is like a theology turned into a gospel and a gospel turned into a dogma. In it 'the primitive passion for analogy is almost unchecked, and the result is a mystical and esoteric philosophy which can be paralleled perhaps only in the writing of the alchemists'. Keynes was consistently contemptuous. He loathed Puritanism and believed that Communism in Britain derived its strength from our innate urge to adopt uncomfortable solutions to our problems. In 1934 he wrote to the *New Statesman* – 'When Cambridge undergraduates take their inevitable trip to Bolshiedom, are they disillusioned when they find it all dreadfully uncomfortable? Of course not. That is what they are looking for.' He was certainly not impressed by Stalin, whom he described in another letter as having produced an environment in which the processes of mind are atrophied and the bleat of propaganda bores 'even the birds and the beasts into stupefaction'. He made it abundantly plain that in any class war, he would be on the side of the educated bourgeoisie and described Marxist economics in the columns of the *New Statesman* as 'an insult to our intelligence'. At the time, this greatly saddened A. L. Rowse, whose *Mr Keynes and The Labour Movement* (1936) advanced the hope that Keynes 'would sit down for a year or two, to embark, as it would appear he has never yet had the patience to do, upon a thorough reading of Marx'. But the liberal in Keynes remained unrepentant. At the beginning of 1939 he berated the Labour Party for not facing the fact that they are not sectaries of an outworn creed 'mumbling moss-grown demi-semi Fabian Marxism', but the heirs of eternal liberalism. Nor was Bertrand Russell anything of an enthusiast for the USSR. He wrote to Gilbert Murray in January 1941 that he had no doubt 'that the Soviet Government is even worse than Hitler's and it will be a misfortune if it survives'.

Nevertheless, it was not wholly unreasonable either to see in Russian Communism a theoretically desirable antithesis to Fascism and Nazism, or to become profoundly disillusioned with capitalism in a society apparently powerless to cope with unemployment at an unprecedentedly high figure. What is much more difficult to understand, particularly after 1933, was the prevalence of pacifism. It can, of course, be argued that the response in 1939 of both senior and junior members of the university to the demands of the war was such that pacifism proved to be ineffective and at most skin-deep. However, its effect on the climate of opinion in the universities, and through them amongst the intelligentsia at large, was catastrophic and has received insufficient attention as a significant element in the history of the drift to appeasement.

A number of different factors contributed to the growth of the movement, enhanced in differing proportion by fear, guilt and idealistic illusions. John Lehmann, who came down from Trinity in 1930, recalled that for him at any rate, the Cambridge he knew was haunted by the shadow of the First War. 'It was always there in the background conditioning the prevalent sensibility.' An enthusiastic member of the university branch of the League of Nations Union, he remembers

being much influenced by a play produced at the Festival,
C. K. Munro's *The Rumour*, in which two Ruritanian states are
manoeuvred into war by the sinister machinations of political
and commercial intriguers. The wicked armament manu-
facturer became a potent figure in left-wing mythology.
From that it was easy to conclude that capitalism itself was
the prime agent of war. Consequently it was not difficult to
attach to anti-capitalist agitation those idealists profoundly
affected by memories of the last war or fears of the next or
uneasy in their conscience about the alleged injustices of the
Treaty of Versailles. Might not a rearmament programme in
the thirties be used to further the interests of the capitalists
and so be secretly aimed against the workers or the USSR,
which, to quote John Cornford, enjoyed 'complete freedom
from any aggressive aims'? An article in *The Girton Review* in
1934 spelt out the new orthodoxy: 'It is possible to conceive
of a government, frightened by discontent and unemployment
at home, welcoming war as a last resort to silence these
murmurs by a stirring call to fight for the fatherland.'

The fiery Ellen Wilkinson, a future Labour minister,
addressed the Cambridge New Peace Movement in 1937.
In her hurried zeal to promote the cause she brought the
wrong speech, but settled down quickly to point out that
under no circumstances could rearmament be justified; war
was one of the inevitable ills accruing from a capitalist form
of society. In Britain, she said, there was no need whatsoever
to support the Government's rearmament programme, since
its purpose obviously was not to protect democracy against
fascism. Then there were the idealistic visionaries like Lord
Ponsonby and Lord Allen of Hurtwood, frequent visitors to
Cambridge. Perhaps the most crackpot performance of all
was that of Ponsonby addressing the New Peace Movement
on 10 May 1935, in which he advocated complete disarmament
for Britain, since a nation that is disarmed would not be
attacked. There were, he said, three sorts of morality in the
world. The first: 'You be good and no matter what I do'
was the morality of the British Empire in the past. The second:
'I'll be good, if you'll be good' – the morality of the League of
Nations. The third was 'I'll be good and I only hope you will
follow my example.' This last was the morality he hoped

would be adopted. The Chairman, Mr Rackham, with a curious choice of metaphor, is recorded as saying that Lord Ponsonby had given them plenty of powder and shot to fight for peace.

Nor were the scientists backward in the matter. Seventy-nine of them, including not only Bernal and Needham but also Snow, Oliphant and F. P. Bowden signed a letter protesting against scientific research being used for rearmament. People believed what they wanted to believe, as for instance the Liberal, R. H. Bernays, who told the Cambridge branch of the League of Nations Union in 1935 that he thought there was no possibility of war within ten years and that disarmament was the foundation of security. Bertrand Russell, an old hand at the game, wrote to the *New Statesman* in August 1935 – 'in all the densely populated countries of Western Europe, it seems almost certain that, within a few days of the outbreak of war, panic will seize the surviving inhabitants of the capitals and the industrial areas, leading to anarchy, starvation, and paralysis of all warlike effort . . . Absolute pacifism, therefore, in every country in which it is politically possible, is the only sure policy both for Governments and individuals.' An anti-war exhibition was mounted in Cambridge in 1934 and there was a great bustle in 1935 to secure signatures amongst the undergraduates for the Reverend Dick Shepherd's Peace Ballot. Cornford urged the faithful not only to sign up, but to add in the blank space: 'War is the outcome of the economic rivalries of capitalist imperialist powers and can only be ended by the abolition of capitalism. The only effective way of fighting against war is mass resistance by the united front of the working class and their allies against all forms of militarism and war preparations.' Dobb was at this time Secretary of the Cambridge Anti-War Council.

Few influential voices were raised in Cambridge in support of the view that it was a paramount moral duty to resist implacably and at all costs the threat to civilized values represented by Hitler, Mussolini and the Japanese. Coulton and W. R. Matthews, Dean of St Paul's were notable exceptions, as was Bishop Hensley Henson, who preached vigorously on the subject in 1937, a year in which Ponsonby took it upon himself to tell the Union how much he disliked

'the humbug and hypocrisy' of the rearmament programme
which thinly veiled 'a pure, unashamed imperialism'. Meanwhile on the Ebro front two Trinity men, Malcolm Dunbar,
Chief of Staff of the XV International Brigade and Peter Kemp,
were fighting each other on opposite sides, and F. L. Lucas
noted that undergraduate pacifists often made good machine-
gunners in Spain. On the whole, few undergraduates were
affected by pacifist propaganda (a notable exception being the
spectacular Gandar Dower, who did however meet his death
as a war correspondent). On the other hand, many of them
were to learn at Dunkirk, in Singapore, in Burma, on the high
seas and in the air what it was like to face a deadly and highly
equipped enemy, while suffering from a gross and unnecessary
inferiority in equipment and warlike preparedness. Any of
them who remembered reading *Granta* in 1936 might have
recalled somewhat ruefully a commentary on a discourse of
Russell's entitled 'Which Way to Peace?' – 'with that ruthless
yet graceful logic which makes his books such a pleasure to
read, Mr Russell analysed the present situation and decided,
not on emotional nor religious grounds, but from a strictly
rationalistic point of view, that absolute pacifism is the only
policy'. That could accurately be described as appeasement
with a vengeance.

Against the sombre background of an ever-increasing threat
of war and with an unprecedented depth of ideological
differences developing, the Union and the political clubs and
societies became in this period a much more significant and
interesting index of Cambridge opinion. The Union was on
the whole more serious than it had ever been since the days
when Bulwer Lytton described it as:

> That club-room, famous then,
> Where striplings settled questions spoilt by men,
> When grand Macaulay sat triumphant down,
> Heard Praed reply, and long'd to halve the crown.

History has added a number of ironic footnotes to statements
made in debate in the full flush of confident youth, as when
F. Elwyn Jones of Caius described the House of Lords, over

which he would one day preside, as the caterpillars of society, the watchdogs of Conservatism and a gilded sepulchre for the superannuated, standing between the worker and the fruits of his work.* Of two visiting Oxford Presidents, E. R. G. Heath of Balliol excused his strangeness at finding himself in Cambridge by describing himself as a glittering solitaire outside his setting, while M. Foot of Wadham began a speech 'with a severe condemnation of the vote-catching demagogues in the Labour Party'.

Since the prevailing mood was such that the Marxists and fellow-travellers found themselves not infrequently on the winning side, it was not, as it now is, official party policy to boycott the Union and consequently debates ranged widely and fiercely. In the same way, the battle lines in the political clubs were more clearly drawn. As *Granta* observed in an editorial in November 1933 – 'the sports field, the beer glass and the loud guffaw still play a part in an average under-graduate's life. But there has grown up alongside of these interests a very real concern for, and understanding of, contemporary problems and events'. It would be in vain for Lord Lloyd to tell the Cambridge Conservatives in 1930: 'God preserve our politics from the highbrow.'

In that same speech, Lord Lloyd expressed the view that Egyptian minds were unsuited to modern democracy. Be that as it may, it became increasingly clear that a great many Cambridge undergraduates were becoming increasingly scepti-cal about the morality and efficacy of the British Empire, although recruitment for the Colonial Service remained decidedly competitive. Surprising as it may seem to those who only knew him at the very end of his life, Krishna Menon, as well as being a tireless and persuasive campaigner for Indian independence, was at that time a man of considerable personal charm. So that he had a ready hearing when he told the Union that repression in India was worse than in Russia under the Tsars or that 'the only sign of the Englishman in India is the policeman armed to the teeth'. In November 1937 R. Palme Dutt explained to the Union that British withdrawal

---

* *Granta* predicted a brilliant future for him believing that he would not be the first, as he would be the greatest, of Puritan Welsh lawyers to make a name in politics.

from India would not be accompanied by civil strife. No wonder Mr George Pilcher, General Secretary of the Royal Empire Society, talking on 'The Indestructible British Empire', viewed with alarm the aloof attitude of 'undergraduates today to the word Empire'. In 1933 the Union voted by 146 to 54 that it had no faith in the conception of a strong and united British Empire as the mainstay of world peace. Mr Lakshmi Ja of Trinity may have had a point when he explained in 1937 that God had given Englishmen three qualities – intelligence, sincerity and conservatism, but in His infinite mercy had decreed that no Englishman was to have more than two.

However, the argument was not invariably one sided. Percy Cradock, the historian of the Union, recalls how just before the outbreak of the war a celebrated exchange took place between the poet and civil servant Humbert Wolfe and one of the brightest oratorical stars of the Union, Pieter Keuneman. Keuneman of Pembroke was a Communist, scion of a bourgeois family in Ceylon, and had been to Bertrand and Dora Russell's experimental school. He would eventually become one of the chief architects of Communism in Ceylon. His speech was a brilliant denigration of the British Empire, full of witty sallies, which convulsed the house. Nobody listening felt that Wolfe had a hope of replying adequately. He had, however, a considerable reputation as a wit. He was all the more effective in consequence when he rose and spoke with deadly seriousness – 'I suppose it's strange that I am the only person in this hall who doesn't find all this very amusing. Perhaps if you belonged to a race as I do – look at my nose if you want to know which – that has been hounded across the face of the earth and found refuge and decency only in the British Empire you would not find it so amusing to hear it derided, scorned. If you don't like it, why don't you get out?' To a hushed assembly, he went on: 'It's too bad of me to spoil an amusing party. I had to say these things, but you really came to be amused, so I will amuse you.' Which he apparently did. Keuneman duly became President of the Union in the first term after the outbreak of the war.

An ever increasing interest was evinced in the affairs of Russia. A local branch of the Society for Cultural Relations with the USSR, which had fallen into disuse, was revived in

1936, the year in which Kamenev and Zinoviev were liquidated. Potential subscribers were told, as usual, that 'the society has always been purely non-political'. They could, nevertheless, look forward to hearing the Soviet press attaché and talks by Bernal and Dr Edith Summerskill, respectively on Science and Health Protection in the USSR. As far as the Union was concerned, the most celebrated debate, though not by the standards of the day heavily attended, was in May 1932, when the house voted that it saw more hope in Moscow than in Detroit, Dobb prevailing over Kitson Clark, and doing his cause no harm by denying the existence of forced labour or religious persecution in Russia. Indeed, he felt that the most hopeful sign of all was the progress in those things which could not be expressed in figures; in the type of man and the type of values which were being developed. The Union shook off some understandable suspicions about the authenticity of the Metro-Vic engineers' trial in 1933 by negativing easily the motion that recent events in Russia had shown the USSR to be unworthy of the respect of the civilized world, with Dobb again very persuasive. That same year, a future Lord Justice of Appeal, J. R. H. T. Cumming-Bruce of Magdalene, told the Union that 'hope lay in the adoption of the Soviet system – a system which combined the spirit of democracy with swift and certain action'.

On the extreme Right, Fascism had few supporters. There was a small Fascist organization, which according to *Granta* was presided over in 1933 by yet another future Lord Justice of Appeal sowing his political wild oats, F. H. Lawton of Corpus Christi. It was predictably addressed by Major-General J. F. C. Fuller in 1935, but otherwise seems to have amounted to nothing much, though indirectly it was involved in a massive debate in February 1933 on the motion that 'This House prefers Fascism to Socialism'. All accounts agree that Sir Oswald Mosley gave a scintillating performance before a house 'packed from floor to ceiling'. 'A section of the House had hissed Sir Oswald Mosley when he entered; the way he crushed his opponents and interrupters and his magnificent oratory carried an enthusiastic House off its feet, although there were probably, at the most, a score of believers in Fascism present.' Mosley's opponent was Clement Attlee, who had had to replace Aneurin Bevan at the last minute. His quiet advocacy, characteristically interspersed with waspish comments such as 'the Fascist party is a party to do the dirty work of Big Business, if ever the National Government fails us in that respect', was enough for his supporters to win by a large majority, despite Mosley's pyrotechnics – an admirable outcome for the good name of the University.

The balance of opinion in Cambridge certainly favoured the National Government until 1935, the year of its sweeping General Election victory, though its foreign policy and the whole question of rearmament began thereafter to tell increasingly against it. An article in *The Cambridge Review* in the run up to the election, signed 'J. N.' and perhaps written by Needham, defined the voters' choice as one between a 'National' (Conservative) British government, armed to the teeth and restricting step by step the civil liberties of its subjects, and a Socialist England, standing side by side with the Soviet Union and the smaller countries to the deterrence of aggression. A few days later the Union voted against the return of the National Government by 163 votes to 149, Professor Laski perhaps persuading some of the waverers that 'every vote for the Labour party was a vote for international peace'. As far as the University vote was concerned, the National Government candidates Sir J. J. Withers and Pickthorn polled between them 14,519 to the 3453 of H. L. Elvin, the Labour candidate. And as we have seen, Charles Fletcher Cooke, a future MP, described as varying according to his mood between shell-pink and pillar-box red, made little or no impact on his Conservative opponent in the undergraduate poll, which took place just before the General Election. But in 1936 the Spanish Civil War started and the Hunger Marchers came to Cambridge. In November of that year there is an interesting record of a meeting in the Arts School to launch 'A People's Front for Britain' with G. D. H. Cole and Captain Harold Macmillan sharing a platform, the latter welcoming the idea as being the genesis of a National Government of the Centre and Left. Harold Macmillan had been much involved in 1935 in producing the pamphlet *The Next Five Years*, urging a public works programme with a National Development Board and a far greater measure of social justice. Among 150 signatories, there were few prominent Cambridge names, although Rutherford, Raven, Barker and Miss Wodehouse signed. As far as Spain was concerned, the Republican cause immediately aroused great sympathy. G. B. Croasdell, President of the Union, visited the Spanish government in the Christmas vacation and proclaimed that this was no war of Fascism against Communism, but one of Fascism against the people. Almost nothing was heard of the other side of the coin, although H. D. Maidment of Pembroke, whose home was in Republican Huelva, testified that he had 'seen the prisons in two local towns, in one the prisoners were sprayed with petrol and then set on fire, in the other the prisoners were herded together and bombs and sticks of dynamite were thrown in amongst them. In many towns the prisons were burnt over the heads of the helpless occupants and in one town they were taken out one by one and told to run for their lives; meanwhile a stick of dynamite had been tied to their back and the fuse lit. There was no need to dig graves.'

A vote of no confidence in the National Government was surprisingly defeated towards the end of 1936 by 394 votes to 316, possibly because Walter Elliot was a more compelling orator than Attlee. Thereafter among the politically active the Conservatives increasingly had their backs to the wall. Their most effective performer was John Simonds of Magdalene, son of a future Lord Chancellor, who was later killed at Arnhem. For a time he held his own well against the rising stars of the Left, A. S. Eban of Queens', a future Deputy Prime Minister of Israel, the Trinity Hall lawyer and cricketer Sam Silkin and Matthew Hodgart of Pembroke, who described himself as Marxist-Leninist-Stalinist-Dimitrovist. Simonds wrote an article called 'The Cambridge Society for the Prevention of Cruelty to Conservatives' – 'We ask kind words for the poor political endeavours of Conservatives; for their fantastic desire to prevent the Spanish bonfire from becoming a European conflagration, even at the fearful cost of allowing it to burn itself out; for their laughable belief that the country must be strong to defend itself and to fulfil its obligations in helping to impose the law of peace; for their stubborn insistence that just because there is no defence against the air the best defence must be potential offence; for their short-sighted refusal to commit the nation to general obligations which in particular circumstances it may not be willing or able to perform.' However, he eventually fell under the spell of the most glamorous figure of the Cambridge Far Left, the immensely wealthy American Michael Whitney Straight of Trinity, brother of the celebrated motor-racing driver.

With the prestige of a double first in economics to add to his reputation as Cambridge's leading socialite, Straight was a very potent influence on his generation. Having visited the Kremlin, he was widely assumed to know what he was talking about. John Simonds came back from a shooting holiday with him in the Alleghanies a confirmed Socialist and, calling himself a Left indeterminate, symbolically crossed the floor of the house in the Michaelmas term of 1937 to be warmly greeted by Eban with the words – 'allow me, Mr President, to be the first to enfold in a wide embrace of welcome the un-expected form of the Vice-President'. In that depressing era of spineless appeasement of the dictators it was not easy for the intelligent and spirited young to adhere to the Government cause. Whatever the merits of Neville Chamberlain, his personality was not one to fire the enthusiasm of youth. To the chorus of political discontent was added the heady influence of the popular poets of the day, who became more and more militant. It was very much contrary to the general mood for J. H. Plumb to write in 1935 – 'it appears that there are three young major poets in England today. They are Stephen Spender, W. H. Auden and C. Day Lewis . . . their voices are full of propaganda, their images drawn from turbines, pit disasters and sweated labour underlying it. This accounts for their popularity amongst the left wing youth, who feel that only stars and lilies are sentimental, for they forget that poverty and industry have had as much slush written about them as cottages with roses round the door.' Spender early in 1938 raised a few remaining conventional eyebrows by entering the Union as a guest speaker in an ordinary suit smoking a cigarette, it being explained that two days before he had been invited to speak his wife had sent his dinner jacket away to a *Daily Worker* bazaar, believing he had no use for it.

The national situation in 1938 was so pitifully confused that it is not surprising that by then Union debates degenerated into utter irrationality as, for instance, when the Communist E. A. Nahum of Pembroke observed that, while under Capitalism a few men control industry, under Socialism everyone does, or C. V. Wintour of Peterhouse, a future editor of the *Evening Standard*, 'stressed that the real menace to British interests lay in the undemocratic measures this country has to take against a strengthened Germany'. To be fair, this last was almost certainly 'a debating point', but it was a common neurosis, continually cropping up in the *New Statesman*. In May a letter appeared signed by the Presidents of the Cambridge University Democratic Front, the League of Nations Union, the Liberals and the Socialists, deploring the growing crisis over Czechoslovakia, urging the League Council to be summoned and the Government to make an unambiguous guarantee with France and Russia of Czech independence.

It was now of course illogically late to will the way if you had consistently opposed the means. In 1930 the Union had voted for the abolition of military training in schools, despite the advocacy of the hero of Gallipoli, General Sir Iain Hamilton; in 1932 they had voted by a huge majority for disarmament, despite Leo Amery telling them that 'the great fallacy of modern times is that armaments are the real cause of war . . . on the one hand England is asked to disarm and on the other she is asked to bell the Japanese cat'; in 1933 there was another massive vote for disarmament, with D. N. Pritt inevitably in the van; in 1934 a letter was published from the Presidents of the Labour Club, the Anti-War Movement and the Christian Peace Society complaining that 'scandalous campaigns for a larger Air Force are allowed to appear in the Press'; in 1936 they voted against rearmament; in 1937 they incongruously approved military intervention in Spain, while also allowing Ponsonby and D. R. Wainwright to persuade them to pass by a narrow majority the motion that 'true national defence can only be effectively secured by individual refusal to bear arms and by complete national disarmament'. Simonds (before his conversion) pointed out that the will to war can only be combated by the will to resist war. Rupert Brooke had described himself as 'magnificently unprepared'.

There was nothing magnificent about the unpreparedness of the British at the time of Munich, though, as events were to prove, it had little or nothing to do with decadence or cowardice. It was due rather to a combination of wishful thinking and sustained disregard for the facts of human nature.

Epilogue

SI VIS PACEM PARA BELLUM

The New Conscripts

We were the first. They called us from our business
To train to fight the men our fathers fought:
We, who were born when life was at its lowest,
Must earn again the liberty they bought.

Richard Sutton, May 1939

Berchtesgaden, Bad Godesberg, Munich, Heston airport; guilt, shame, foreboding, fear, relief – 'this is the second time in our history when there has come back from Germany to Downing Street peace with honour. I believe it is peace for our time.' The day after the Munich agreement, as the university settled down for the Michaelmas term of 1938, the Vice-Chancellor, H. R. Dean of Trinity Hall, echoed the mood which would prevail in the country at large for the next few months. 'The stress and anxiety which have overwhelmed us all during these last days make it hard to review in true perspective the peaceful happenings of the academic year . . . To all during the last weeks of vacation who by wise counsel and hard work have made preparations to face the dangers with which we were threatened, I wish to express my most sincere gratitude. Yesterday, in common with the rest of the world, we awakened from the horrors of a dream to face the new day with thankfulness and courage. The university, freed from the threat of imminent war, looks forward today with hope and confidence, recently beyond expectation, to the peaceful and productive labours of another year.'

Air-raid shelters had been dug and Girton, which had been planned to open as a dormitory for London babies, was still a college. F. L. Lucas in his diary described the temporarily triumphant Prime Minister as resembling some country cousin whom a couple of card-sharpers in the train have just allowed to win sixpence to encourage him. A passionate critic of Chamberlain, he went round collecting protest signatures. Among those who responded was Coulton, whom he found sitting like an aged monk in dressing gown and slippers, a plate with the remains of lunch under his chair and his table covered to a height of two feet with books and papers, interspersed with wooden boxes (labelled 'Fry's Chocolate') and objects of clothing. E. M. Forster told his readers in the

London Mercury that part of his credo was that he hated causes and if he had to choose between betraying his country and betraying his friend he hoped he would have the guts to betray his country.

Soon *The Cambridge Review* was able to report that while a few meetings had been abandoned and some lecturers would have to practise an unwonted compression, already the course of university life seemed to be running as smoothly as ever. No more recruits were accepted for the horsed troops of the OTC cavalry squadron and Sergeant R. E. Jordan of the Royal Tank Corps, no doubt assisted by the Adjutant, was to instruct those undergraduates who wished to be mechanized in the two Light Tanks Mark II available, which were never simultaneously in working order. The Heretics were revived and listened to Eddington on the limitations of physical science. One of their former heroes, Haldane, who for the past few years had been charging round Spain advising the Republicans on air-raid shelters, was planning to have himself experimentally bombed in an ARP shelter. An address by Mr Attlee to the Socialist Club in the Corn Exchange was reported to have been disturbed by the Marquis of Granby (Trinity) and fireworks were let off. There was a meeting of eminent but by now rather less confident pacifists – Lansbury, Eddington, Raven, Vera Brittain. In November the Union, under the Presidency of the Left-wing Mohan Kumaramangalam of Eton and King's, voted by 233 to 107 that the defence of Britain was not safe in the hands of Mr Chamberlain, an opinion in which they showed themselves a great deal more prescient than their seniors at Westminster. During the debate Matthew Hodgart 'quoted some very revealing shares held by the Prime Minister and members of the Cabinet and linked them up with the Government's policy on defence'.

By the end of the term the post-Munich euphoria was wearing thin. Although the Newnham girls were cooking sausages outside the Marshall Library for Spanish relief; the Republicans were evidently losing. J. A. Ryle, the Regius Professor of Physic, suggested that the colleges should cease spending £5000 a year on feasts while children starved in Spain and King's agreed to waive their next feast. More and more ghastly details emerged of the Nazi persecution of the

Jews. An awful sense of political powerlessness pervaded thought and conversation. Lucas, digging in his garden, was wont to reflect what it would feel like to be digging one's own grave before a firing party. Keynes, finding little ground for optimism in the short term, turned his gaze towards the long-term future: 'The question is whether we are prepared to move out of the nineteenth-century laissez-faire state into an era of liberal socialism, by which I mean a system where we can act as an organized community for common purposes and to promote social and economic justice, whilst respecting and protecting the individual – his freedom of choice, his faith, his mind and its expression, his enterprises and his property.'

In February 1939 there appeared a remarkable letter signed by the Bishop of Ely, the Mayor of Cambridge, the Chairman of the County Council and the Vice-Chancellor. It began by pointing out that 1939 would be a critical year in world history. There was a fear of war, poverty and insecurity and a great yearning for a practical solution to these problems. With that in mind, the signatories wished to draw attention to the gathering international momentum of Moral Rearmament. They recalled a letter signed in September by Lord Baldwin, Lord Birdwood and others, emphasizing that the real need of the day was for moral and spiritual rearmament. They proposed therefore to draw their readers' attention to an anthology of statements on this subject drawn up by H. W. Austin, the great lawn tennis player, himself a Cambridge man, called *Moral Rearmament, the Battle for Peace*, obtainable at all booksellers, price 6d. P. F. D. Tennant of Queens' declared himself impressed. He pointed out, however, that what impressed him was the *disarming* morality of the moral rearmament which was advocated. 'It is no doubt a very stimulating experience to listen to the good resolutions of international tennis players, or bishops, or business men, but none of them for all their publicity have succeeded in competing with the simple practical principles suggested by a certain popular agitator in the first century of his own era. It is practical principles of this nature which are required, no new movement need be launched and moral rearmament should remain the monopoly of the gentleman [Dr Buchman] who coined the slogan and be incorporated in his newly patented religion, which has just paid a doubtful compliment to our sister university by being registered as a limited liability company under her name.'

Similar diversity of opinion surrounded the problems of secular rearmament. The Union at the end of April voted against compulsory National Service by 204 votes to 144, despite Mr Amery's very reasonable observation that to send out half-trained troops was murder. The opponents of conscription had a prestigious ally in Captain Liddell Hart, presumably because like one of his most celebrated disciples he preferred *l'armée de métier*. Charles Wintour declared himself understandably puzzled by the seemingly inconsistent attitude of the Left which called for a strong foreign policy, but opposed compulsory service. However, P. W. Kemmis of Queens' may well have been more persuasive in asserting that the defence of liberty meant no more than the defence of vital British interests as interpreted by the Conservative Party. Arnold Kettle, another luminary of the Pembroke far Left, argued in a pamphlet that instead of conscription there should be a system of voluntary military training organized democratically through the trade unions. Canon Raven with others signed a letter to *The Times* stressing that if war came it would not be right for Parliament to introduce conscription. The Festival, revived under new management, appropriately produced Shaw's *Arms and the Man*. Sir Will Spens, who had just completed his massive Government report on education, became Commissioner for the Eastern Region under the Civil Defence scheme.

With so many sombre preoccupations in the air, the *Granta* editorial, which announced the beginning of the last pre-war term, is worth quoting at length as evidence of the resilience of youth and Cambridge's inflexible determination to maintain its traditional social programme. Entitled 'We're back', it runs: 'The Vice-Chancellor blows his whistle, and everything starts. The Term surges forth. The Spring Term, the May Term, the Summer Term. Call it what you wish – the best Term of all. The Term of Grantchester Meadows and The First and Third [Trinity's Boat Club]. A grimy train trundles in from Bletchley bringing an assortment of popular-fronters and academics. An exotic 1939 Zephyr slides suavely up to Trinity Gate bringing a bit of Debrett's peerage and a quarter bottle of Bollinger Special Cuvée. Deanna [Durbin, an ingénue film star of great celebrity] is here thrilling the evening multitudes, and King's dons can see *Snow White* another dozen times this week. May Week gets nearer . . . Mozart's *Idomeneo* fills the pentagonal Arts [Theatre], Cambridge is having another English première, producer Camille Prior sits in a box justly proud. The May Sunday excursions* are crowded with purple lovelies. They walk down through King's and back through Trinity and the sun glows. A cape of pale Russian lynx. An off-shoulder dress of emerald tulle . . . A world of lawns and punts, neckties and shirting-patterns, *crème brûlée* and paprika salad. The Vice-Chancellor blows his whistle. What a term it's going to be . . .' Peter Studd, the captain of the university cricket XI, a future Lord Mayor of London, told an interviewer that he hoped to God that Hitler wouldn't declare war before the cricket season was over. A very different tone was adopted in a letter to *The Cambridge Review* from Ebenezer Cunningham of St John's, who as well as having written an exceptionally influential book called *The Principle of Relativity* in 1914, was a devout Congregationalist and had been a convinced pacifist since the Boer War. He informed his readers, in sharp contrast with the levity of *Granta*, that while the world had been holding its breath and crisis headlines filling the press, two hundred professors and students from twenty-five universities in European and other countries had assembled at Undersaker in the Swedish mountains to consider how Moral Rearmament through education could bring stability and security to a world whose foundations were trembling.

Morally rearmed or not, the university was determined to go on with its proper business. There were important academic changes during the year. Glover ceased to be Public Orator; Cornford retired from his chair, as did Barker, who was replaced by a sharply contrasted type of scholar in the person of D. W. Brogan. Raven succeeded Sir Charles Darwin as Master of Christ's; and Temperley succeeded Lord Birdwood at Peterhouse only to die within the year. Gray, well over

---

* Four shillings and twopence return third class, but of course rather more for the type of clientele described.

eighty, was still Master of Jesus. Moore, who had followed James Ward in 1925 as Professor of Philosophy, was succeeded in his turn by Ludwig Wittgenstein. For forty years Moore had contributed almost annually to the *Proceedings of the Aristotelian Society*, so that McTaggart was alleged to have said that he was always glad to pay ten and sixpence for his copy, as Moore's article was always worth the ten shillings and the rest often worth the sixpence. Moore would live for nearly another twenty years, surviving his successor. On 20 April the Ancient, Medieval and Modern Cambridge Histories were finally completed after more than forty years' editing. Cockcroft, the new Jacksonian Professor of Natural Philosophy, was procuring a cyclotron for the university. And more freshmen had come up than in any year since 1919.

While an honorary degree was conferred on the United States ambassador, Joseph Kennedy, no great admirer of the country to which he was accredited, and T. S. Eliot was made an honorary fellow of Magdalene, Cambridge had a visitor that summer, who may have been felt by those who remembered his impact on a previous Cambridge audience not quite to have fulfilled his earlier promise. Winston Churchill addressed a meeting in the Corn Exchange on 19 May, specifically to counter the Union vote against conscription. An undergraduate poll on 15 May had evoked a 55 per cent response, i.e. roughly 3000. 59·9 per cent of those voting declared themselves in favour of conscription and 40·1 per cent were against. 74·1 per cent were for an alliance with Russia and 25·9 per cent against. Significantly, 770 declared that they opposed conscription because they opposed Chamberlain, while 440 did so because they were pacifists. Churchill's meeting was a lively one, at the end of which the chairman declared that a show of hands indicated a 10 to 1 majority in favour of conscription. This information was duly passed on to the correspondence columns of *The Times*, but was hotly contested by Arnold Kettle, who claimed it grossly overestimated the size of the majority. Three days after the Corn Exchange meeting Hitler and Mussolini signed their so-called Pact of Steel.

The Union debating chamber was, as usual, emptier in the summer and the proceedings more desultory. Successively, the house decided (understandably) that it was not glad it was born when it was; that it was tired of politicians; but that it was not yet tired of books, if only by a majority of 26 votes to 20. The tripos completed, the concluding Presidential debate, the last of the pre-war years, took place. Since the outgoing President, a Left-wing Conservative from a northern grammar school, Peter Hague, was killed in the war it is pleasant to recall that it was a rather brilliant occasion. The chief gladiators were the two most prominent advocates of the day, Sir Patrick Hastings and Sir Norman Birkett, the latter observing of his opponent that 'a thousand guineas in his sight are like an evening gone'. Birkett secured a majority of 305 to 203 against the motion that there was still one law for the rich and another for the poor. May Week came and went and the university team made 531 against Leicestershire.

The September editorial of the St Catharine's magazine included the following:

'In the carved oak panels of the War Memorial, on the south wall of the Chapel, there has been added during the past year a new name. The St Catharine's Society at a recent meeting had asked that the record for 1914–18 should be made complete so that honour might be given.
HOSTIS AMICUS
L. H. JAGENBERG
It is perhaps consistent with the irony of things that, some twenty years after the end of the war, the friend and enemy should not be altogether forgotten; and something of that irony might be thought to be, in a sense, a commentary on Cambridge during the last year. Jagenberg, his contemporaries tell us, was loved and respected. It is right that all members of a College, whatever their nationality, should share equally the fellowship of the living, and the honour of the dead. Now, when scholarship is prostituted to politics or creeds, it is more necessary than ever that Universities should revert to the medieval tradition that recognized no such barriers, and the College must welcome the strangers among us . . .'

The war against Hitler started very well for Kingsley Martin and the *New Statesman,* the opening words of its first war editorial reading: 'To have begun the war by dropping leaflets instead of bombs on the towns of Germany is a right and imaginative stroke, of good augury for the future.' But the going got a bit rougher when the Red Army occupied a large part of Poland. Haldane inaccurately remarked that the Russians would start with one advantage, in that many of the Poles in the occupied districts, while hating the Russians, would hate the Germans more. Rowse took a more positive line – 'fancy preferring the Poles to the Russians; the ineptitude of it! . . . Isn't it better than an integral Poland shall become part of a federation of Soviet Republics?' The last word, however, was surely that of Keynes writing from King's on 14 October – 'the intelligentsia of the Left were the loudest in demanding that the Nazi aggression should be resisted at all costs; when it comes to a showdown, scarce four weeks have passed before they remember that they are pacifists and write defeatist letters to your columns, leaving the defence of freedom to Colonel Blimp and the Old School Tie, for whom three cheers.'

Portway was by then back in military harness, as were many dons much younger than he. But this time, the authorities were far more skilful in matching individual talents to war-time exigencies. With Adcock as recruiting sergeant, a for-midable team of Cambridge intellectuals took the train to Bletchley over the next year or two and applied their minds there with great success to the unravelling of German ciphers. They included as well as Adcock, F. L. Lucas, D. W. Lucas, L. P. Wilkinson, J. Saltmarsh, G. C. Morris, F. L. Birch, A. M. Turing, A. J. H. Knight, G. Barraclough, Max Newman, F. H. Hinsley, J. H. Plumb, H. O. Evennett, T. D. Jones, R. J. Getty, D. R. Taunt, W. G. Welchman, L. W. Forster, D. W. Babbage, R. F. Bennett, E. R. P. Vincent, D. Parmée, and F. J. Norton. F. L. Lucas commanded the Bletchley Home Guard. The older men fire-watched in Cambridge or looked after the black-out and other air raid precautions and often, like Housman's biographer A. S. F. Gow, wrote letters to their former pupils. Pigou wrote to the Headmaster of Eton offering to teach 'Hun, Frog and Wop' without accent, if allowed to keep a day ahead of the class. F. A.

Simpson, as his war effort, collected honey to such an extent that he could not think what to do with it and did not altogether appreciate it when an exasperated colleague suggested that he could always be embalmed in it. In the event, Cambridge suffered very little from the attentions of the Luftwaffe. One bomb exploded in Jesus Lane, and killed Mr Nahum of Pembroke. Few of the millions of tourists who visit Cambridge look closely enough at the daunting eastern façade of Whewell's Court, Trinity, to notice that it was and is slightly chipped as a result.

Sources

A historian of the University in this period is fortunate to have available in *The Cambridge Review* a weekly journal of record, comment and criticism, which maintained a remarkably high and consistent standard throughout the inter-war years. Among official publications of the University, *The Cambridge University Reporter*, *The Cambridge Historical Register* and *The Student's Handbook for the University and Colleges of Cambridge* are indispensable. Most of the university undergraduate journals are marred to the point of unreadability by heavy-handed jocosity, but nearly all contain some serious literary criticism and extended reporting of acting and debating. Especially useful in this connection are *Granta*, the *Old Cambridge*, the *New Cambridge* and *The Cambridge Gownsman*. Important undergraduate literary magazines were *The Venture* and *Experiment*. For the politics of the thirties *Cambridge Left* and *The Democrat*, though short-lived, are interesting. C. K. Ogden's the *Cambridge Magazine* and F. R. Leavis's *Scrutiny* are both central to the Cambridge scene in the period, though both deal with wider issues.

There is a considerable range of significant material to be found in the publications of the various colleges. Quite outstanding in quality and interest are the obituary memoirs prepared by direction of the Council of King's College, particularly associated with L. P. Wilkinson and J. Saltmarsh, and *The Eagle*, the Saint John's College magazine. I have also found useful the *Saint Catharine's College Magazine*, *The Trinity Annual Record*, *The Trinity Magazine*, *The Magdalene College Magazine and Record*, *The Sell*, *The Pem*, *The Letter of the Corpus Association*, *The Dial*, *The Caian*, *The Christ's College Magazine*, *The Lady Clare*, *The Girton Review*, *Thersites*, *Basileon*, *The Sidney Sussex Annual*, *Gonville and Caius College Biographical History* and *Admissions to Peterhouse 1931–1950*.

I have had frequent recourse to *The Proceedings of the British Academy*, *The Proceedings of the Royal Society*, *The Times* (including especially the volume entitled *Obituaries from The Times 1961–1970*), the *New Statesman and Nation*, *The Listener* and *Encounter*.

Unpublished sources are largely drawn from the collection to be found in the University Library known as the Cambridge Papers

Classification. These include, inter alia, memoranda and notes of evidence submitted to the Royal Commission and material on The Heretics and the Unemployed Camps. I have been particularly fortunate, as I have acknowledged in the preface, to have had access to the papers relating to the Haldane case and to the diaries of A. C. Benson. Benson died in 1925. He allowed his friend Percy Lubbock to publish a volume of extracts selected from his diaries, which amount to some four million words. Apart from this, the diaries were embargoed and shut up in a wooden box for fifty years. In the summer of 1975 this was opened in accordance with Benson's will by the Master and Fellows of Magdalene. Sir Desmond Lee allowed me to use his unpublished reminiscences of Wittgenstein, and Mr T. C. Nicholas his private records of the Royal Commission. The Faculty of Philosophy allowed me to examine the minutes of the Moral Sciences Club. I am indebted to Miss H. E. Peek, the Keeper of the University Archives, for valuable assistance. The minutes of the Committee of Tutorial Representatives contain some useful information.

A LIST OF PRINTED SOURCES

ed. A. J. Ayer   The Humanist Outlook

E. H. F. Baldwin   Gowland Hopkins

E. Barker   Age and Youth

ed. C. Barrett   L. Wittgenstein – Lectures and Conversations

C. H. W. Beaton   The Wandering Years

J. Bell   Essays, Poems and Letters

W. Blunt   Cockerell

M. C. Bradbrook   That Infidel Place

M. C. Bradbrook   Malcolm Lowry

F. Brittain   It's a Don's Life

F. Brittain   Bernard Lord Manning

F. Brittain   Arthur Quiller-Couch

ed. R. Brower, H. Vendler, J. Hollander   I. A. Richards – Essays in his honour

ed. A. Bullock   The Twentieth Century

H. M. Burton   There was a Young Man

R. A. Butler   The Art of the Possible

H. Butterfield   The Whig Interpretation of History

Cambridge University Air Squadron – A History

S. Campion   Father, a Portrait of G. G. Coulton at home

D. Caute   The Fellow-Travellers

Old Patterns in Perilous Times, An Account of the Cambridge Inter-Collegiate Christian Union

R. Clark The Life and Work of J. B. S. Haldane

T. E. B. Clarke This is where I came in

P. Cradock Recollections of the Cambridge Union 1815–1939

J. G. Crowther The Cavendish Laboratory

G. Daniel The Backward Looking Curiosity

ed. C. Day Lewis Mind in Chains

F. W. Dillistone Charles Raven

M. Dobb Soviet Russia and the World

M. Dobb Russia Today and Tomorrow

A. V. Douglas The Life of A. S. Eddington

R. A. Downie James George Frazer

R. A. Downie Frazer and The Golden Bough

T. Driberg Guy Burgess – A Portrait with Background

R. Duncan All Men are Islands

E. Eshag From Marshall to Keynes

A. S. Eve Rutherford

E. M. Forster Goldsworthy Lowes Dickinson

E. M. Forster Abinger Harvest

ed. R. Gill W. Empson, the man and his work

T. R. Glover Greek Byways

T. R. Glover Cambridge Retrospect

A. S. F. Gow A. E. Housman

M. Grant Cambridge

V. H. H. Green Religion at Oxford and Cambridge

J. Gross The Rise and Fall of the Man of Letters

C. Haden Guest David Haden Guest. A Memoir.

C. Haldane Music, my Love

C. Haldane Truth will out

A. R. Hall The Cambridge Philosophical Society

M. A. Hamilton Newnham: an informal biography

G. Harding Along my Line

G. H. Hardy A Mathematician's Apology

G. H. Hardy Bertrand Russell and Trinity

R. F. Harrod The Life of John Maynard Keynes

R. Hayman Leavis

T. J. N. Hilken Engineering at Cambridge University

ed. E. Homberger, W. Janeway, S. Schama The Cambridge Mind

K. B. Hoskins Today the Struggle

E. C. Hoskyns Cambridge Sermons

Housman Society Journal, 1974 Vol. 1

C. Isherwood Lions and Shadows

J. M. Keynes Collected Writings

ed. M. Keynes Essays on John Maynard Keynes

A. Koestler The Yogi and The Commissar

E. Larsen The Cavendish Laboratory

J. Lehmann The Whispering Gallery

R. Lehmann Dusty Answer

ed. F. Lincoln Ralphs New Minds for Old

J. Lindsay   A Cambridge Scrapbook

G. Lowes Dickinson Autobiography (*ed.* D. Proctor)

F. L. Lucas   The Greatest Problem

F. L. Lucas   Journal under the Terror

F. L. Lucas   Critical Thoughts in Critical Days

ed. H. Maas   The Letters of A. E. Housman

I. Macartney   Break of Day

R. McWilliams-Tulberg Women at Cambridge

N. A. Malcolm   Ludwig Wittgenstein

F. G. Mann   Lord Rutherford on the Golf Course

B. K. Martin   Father Figures

ed. D. E. Moggridge   Keynes – Aspects of the Man and his Work

I. Montagu   The Youngest Son

N. J. T. M. Needham   Hopkins and Biochemistry

ed. N. J. T. M. Needham Background to Modern Science

N. J. T. M. Needham   History is on our side

ed. C. K. Ogden   Psyche

C. K. Ogden and I. A. Richards The Meaning of Meaning

T. Okey   A Basketful of Memories

M. Oliphant   Rutherford

B. Page   Philby; the Spy who betrayed a Generation

M. Paley Marshall   What I remember

J. Passmore   A hundred years of Philosophy

N. Pevsner   Cambridgeshire

J. H. Plumb   G. M. Trevelyan

D. O. Portway   Militant Don

D. O. Portway   Memories of an Academic Old Contemptible

J. B. Priestley   Thoughts in the Wilderness

J. B. Priestley   Margin Released

K. Raine   Land Unknown

Report of the Royal Commission on Oxford and Cambridge Universities 1922

Report of the Prime Minister's Commission on Classics in Education 1921

I. A. Richards   Practical Criticism

I. A. Richards   Complementarities

I. A. Richards   Internal Colloquies

S. R. Riedman   Portraits of Nobel Laureates in Medicine and Physiology

ed. J. P. C. Roach   Victoria History of the County of Cambridge and Ely

S. C. Roberts   Adventures with Authors

S. C. Roberts   The Family, the History of a Dining Club

D. S. Robertson   The Future of Greek Studies

J. Robinson   Essays in the Theory of Employment

J. Robinson   Collected Economic Papers

C. H. Rolph   The Life, Letters and Diaries of Kingsley Martin

A. L. Rowse   Mr Keynes and the Labour Movement

B. Russell   Autobiography

D. Russell   The Tamarisk Tree

R. Salisbury Woods   Cambridge Doctor

P. A. Schillp   The Philosophy of G. E. Moore

P. A. Schillp   The Philosophy of C. D. Broad

P. Seale and M. McGonville   Philby – The Long Road to Moscow

G. L. S. Shackle   The Years of High Theory

P. Sloan   John Cornford A Memoir.

C. P. Snow   The Masters

C. P. Snow   Varieties of Men

S. Spender   Forward from Liberalism

B. Stephen   Girton College, 1869–1932

D. R. Stoddart   The R.G.S. and the foundations of Geography at Cambridge

H. Strachan   History of the Cambridge University Training Corps

J. Symons   The Thirties

E. M. W. Tillyard   The Muse Unchained

G. M. Trevelyan   Clio, a Muse and other Essays

G. M. Trevelyan   An Autobiography and other essays

J. A. Venn   Alumni Cantabrigienses

B. Willey   Spots of Time

B. Willey   Cambridge and other Memories

C. Winter   The Fitzwilliam Museum

L. Wittgenstein   Letters to Russell, Keynes and Moore (*ed.* G. H. von Wright)

H. G. Wood   T. R. Glover

N. Wood   Communism and the British Intellectuals

T. C. Worsley   Flannelled Fool

ed. G. H. Wright   Cambridge University Studies

Index

Index

Cole, G. D. H., **225**
Colville, J. R., 156
Compton, A. H., 94
Connolly, Cyril, 198
Conservative Association, 150–1
Conway, G. S., 42
Conway, R. S., 133
Cook, A. B., 116, 133–4, 183
Cook, S. A., 90
Cooke, Alastair, 62, 156
Cooke, Charles Fletcher, 156, 225
Cornford, F. M., 28; supports women's
    cause, 36; on religion, 52; 91, 141;
    as Professor, 183; 212, 237; *Micro-
    cosmographia Academica*, 172
Cornford, Frances, 212
Cornford, John, 158, 209, 212–13,
    215–16, 219–20
Cornforth, Maurice, 158, 201, 212
Corpus Christi College, 164–5
Coulton, G. G., on Christianity, 50;
    eccentricities, 78–9, 233; 107–8,
    118; on arming for war, 220; 233
Courtauld, Miss Sydney Renée, 169
Cradock, Percy, 223
Crane, Gladys, 46
Crawley, Charles W., 106, 148, 177
Crawley, L. G., 160
Creed, J. M., 175
Crewe, R. O. Ashburton Crewe-
    Milner, Marquess of, 87, 169
Croasdell, G. B., 226
Crowther, Geoffrey, 144–5, 151
Cruso, Francis, 52
Cumming-Bruce, J. R. H. T., 224
Cunningham, B. K., 178
Cunningham, Ebenezer, 237
Cunningham, William, 105, 108

Dalton, Hugh, 22
Danby, I. W., 179
Dangerfield, George, 22
Daniel, Glyn, 132, 204
Darby, H. C., 86, 134
Darlington, W. A., 118
Darwin, Sir Charles Galton, 56, 176,
    237
Davenport, John, 166
Davey, F. N., 165
Davies, Hugh Sykes, 46, 73, 166, 203
Davies, J. G. W., 161
Dawson, E. W., 58
Day Lewis, Cecil, 210, 212n, 227
Dean, H. R. (Vice-Chancellor), 233,
    235
Debenham, Frank, 134–5
Dent, E. J., 74
Devlin, P. A., 144–5, 147
Dial, The, 49, 148
Dialectical Materialism, 201, 217; *see*

also Marxism
Dickinson, Goldsworthy Lowes, 20–1,
    51, 163, 167, 182
dining clubs, 81–2
Dirac, P. A. M., 98, 105, 189
disarmament, 228; *see also* pacifism
Dobb, Maurice, Union activities, 24,
    146; 53; politics, 144–6, 211; visits
    Russia, 151, 188; pacifism, 220; 224
Doggart, James, 52
Donat, Robert, 77
Downing College, 59
Doyle, Sir Arthur Conan, 64
dress, 60–1, 76, 139
Driberg, Tom, 51
Drury, Thomas Wortley, Bishop, 82
Dudden, F. Homes, 155
Duff, P. W., 192
Duff, R. B., 169
Duleepsinhji, K. S., 160
Duncan, Ronald, 196
Dunn, Sir William, 99
Durnford, Sir Walter, 48
Dutt, R. Palme, 222

Easton, Murray, 167
Eban, A. S., 226–7
Eberhardt, Richard, 73, 193
Economic Journal, The, 138, 140
Economics, 136–40, 205–8, 216
Eddington, A. S., 28, 97–8, 186–7,
    190, 201, 234
Eddison, Robert, 77
Eden, Anthony, 152
Edward, Prince of Wales (*later*
    Edward VIII), 57
Edwards, Trystan, 167
Einstein, Albert, 103–4
Eliot, T. S., poetry, 70, 73, 166;
    reviews Benda, 146; 166, 193;
    praises Duncan's *Abelard*, 196; 238
Elliot, Walter, 226
Elliott, Claude, 37, 41
Elvin, H. L., 144–5, 225
Ely, B. O. F. Heywood, Bishop of, 235
Empson, William, 46, 52, 72–3, 123,
    157, 193; *Seven Types of Ambiguity*,
    193
Engineering (Mechanical Sciences),
    102–3, 168, 211
English Historical Review, 107
English literature, 116–24, 193–8
Epstein, Jacob, 166
Eton, 80–1
Evennett, H. O., 240
Experiment, 72–3

Fairbairn, Steve, 59, 160
Family, The (dining club), 81, 185
Fay, C. R., 22, 36, 38–9

Index

Hastings, Sir Patrick, 239
Hawkes, Jacquetta (née Hopkins), 171
Hazeltine, H. D., 55, 135
Heath, Edward R. G., 222
Helpmann, Robert, 160
Henderson, Arthur, 84
Henderson, Hubert, 140
Henn, T. R., 166, 196
Henson, Hensley, Bishop of Durham, 220
Herbage, Julian, 61
Heretics, The, 50–3, 235
Higgins, Norman, 159–60
Hinsley, F. H., 200, 240
History, 91, 105–14, 122, 198–201, 216; see also Ancient History
Hoare, Sir Samuel, 147, 151
Hobsbawm, Eric, 158, 162, 199
Hodgart, Matthew, 226, 234
Hollond, Harry A., 26, 28–9, 41, 86, 136, 141
Hopkins, Frederick Gowland, 36, 53, 56, 98–100, 102, 171, 189, 216
Hopkins, Gerard Manley, 193
Hoskyns, Sir Edwyn Clement, 165, 174, 176–7
Housman, A. E., 13, 27; on Russell, 29; on eccentrics, 78; 79; character, 80; 81; as classicist, 88–90, 191; 89, 91; on Frazer's *Golden Bough*, 131–2; in General Strike, 141; Bronowski dismisses, 166; 183–4; death, 185
Housman, Laurence, 185
Hulbert, Claude, 69
Huxley, Aldous, 53, 166

Inge, W. R., Dean of St Paul's, 48, 81, 142, 177
Ingle, R. G., 15
Inglis, Charles Edward, 102–3, 180
Institute of Biochemistry, 99
Isherwood, Christopher, 64
Italian, 115, 203

Jackson, Henry, 36, 117, 182
Jagenberg, L. H., 239
James, M. R., 56, 84
Jennings, Humphrey, 73
Jesus College, 17, 50, 59, 76, 160
Jex-Blake, Katharine, 18, 39
Johnson, Hewlett, Dean of Canterbury, 216
Johnson, W. E., 124–7, 130, 201; *Logic*, 127
Jones, Ernest, 52, 70
Jones, F. Elwyn, 221
Jones, T. D., 240
Joseph, H. W. B., 127

Kahn, Richard, 206

Kapitsa, Peter L., 95–6, 187–8
Kemmis, P. W., 236
Kemp, Peter, 221
Kendon, Frank, 117
Kenny, C. S., 55, 57
Kettle, Arnold, 158, 236, 238
Keuneman, Pieter, 158, 217, 223
Keynes, J. N., 36, 56
Keynes, John Maynard, 26; on Russell's pacifism, 28; supports women's cause, 36; marriage, 50; member of Apostles, 51; 104, 125–7; supports Wittgenstein, 129; 136; and Economics, 136–41, 156, 205–7; 139, 140; in General Strike, 141; politics, 141, 151, 234; on Russian visit, 146; 155, 160, 162; anti-Marxism, 217–18; 240; *The General Theory of Employment, Interest and Money*, 207–8; *Treatise on Probability*, 126
Kiernan, Victor, 158, 213
King and Country vote, 179
King's College, 162–4
Kitson Clark, George, 111–12, 199, 224
Klugmann, James, 158
Knight, A. J. H., 240
Knights, L. C., 119, 197
Knox, Ronald Arbuthnott, 111
Koestler, Arthur, 189, 213
Krishna Menon, V. K., 222
Kumaramangalam, S. Mohan, 234
Kun, Bela, 213

Labour Club, 145–6, 152, 228
Labour Party, 21–2, 24, 216–18
Lambert, Constant, 160
Languages (modern and medieval), 114–15, 126, 203–4
Lansbury, George, 21, 147, 151, 234
Lapsley, Gaillard, 80, 109, 192, 199
Latin, 87, 91
Laski, Harold J., 106, 225; *Law and Justice in Soviet Russia*, 188
Laslett, Peter, 200
Laurence, R. V., 28, 37, 48, 81–2, 106, 141
Law, 135–6, 192
Lawrence, D. H., 71, 166
Lawton, F. H., 156, 224
League of Nations, 23–4, 219
League of Nations Union, Cambridge Branch, 24, 218, 220, 228
Leavis, F. R., 117, 121, 124, 165, 185n, 194–8; *Revaluation*, 196
Leavis, Queenie D. (née Roth), 195, 198
Lee, Desmond, 129, 165
Lee, Jennie, 152